Today, most thoughtful Americans agree that the growing challenge of foreign competition requires some major structural shifts in the U.S. economy—in our capital markets, our workplaces, our schools—to name but a few. The hitch: the things we must do to retain our longstanding technological advantage in world trade—dollar devaluation, an expanded program of public investment, and the growth of high-income, hi-tech jobs, for example—are all likely to prove inflationary and therefore, in the long run, self-defeating.

This genuinely original book by a young economist (and former executive director of the Joint Economic Committee of Congress) not only defines the problem but suggests a politically viable way out of the dilemma. The key to a noninflationary industrial policy, he suggests, involves a balancing act whereby the timing of our bargaining and pay system is coordinated in such a way as to minimize inflationary expectations. This lucid and tough-minded book will be widely recognized by economists and policymakers alike as providing the basis upon which a workable industrial strategy must be built.

Balancing Acts

BALANCING ACTS

Technology, Finance and

the American Future

James K. Galbraith

92-1110

Basic Books, Inc., Publishers   *New York*

Library of Congress Cataloging-in-Publication Data

Galbraith, James K.
  Balancing acts.

  Includes index.
  1. Industry and state—United States.
  2. United States—Economic policy—1981–
  3. Inflation (Finance)—United States.
  4. United States—Economic conditions—
  1981–   . I. Title.
  HD3616.U46G27 1989   330.973'0927   88–47906
  ISBN 0–465–00584–5

For John Kenneth and Catherine Atwater Galbraith

CONTENTS

ACKNOWLEDGMENTS

THIS BOOK arrives under an agreeably heavy load of debts. It is the product of work, thought and conversation on topics that have been my major preoccupation for more than half a decade and in the writing for three years.

During the early stages at the Joint Economic Committee I enjoyed the sponsorship of a great congressman, Henry S. Reuss, and then that of his distinguished successor, Lee H. Hamilton. And I benefited from the company of inspired colleagues on the Committee's staff, among whom William Buechner, Mary Eccles, Richard Kaufman and David Smith especially stand out.

Since my arrival at the University of Texas in 1985, my work has received support, criticism and strong encouragement from my colleagues at the Lyndon B. Johnson School of Public Affairs, notably Sidney Weintraub, Ray Marshall and Norman Glickman. Unstinting institutional support from the dean of the LBJ School, Max Sherman, has made my research easier than it would otherwise have been. Elsewhere on the Texas campus, I have learned especially from my colleagues Steve Magee (business), Jim Rebitzer (economics) and Tom Ferguson (government), each of whom has read and given help with working papers that were later blended into the present book. My research assistants at various times, Robin King, Gustavo Perochena and John Horrigan, have been excellent and indispensable. For research support I thank the Brookings Institution, the Economic Policy Institute, the Sunshine Foundation and the IC² Institute of the University of Texas.

In the wider world, I wish to acknowledge conversations and assistance in various forms, witting and otherwise, from the following friends, colleagues and erstwhile co-authors: Andrew Bartels, Francis Bator, Albert

Acknowledgments

Bressand, José Casar, Stephen Cohen, David Colander, William Darity, Jr., Paul Davidson, David Dreyer, Robert Eisner, Gail Fosler, Benjamin Friedman, Heidi Hartmann, Robert Johnson, the late Nicholas Kaldor, Anatole Kaletsky, Pentti Kouri, Robert Kuttner, Steven Marglin, Richard Medley, Edward Nell, Lee Price, Steven Quick, Robert Reich, Derek Shearer, Lance Taylor, Martin Weitzman, Toru Yanagihara, Robert Zevin and John Zysman. Special thanks are due to Richard Bartel, editor of *Challenge,* in whose pages some of the central ideas of this book received an early hearing, and to Gar Alperovitz and Roger Skurski, editors of *American Economic Policy,* where an ancestral version of my thoughts on industrial intervention appears.

Martin Kessler, president of Basic Books, has been very patient throughout a process that was far longer than originally promised. Charles Cavaliere, my editor, has done a fine job polishing prose and grammar and supervising the preparation of the manuscript, and Helen Greenberg copyedited with exemplary speed and skill.

The most serious debts, however, are owed to those who read this manuscript at various stages and gave extended attention to it. There were four who did so.

Alfred S. Eichner took an early version utterly to pieces, and without him the final version would never have reached a publishable condition. Al's sudden death in the winter of 1988 is a fresh and bitter blow.

Walt W. Rostow is the most constructive colleague one could hope to have. He read the penultimate draft from end to end, giving comments on virtually every page. Innumerable historical points, particularly, have been sharpened or corrected with his help. And if in the end I do not ascribe to the shifting commodity terms of trade all of the importance that I should, that is my fault and not his.

John Kenneth Galbraith, my father, read the penultimate draft with an eye especially to language and style. Again, there were comments on virtually every page. If the final result displays any degree of clarity and grace, and any consistency of tone, he must get much of the credit.

Robert L. Heilbroner, finally, read the entire manuscript through on two separate occasions. On each, he supplied a long, piercing commentary, chapter-by-chapter as well as chapter-and-verse. It has been Bob's unique ability to see the whole work, to understand its defects of structure, and to say, with unerring judgment, how to make it go where I wanted it to go, to do what it should be made to do. To this, any overarching logical sequence that the book now possesses is owed.

Acknowledgments

Lucy Ferguson Galbraith provided love, counsel and patience throughout. Douglas and Margaret, whose lives almost entirely overlap the preparation of this book, provided a powerful incentive to get it finished.

With the help I have had, there is no reason why this should not be in all respects an excellent book. Except, of course, for defects in the raw material with which my friends, assistants, colleagues, teachers and editors have had to work. These are the unavoidable responsibility of the original author.

Austin, Texas
April 7, 1988

Balancing Acts

I call attention to the nature of the problem, because it points us to the nature of the remedy. It is appropriate to the case that the remedy should be found in something which can fairly be called a *device*. Yet there are many who are suspicious of devices, and instinctively doubt their efficacy. There are still people who believe that the way out can only be found by hard work, endurance, frugality, improved business methods, more cautious banking and, above all, the avoidance of devices. But the lorries of these people will never, I fear, get by. They may stay up all night, engage more sober chauffeurs, install new engines, and widen the road; yet they will never get by, unless they stop to think and work out with the driver opposite a small device by which each moves simultaneously a little to the left.

—JOHN MAYNARD KEYNES, 1933

INTRODUCTION

THERE IS A LEGEND that on one occasion, perhaps in 1859, the aerialist Blondin, crossing on his tightrope in front of Niagara Falls, met with the supreme crisis of his career. A guy rope behind him, essential for stability, frayed and gave way. This sent a visible, deadly shock wave down the main line. Blondin's reaction was instant and effective: he *ran*, gripping his balance pole, ahead of the tremor, until he had reached safety on the far shore.

The legend is improbable and may well be false. But it illustrates two true propositions. The first is that good policy sometimes requires quick action. The second, closely related, is that equilibrium is more easily maintained at high speed.

Since 1982, the steady growth and price stability enjoyed by the U.S. economy have been purchased, as all know, by federal budget deficits approaching $200 billion per year and by corresponding deficits on trade and the current account. These have transformed the financial position of the country. They are undoubtedly unsustainable for that reason. The question is what to do about them, and when.

I will argue that the answer must turn on two choices. The first is a choice of industrial direction for the United States. The second is a choice of institutions to replace tight money and periodic recession as the guaran-

tors of a reasonably stable price structure and currency. I further argue
that the decision to make these choices should come quickly, followed by
action at all deliberate speed.

The choices are made necessary by a contradiction that has emerged
forcefully during the Reagan years. On the one hand, the steady development of U.S. industry along its lines of historic advantage requires high
rates of investment in the global economy, and specifically, high rates of
growth in the developing world. Yet, with global integration of financial
markets, the intermittent application of tight money and high interest
rates makes rapid development impossible. Thus price stability is now
purchased at the cost of increasing international comparative *dis*advantage in the most advanced industries, which yield the highest standard of
life. To stick with the old stabilization methods is, in a word, incompatible
with competitive success.

Industrially, the United States faces a choice between what may be
described as alternative programs of industrial development. An inward-
looking program can emphasize expanded production of import-competing consumer goods, ranging from automobiles to televisions. It would
therefore rest on achieving competitive real wages and improved quality
and consumer appeal for American products. The alternative is an outward-looking program, which emphasizes export performance in global
markets, mainly for investment goods, and which therefore focuses on the
expansion of those markets and on reinforcing the long-standing American comparative advantage in the production of those goods.

The inward-looking program would seek sustained recovery for such
older industrial sectors as automobiles, steel, consumer electronics and
textiles. Above all, it would seek the preservation of manufacturing jobs
in those sectors. The outward-looking program places its priority instead
on extending U.S. technological and scientific advantage in world markets. Above all, it is a program for rapid transition and for growth in such
advanced sectors as computers, chemicals, aerospace, energy and industrial equipment.

This is no academic distinction. It has been, indeed, at the heart of the
recent presidential campaign and will be at the heart of future struggles
over both macroeconomic direction and trade policy. Advocates of one
program threaten Korea and Taiwan; advocates of the other urge relief
of the Latin American debt. Advocates of one draft trade legislation and
stress the need to cut American imports. Advocates of the other stress

4

Introduction

interest rates and the need to stimulate the growth of exports. Advocates of one seek job preservation; advocates of the other emphasize programs to provide for smooth modernization and transition.

The inward-looking program is more easily launched and possesses, no doubt, a better-developed political constituency. Given strong U.S. demand growth, dollar depreciation makes American-made consumer goods comparatively attractive and encourages increased U.S. labor content in imports. Selective trade protection has the same effect and so forms an element of some inward-looking proposals. An incomes policy to help keep manufacturing real wages competitive in the face of rising living costs, if necessary, will return as a political possibility now that the Reagan years have ended. Further, the technical difficulties of expanded U.S. consumer goods production are not large. Where U.S. know-how has weakened in certain industrial spheres, the necessary capital goods and the best-practice techniques can be imported from the Germans and the Japanese. The expanding practice of U.S. assembly of Japanese automobiles, motorcycles, videocassette recorders and other consumer products is an adaptation to recent macroeconomic conditions that have favored inward-looking development (as well as to the threat of protection).

Against this, the outward-looking program has three large advantages. First, as noted, it exploits the long-standing and still valid pattern of U.S. comparative advantage in advanced technologies and investment goods. Second, it is the area of greatest continuing potential for expansion: real U.S. exports returned to 1981 levels only in 1987, while by that time domestic production of consumer goods already stood close to capacity limits. Third, it is the area of increasing returns, declining costs, dynamic monopoly profits and high incomes to those who secure them. The worldwide competition for such profits is, to some extent, a zero-sum game. And so, if the United States chooses not to compete for the "quasi-rents" of technological leadership, it will find itself, sooner or later, paying out to some other nation's technological "quasi-landlords."

This book is then a brief for the outward-looking program, considered as comprehensively as my analytical imagination permits. Some space must be devoted to the background of the present setting, and some also to a principled reconsideration of the goals of economic policy under an outward-looking program. However, the essential policy steps can be stated briefly.

The first requirement is and remains a fiscal correction. The deficits must be cut. This book tries particularly to define the size and appropriate timing of that correction, for there is a serious danger in attempting too much, too early. Flexible instruments are available, and they should be used: a tax increase of the right general size can be enacted now for implementation at a delayed date. The case for simple adjustment of income-tax rates, as against cumbersome battles over spending or dramatic further changes in the tax structure, rests on the ease with which rate changes can be legislated and then, if necessary, reconsidered as circumstances change.

Corresponding to fiscal correction, there must be a fall in interest rates. The responsibility for this lies with the Federal Reserve, which must act to sustain U.S. growth and a higher rate of investment worldwide. The Federal Reserve's customary politics, as natural ally of the creditor class, must be set aside in this endeavor long enough for the transition to take place.

Internationally, the dollar and the Third World debt are intertwined. Much present reporting holds that the dollar, grossly overvalued until 1985, has already fallen so far as to be undervalued. But this is nonsense, as the monthly trade figures continually reveal. The dollar has indeed fallen in comparison with the yen and deutsche mark. But it has not fallen nearly so far when measured against the whole universe of countries with which the United States actually trades. These include a large proportion of developing countries, which have pursued continuing strategies of devaluation with respect to the dollar, at enormous cost to their capacity to import, in order to keep up partial service on their debts. Thus the debt crisis lies at the heart of a continuing structural overvaluation of the dollar.

The compelling national interest of the United States therefore lies in moving rapidly to a settlement of the debts of Latin America and the developing world. Our choice is between financial claims that cannot be honored and the real production and employment afforded American workers by growth and development in the poor regions of the world. This choice, at least, is plain. The means and modalities of achieving a settlement are perhaps complex, but I argue that the essential and so far missing element is simple. It is nothing more than a determined commitment by the U.S. government to achieve a settlement.

The domestic and microeconomic elements of the program receive less emphasis here than in other works, but they are not less important. They consist mainly of a sustained increase in the traditional public investment

Introduction

activities of the government, particularly in infrastructure, in education and in support for research. These activities have been severely squeezed in the past decade between rising military expenditures and increasing transfer payments to individuals. They now need to be restored to an annual basis at least as large as their previous peak in 1980. This could be achieved, and then some, by a shift out of the military and net interest accounts amounting to only 1 percent of GNP, without increasing the growth rate of federal expenditure beyond well-established trends. At the same time, ventures that seek to funnel public resources for the preservation of specific industries, other than to cushion transitions, work against the mandate of rapid transition and are to be avoided.

Commitment by the Federal Reserve to sustained economic growth rules out the periodic use of tight money to beat back inflation, with its inevitable costs in lost production, unemployment, and interrupted development in the world economy. But this raises the second critical choice mentioned above. What strategy for the control of inflation can be put in the place of periodic bouts of tight money?

This is a most difficult question. Past experience, mainly with guidelines and controls, is uncomforting. Schemes and proposals abound, but suffer defects of design or lack a reliable degree of integration with a broader strategy of export-led, development-led growth. The common attitude of liberal politicians, which is to deny the threat of inflation for as long as possible and then to panic, does not seem acceptable.

My approach is to begin with a fundamental reconsideration of why chronic inflation is a problem. The difficulties center, I think, not in our economy but in our political system. Moreover, they depend not on the extent to which the price level changes, but on the chronic, drawn-out, debilitating character of past peacetime inflations.

Thus the original strategy proposed here is to manage and compress price shocks when, from time to time, international events make them inevitable. The scheme set out has two essential elements. The first is a synchronization of wage bargaining on an annual basis, so as to provide for rapid adjustment of all workers to changes in the external environment. The second is a conversion of all governmental inflation adjustments—in pay, retirement benefits and welfare—to a common, forward-looking, and discretionary basis. This would provide the president with a powerful means of signaling to the political system a national strategy for adjustment.

These new tools would provide a future president with a balancing pole. They cannot substitute for strength, poise and agile footwork. But by using them creatively, a president might better succeed in managing sustained growth without recession and without uncontrolled, chronic, politically destructive inflation. He would thus be freed to pursue the progressive role that an advanced economy can and must play in world-wide development. And in this way, the contradiction at the heart of U.S. political economy can perhaps be reconciled.

CHAPTER 1

Capital Goods

T HE GLOBAL ECONOMY has now become a fixture of American political culture and, especially in electoral seasons, Americans have learned that a competitive challenge defines our economic existence. The prime challenger has been named: Japan, supplemented in some accounts by Korea, Singapore, Hong Kong and Taiwan, with Brazil and perhaps Mexico coming on. But beyond this the character of the challenge, a dim matter of exports, imports, deficits and debt, capital flows and changing patterns of trade, employment and technology, remains surprisingly ill-defined. Just what, if anything, are the Japanese and the others taking from us? In what sense does America lose from a flood of cheap imported goods? Are we really worse off because the process of development seems to be working in the Far East?

In one clear respect we *are* worse off. We have a national government and yet, it is evident, an increasingly international economic policy problem. Hence our fate no longer seems to rest securely in our own hands. There is a growing sense that traditional policies no longer work; that modern economics seems no longer able to offer effective solutions; that politicians and policymakers must increasingly navigate on dark seas without a reliable compass. Loss of control, whether real or only apparent, breeds unease and anxiety everywhere: in the circles of policy, of scholars, and of public debate.

Mass anxiety, in turn, breeds a demand for expert discussion. Business school theorists, left-wing economists, political sociologists and other scholars have moved to meet the demand. Yet these arguments arise from disparate intellectual roots ranging from Marxism to the institutionalist theory of organizations, and so no single coherent policy prescription seems to flow from them as a whole.[1] There has been instead an explosion of new doctrines and programs, some heterodox, others merely eccentric, and many corporatist and mercantile in defiance of the economist's insistence on the virtues of competition and free trade. The policy discussion recalls in some ways that of the Depression, when John Maynard Keynes wrote of the economic "underworlds" of Karl Marx and Silvio Gesell, whose followers were trying to meet the defaulted obligations of the establishment in coping with a crisis that many perceived but for which orthodoxy had no name.[2]

Mainstream professional economists are perhaps the only group with presumed expertise to have stayed so far on the margins, if not completely out of, the debate. The economist, presented with a problem of international competition, seeks as a matter of instinct and training to address the domestic problem of productivity growth. Yet here the mainstream model provides little policy guidance. On the one hand, the slowdown in productivity growth has remained an unsolved mystery to the economics profession. On the other, welfare analysis does not suggest that the United States as a nation is necessarily irrational in tolerating the slowdown.[3] In the final analysis, the mainstream economist must fall back on a basic belief in the efficiency of markets: although conditions may be slowly getting worse, it does not follow that increased intervention by government will make them better. Thus the disputes over unfair trade, deindustrialization, income polarization and industry policy are not the stuff of professional journals within the economics profession.[4]

As it happens, I share the underlying confidence of most professional economists in the mixed market economy of the United States. The reader will therefore not find in these pages a compilation of evidence about the failings of American business, American labor, American government or the American system of education. No doubt such failings exist, and any comparison of actual with ideal institutions can produce grounds for improvement. The literature of the new policy underworld has already contributed much to this task. But the belief that such failings lie at the heart of U.S. economic difficulties in the international sphere must confront, and cannot cope with, the simple fact that less than a decade ago, under sharply different policy conditions than we have since enjoyed, U.S. industry in international trade was a tremendous if uncelebrated success. For this reason, I maintain that recent failures of policy, and not deep faults of character, lie behind the difficulties we experience at present.

Yet I also believe that the power of policy, properly applied, will, if exercised strongly and quickly, prove sufficient to reverse our present course. Mainstream economics, in its present condition, for the most part denies this. Indeed, the passive attitude of economists toward the prospects and possibilities of economic policymaking lies behind the recent explosion of noneconomic policy prescriptions. There is a vacuum. My main quarrel is with those who have created it, and only secondarily with others who seek to have it filled by means that differ from those suggested here.

To be sure, the passive attitude of mainstream economists in matters of policy is not without cause: it stems in part from the apparent traumatic policy failures of the past twenty years. Permanent full employment without inflation seemed within reach as recently as 1965. Then it slipped out of hand, out of reach, and receded from view. There were recessions in 1970, 1974, 1980 and 1981. With each recovery, inflationary pressures got worse as unemployment fell. With each slump, the peak unemployment rate rose higher, until it seemed by 1982 that double digits for both inflation and unemployment might become routine. Keynesianism was discredited first, then, in short order, supply-side economics and monetarism rose and fell.

In this climate, the accomplishments of recovery by the end of 1988—unemployment down to 5.5 percent without serious inflation—were (correctly) seen to have been purchased only by the creation of unsustainable deficits in the federal budget and in international trade. That being so, mainstream economists could offer no clear means even to preserve, let alone to improve on, the favorable economic conditions of this time. Calls for austerity, a polite code word for another intentional recession, were beginning to fill the air as the 1980s closed. The policy imagination of the establishment had suffered a collective failure, whose consequences would inevitably be felt most severely by those least able to protect themselves.

I will argue that this failure is not rooted in impossible difficulties of the actual situation, nor is it a necessary lesson of past bitter experience.

It is instead a trained incompetence, arising from the way the economist is taught and, in turn, teaches others how to look at and think about the world. Macroeconomics, in particular, was framed by the Great Depression, and it matured under the umbrella of U.S. preeminence after 1945. It did not need to have, from the start, a strong consciousness of international competition. Although throughout this period the United States was the largest importer and exporter in the world and the guarantor of world financial stability, trade was only a small fraction of total production, and international financial considerations did not impinge—or seem to impinge much—on domestic policymaking. Hence macroeconomics could, and did, develop as a science of the closed national economy. International trade, finance and development were off the agenda, researched away from mainstream macroeconomics and taught as separate fields in upper-level graduate courses. The two areas simply did not connect.

In the policy traumas of the 1970s and 1980s, the inward orientation of macroeconomics led to explanations that were either inward oriented themselves (e.g., the productivity slowdown) or that, at best, superficially incorporated external events (such as the oil price shocks). It obscured, and still obscures, the critical element introduced by international competition. That element is the cumulative effect of structural changes wrought by macroeconomic policy in open economies, by the fact that technical and industrial substitutions, changes in the pattern of industrial development, occur across countries as time passes and as a consequence of macroeconomic policy actions. Often these changes cannot be easily erased when the policies change, and so, in the world of trade, macroeconomic decisions have permanent structural effects.[5]

By their nature, macroeconomic models abstract from industrial structure. From their perspective, an export of coffee is the same as an export of jet aircraft. When opened to international trade, the models tell of foreign trade multipliers and import leakages from the stream of domestic demand, and otherwise usefully complicate the process of predicting short-run macroeconomic direction. They can, at their best, calculate the effects on prices and incomes of a large shock to, say, import prices or supplies. But there is no room in them for the observation that countries that export coffee are invariably poor, while those that export jet aircraft and computers are without exception rich. Nor do they permit an examination of the consequences for the United States of, say, losing the computer market to Japan, even though the lost trade share might be fully offset by increased exports of, say, soft timber or hard wheat.

The point is simply that the structure of a country's industrial base is the key to its standard of living in the long run. Each nation pursues the accumulation of wealth by tactics corresponding to its resources and capabilities. Economic rent, the search for the marketable products of natural endowments and human skills that yield large surpluses over their cost of production, is a prime source of sustained prosperity. Conversely, any necessity to pay such rents, whether to resource monopolies or to the sources of technological advantage, is a cause of comparative under-development. This point is neither novel nor especially controversial; it is simply omitted from most of mainstream macroeconomics. And to bring it into the discussion in its proper place requires us to rethink macroeconomic problems almost from the beginning.

Resource endowments may be fixed, but the patterns of other types of advantage evolve.[6] And because all countries are evolving all the time, changes in one country are not always strictly reversible. Once a pattern of demand and supply has been altered, the expansion path most favored by private initiative may, and in general will, be different from what it would otherwise have been.

And so, policies affecting demand in the first instance can influence, over periods of years, the pattern of activities and occupations within the United States as compared with the rest of the world, and thus also the social structure and distribution of income in the United States. We can choose, in many respects and in large measure, the kind of country we would like to be. A nation of bankers and clerks will be different from one of farmers, machinists and computer engineers. There is a choice, at the margin, between automobile production and aerospace engineering, between blast furnaces and national laboratories, between data processors and soda jerks. Can we say which of these will make us richer and which poorer? Can we say how national macroeconomic policies affect this choice? Can we change policies so that the outcomes are more to our liking? I think we can.

The Hierarchy of Production

The conventional classification of nations, as developed, for example, by the World Bank,[7] is in terms of per capita national-income levels, and so reflects the economist's orientation to national-income balance sheets and expenditure flows rather than to industrial structure. One might instead propose an alternative qualitative classification, based on the character of technological capacity and industrial development, so as to make a little more clear the sort of distinction that forms the basis for international trade and for patterns of economic rent.

At the top are the leading technological powers (LTPs), with advanced industrial sectors, whose comparative advantage lies in their development of new technologies and in the production and export of technologically advanced goods, often primarily capital goods, often to a world market. The United States, Japan and Germany lead this list, accompanied by the United Kingdom, France and some of the smaller European economies, notably Switzerland and Sweden. Italy has perhaps a claim to membership as well, based, however, more on superior design capabilities than on science-based technological prowess.

Second, the intermediate manufacturing powers (IMPs) are capable of exploiting established industrial niches, often with superior labor relations and quality control, but do not possess the research and development base to develop fundamental new products and processes themselves. They thus possess the trade relations of South Korea, whose multibillion-dollar bilateral surplus to the United States, representing exports of consumer goods to an LTP, is offset by a trade deficit with Japan, representing imports of capital goods (in this case from a different LTP).[8]

Third, the resource-based economies (RBEs), rich and poor, are dependent on agriculture, mining and energy. These countries import both capital and consumer goods, and pay with what David Ricardo once termed "the original and indestructible powers" of the soil.[9] Their fortunes depend on accidents of endowment, world demand, demography and occasional access to cartel power. Such countries may possess their own capital goods and consumer sectors, and so reduce their demand for these imports, but such goods are typically of inferior quality and cannot be sold at a profit in world markets. They exist as a sort of concession, behind trade barriers or capital controls, living, so to speak, on the rents earned by resource exploitation.

Capital Goods

Fourth and finally are the subsistence economies (SEs), backward, miserable, and essentially outside the orbits of world trade. They play little role in the story with which we are concerned here.

Obviously, elements can exist in combination. The United States, notably, is blessed with rent-earning resources and technological power. Brazil, India and China possess the elements of subsistence, resource-based exploitation and IMP status side by side. The Soviet Union exports resources for hard currency and imports food, while generating most of its capital and consumer goods outside the ambit of world trade.

Allowing for such mixed cases, this classification provides more than a hierarchy of available standards of living. It also gives some sense of the available paths of development. Nations at each level (like families in the labor market) aspire to move up to the next level. SEs search for bauxite, cobalt and oil. RBEs seek to build a manufacturing sector capable of breaking into advanced-country markets for consumer goods. IMPs seek to graft onto their industrial successes a self-starting research capability. At the top, suppliers of technical innovation and the capital goods which crystallize such innovation seek to maintain their lead if they are wise.

The late-twentieth-century United States clearly falls primarily in the LTP category, despite the strong presence of middle-technology manufacturing and a rich endowment of resources. It also, and not by coincidence, enjoys the world's highest average living standard, certain small economies of Europe and Middle East sheikhdoms after 1973 excepted. The means of doing so can be thought of at least partly in Schumpeterian terms: as the dynamic monopoly profits that we have reaped by being the prime supplier to the world of innumerable pieces of tangible and intangible capital equipment.[10] The postwar Americanization of the world economy and culture reflects not the insularity in terms of which Americans sometimes conceive their lot but their immense influence over the opportunities for development open to everyone else and over the paths of development freely chosen as incomes and opportunities have risen.

We may thus pose a crucial question facing the United States in a tidy way. Do we aspire to sustain the living standard available to the LTPs and avoid falling back to the standards generally available to the IMPs, diminished as they are by the necessity of paying out rather than being paid the quasi-rents that accrue to the technological leaders? If so, how do we maintain the position of comparative advantage in advanced technology and advanced service trade that secures to us the rents earned by the holder of that particular world role? And specifically, what macroeconomic policies are required?

The Key Role of Capital Goods

Almost any activity can be pursued in a more or less efficient way, so that in all industries cost differentials exist for comparable products or quality differentials for products of comparable cost. Certain activities, however, promise greater and more durable scarcity rents than others. U.S. banking, for example, may enjoy a worldwide comparative advantage due to its more efficient access to capital markets and its use of telecommunications and computer equipment.[11] But how large and how durable can such an advantage be? The fundamental fact is that banking services are users, not creators, of technology. Bankers can therefore be readily replaced, and bankers of one nationality can displace those of another. This is now clearly happening with Japan's rise in financial power.

Likewise automobile assembly, a traditional American behemoth, may remain an industry in which U.S. workers are comparatively well paid, so that to create an auto job at the expense of (say) a janitorial job raises national income. But how durable can high U.S. auto wages be in the long run, when we increasingly import the basic technology from Japan and compete for sales with functionally identical vehicles produced with far cheaper labor in Korea? It seems clear that much standardized activity must be subject to inexorable pressures of worldwide cost competition, even if its capital equipment is vigorously upgraded and renewed, which under the circumstances is unlikely. With free trade, only a rapidly growing world economy and market can even partly offset these pressures and keep a high-wage producer of standardized products profitable in the medium run.

It is activities that exploit scarcity value—and, above all, the transitory but massive scarcity value of technological advantage—that yield supernormal incomes to their owners. Any country with a wide range of embodied technological advantages is likely to become comparatively and absolutely prosperous. It becomes so partly by persistent hard work that sustains confident expansion and partly by superior diligence, attention to

16

Capital Goods

costs and efficiency in production. But there is also the way that great individual fortunes are made, the way of creating seemingly instant wealth: by capitalizing on a transient advantage, by creating an indispensable product and reaping the surplus that others are willing to pay—so long as the monopoly holds—in order to own it.[12]

This leads in a straightforward direction. The U.S. position in the global economy and its standard of living have depended on its ability to continue substantially to dominate world production of *capital goods*, of the machinery and equipment that flow into the industrial process. Further, that ability depends on its capacity to generate and sustain the expansion of an investment goods–producing sector serving a world market.[13]

Why capital goods? Because capital goods embody design, and unique design is the essence of scarcity value. The machinery and equipment used in the production of goods and services—and not the final act of production itself—are what determine which technologies, which systems, become the basis of consumer life in the industrial world. For this reason, technical superiority in capital goods is the quintessence of advanced development, the ultimate rent-yielding economic activity. Superiority here is the one thing that cannot be emulated by a developing or industrializing nation or even by a second-rate industrial power, nor can it be undercut by low-wage competition. It is therefore the one thing that guarantees an advanced nation a high standard of living.

In capital goods the United States has in fact dominated for half a century—the American Century, the century of the assembly line, of the airplane, of the automobile and the electrified household. Substantially, we still dominate today, as our trading patterns reveal. Today we export jet aircraft, not passenger cars; computers, not pocket calculators; looms, not shirts; oil drilling equipment and refinery technology and resins, not gasoline or plastic toys. Throughout the world, mines, factories, transportation systems and power plants operate to specifications and with machinery that originated in the United States.

In a survey of long-range trade developments published seventeen years ago, William Branson and Helen Junz noted the following:

Capital goods have had a surplus in every year of the period 1925–70. . . . Imports were very flat before World War II, varying in the range of $10 to $40 million, while exports were generally in the $400 to $600 million range. After the war, capital goods exports showed the typical bump in the late 1940s, yielding a much higher surplus than in the prewar years. That surplus has grown rapidly and remarkably consistently to the present, exceeding $10 billion in 1970.

Consumer goods (excluding food and beverages) describe a pattern completely different from that of capital goods. . . . Before World War II, the United States typically was a net importer of consumer goods by a small margin. Immediately after the war, a sizable surplus emerged as exports quadrupled from around $250 million to $1 billion. After this postwar bulge disappeared, exports grew slowly but steadily. Imports of consumer goods, on the other hand, have expanded at an increasingly rapid pace, overtaking exports in 1959. With the exception of a slight decrease in 1961, the deficit has increased ever since.[14]

The extent of U.S. reliance on capital goods exports even today bears emphasis. In 1986, merchandise accounted for about two-thirds of all exports, and manufactured products for nearly 90 percent of that—agricultural products amounted to only 12 percent of merchandise exports. Capital goods and industrial supplies together accounted for over 60 percent of merchandise exports, and the proportion rises to nearly three-quarters when automotive exports—which consist mainly of parts traded with Canada, and trucks, a capital good—are added in. Finished consumer goods probably account for less than 15 percent of merchandise exports. Finally, over half of exports of services, a nonmerchandise category accounting for one-third of all exports, reflect factor income, mainly profits, on past overseas capital investments. The 1971 Branson-Junz conclusion can be repeated: ". . .one might say that the United States does not export mass-produced, physical-capital-intensive goods; it exports custom-made, human-capital-intensive goods."[15] Figure 1–1 provides a picture of the structure of U.S. exports and imports by major industrial grouping.

The global nature of the capital goods market also bears special emphasis. There are more than a score of large, profitable automobile producers in the world today whose products can be found readily in the U.S. market, and for a dozen or more of them, the U.S. market represents a major share of total sales. In almost any other consumer goods field, the same observation applies: a plethora of companies, all efficient and profitable, and yet dwarfed by the scale of the largest national market to which they sell.

In capital goods this is not so. In computers, in aerospace, in electrical

FIGURE 1-1

Structure of U.S. Trade

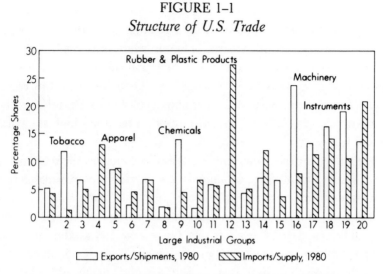

Large Industrial Groups

☐ Exports/Shipments, 1980   ▨ Imports/Supply, 1980

SOURCE: *U.S. Industrial Outlook*, DOC, 1986. Ratios based on 1980 data.

TABLE 1-1

Trade in Twenty Large Industries, 1984, in Billions of Dollars (Two-Digit SIC Codes)

	Exports	Imports
1. Food and kindred products	11.1	12.0
2. Tobacco manufactures	1.1	0.1
3. Textile mill products	1.5	3.5
4. Apparel and other textiles	1.0	13.9
5. Lumber and wood products	2.7	4.8
6. Furniture and fixtures	0.5	2.5
7. Paper and allied products	4.3	7.6
8. Printing and publishing	1.4	0.9
9. Chemicals and allied products	22.2	11.9
10. Petroleum refining products	5.1	21.2
11. Rubber and plastic products	2.9	4.4
12. Leather and leather products	0.5	6.8
13. Stone, clay and glass products	1.9	3.8
14. Primary metal products	4.0	20.3
15. Fabricated metal products	6.5	6.8
16. Machinery, except electrical	37.3	26.0
17. Electrical and electronic equipment	20.2	35.0
18. Transportation equipment	32.2	55.7
19. Instruments and related	8.6	7.7
20. Miscellaneous manufactures	1.9	9.7

SOURCE: Virgil Ketterling, "Industry Trends in International Trade," *U.S. Industrial Outlook 1986* (Washington, D.C.: DOC, 1986), 14–21.

machinery, in farm equipment, in road-building equipment, and in advanced machine tools we do not find a great diversity of firms. We find at most a few, and in many cases only one whose profitability would be assured without hidden or direct subsidization. Boeing and IBM build from American designs for global markets. Their fortunes thus rise and fall with world as well as domestic economic conditions. And the surpluses they earn in world trade are the surpluses that pay for a high standard of U.S. consumer goods imports.

The global scale of investment goods markets enables the technological leader to take advantage of economies of scale that are unavailable to the followers, who are left to struggle with higher costs, lower margins, smaller markets and—in general—a cushion of resources that is inadequate to maintain the pace that the leader sets. Once a country establishes technological leadership, it earns scarcity rents which, properly reinvested, make leadership relatively easy to sustain. But once technological leadership is lost, to regain it requires effort and sacrifice of a wholly different order.[16]

For twenty years, U.S. domination of world capital goods has been under challenge, first by the Europeans and now by the Japanese. Periodically we have lost elements of our position—but then we have shown an ability, with the right policies put in place quickly enough, to regain them. During the 1970s, as will be discussed in depth in the coming chapters, after the Vietnam War and the dollar devaluations of 1971, we were on the world trading offensive. This was due to a sharply falling exchange rate and the post–Vietnam War demobilization, which shifted crucial advanced resources from the military to the civilian sector. U.S. policy worked, wittingly or otherwise, to promote economic growth and purchasing power in those foreign countries, notably in Latin America, that provided strong markets for U.S. capital goods suppliers. This was helped by the concentration of financial resources in the hands of national governments that was achieved first directly by the Organization of Petroleum Exporting Countries (OPEC) and then through petrodollar recycling to the IMPs and RBEs. These policies stimulated a burst of development throughout the world, rapid growth of trade and a boom for advanced U.S. exporting industries.

It is true that the perception of a trade crisis arose while these changes were going on, but this perception was misplaced. Throughout the 1970s, the Japanese concentrated on the immediate profits to be earned in their established niche: the sale of manufactured consumer goods (such as

Capital Goods

automobiles, TVs, radios, and cameras) and steel to the United States. Such imports surged, threatening in particular the market shares of certain prominent U.S. consumer goods industries, but it was not then perceived clearly that there was an obverse to this story. The displacement of U.S. consumer goods with imports was the counterpart of U.S. success in stepping up the flow of advanced technology exports, especially to the developing world. Figure 1-2 shows that the growth rate of U.S. exports from 1973 through 1979 was no worse than the average for all industrial nations, and was higher than that of Germany by a small amount. The erosion of our automotive and steel industries was highly visible, yet we overlooked the offsetting successes of Caterpillar, of Boeing, of Deere, of Allis-Chalmers, of our energy equipment producers, and of IBM. As a whole, throughout this period the United States was paying its way.[17]

Thus the United States could and did roll up vastly increased surpluses on capital goods trade after 1974, and also on capital transactions (the profits of U.S. companies overseas), completely offsetting the rising bill for manufacturing imports (mainly Japanese) and for oil (due to OPEC). Robert Z. Lawrence has shown that the U.S. trade *surplus* in R&D-intensive goods rose by $40 billion from 1973 to 1980, completely offsetting an equivalent rise in the trade deficit in non-R&D-intensive goods (such as oil).[18] Despite the perception of a crisis in the late 1970s brought on by adjustment problems[19] and the failure to cope with other issues

FIGURE 1–2
Growth in Real Exports

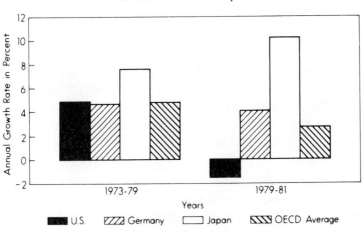

Source: Organization for Economic Cooperation and Development.

(especially inflation), the underlying story was one of success. U.S. industry remained at the forefront of world economic and technological development until roughly 1981.

The Reagan Regress

We are now at the end of the 1980s, and the gains in world markets of the previous decade have been substantially squandered. This was done, in a sense, deliberately, because of the political imperatives created by an inward-looking set of macroeconomic goals focused on aggregate real growth, price stability and the unemployment rate. The adverse international consequences far outweigh these matters in their long-range importance. Our fundamental comparative advantage as an advanced industrial nation—in technology- and knowledge-intensive capital goods—eroded to the point where surplus in these most vital areas evidently turned to deficit on our current account.[20] As this happens, we stand to lose the income that our dominant share of trade in this area previously supported.

The danger is not, unfortunately, an unambiguous threat to all segments of American society; indeed (as was true in Britain), there are strong elements who actively favor continuing down the present path. A high-interest, stable-money policy is good for the role of the dollar and hence, for a while, for the international role of U.S. banking. There are more tangible benefits in some industries and regions: traditional consumer goods–producing corporations (such as automobile manufacturers) have regained strength. Lee Iacocca owed his vogue—and the survival of Chrysler (which buys inputs from Canada and Japan and sells its products mainly in the United States)—in no small part to President Reagan's deficit/exchange rate mix and its consequences for our patterns of trade. Ford Motor's more recently celebrated success is to some extent of the same kind. So too certain advanced sectors—particularly those with a military application—may prefer the sheltered market of the U.S. government to the rigors of direct commercial competition with the Japanese. But every policy that made for continued capital goods domination in the long term was changed. Growth in traditional foreign market areas for U.S. goods collapsed; growth has remained

FIGURE 1–3A
The Export Boom in Capital Goods

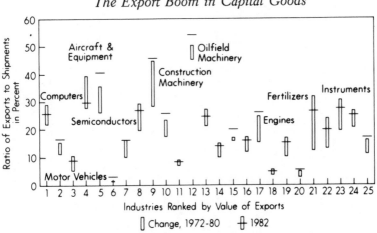

SOURCE: *U.S. Industrial Outlook*, DOC, 1986.

FIGURE 1–3B
Growth of Leading U.S. Imports

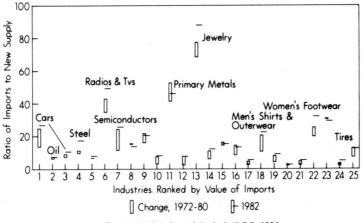

SOURCE: *U.S. Industrial Outlook*, DOC, 1986.

NOTE: Figures 1–3A and 1–3B trace the increases in export and import orientation, respectively, of the twenty-five largest U.S. exporting and importing industries for the transition decade from 1972 to 1982. The industries are tabulated by four-digit SIC codes and are arrayed in the order shown in the accompanying tables. In figure 1–3A the bottom of the bar marks the share of exports in all shipments of each large exporting industry in 1972. The top of the bar represents the export share in 1980, at the peak of the export boom. The horizontal line represents the share in 1982, after two years of domestic and global recession. The chart shows how world development caused a marked increase in the outward orientation of major U.S. advanced technology and capital goods manufacturing in the 1970s, and reflects the effects of the high dollar and the severe global recession on U.S. exports in 1981–82.

In figure 1–3B similar data are given on the share of imports in all sales for the twenty-five largest importing industries. The chart shows that the rise in imports continued into the 1980s as the high dollar cheapened imports, even though domestic demand fell in the recession. Note that the import industries include a far larger proportion of low- and medium-technology consumer goods and fewer advanced capital goods than do the large export industries.

TABLE 1-3A

Twenty-Five Leading Export Industries, 1984, in Billions of Dollars (Four-Digit SIC Codes)

1.	Electronic computing equipment	13.3[a]
2.	Motor vehicle parts and accessories	8.8[b]
3.	Motor vehicles and car bodies	8.1[b]
4.	Aircraft	5.7[a]
5.	Aircraft equipment, n.e.c.[c]	5.1[a]
6.	Petroleum refining	4.7
7.	Industrial organic chemicals	4.7[a]
8.	Semiconductors and related devices	4.6[a]
9.	Construction machinery	3.4[a]
10.	Industrial inorganic chemicals, n.e.c.	3.0[a]
11.	Radio and TV communications equipment	2.9[a]
12.	Oilfield machinery	2.8[a]
13.	General industrial machinery, n.e.c.	2.7[a]
14.	Plastics materials and resins	2.7[a]
15.	Aircraft engines and engine parts	2.5[a]
16.	Photographic equipment and supplies	2.4
17.	Internal combustion engines, n.e.c.	2.3[a]
18.	Miscellaneous plastic products	2.3
19.	Electronic components, n.e.c.	2.2[a]
20.	Meatpacking plants	2.1
21.	Phosphatic fertilizers	1.9[a]
22.	Cyclic crudes and intermediates	1.8[a]
23.	Instruments to measure electricity	1.7[a]
24.	Soybean oil mills	1.7
25.	Farm machinery and equipment	1.6[a]

[a]Capital goods and intermediates.

[b]A significant part is intracompany shipments under the U.S.–Canada automotive agreement.

[c]n.e.c.: not elsewhere classified.

SOURCE: Virgil Ketterling, "Industry Trends in International Trade," *U.S. Industrial Outlook 1986* (Washington, D.C.: DOC, 1986), 14–21.

TABLE 1-3B

Twenty-Five Leading Import Industries, 1984, in Billions of Dollars (Four-Digit SIC Codes)

1.	Motor vehicles and car bodies	38.4[a]
2.	Petroleum refining products	21.1[a]
3.	Motor vehicle parts and accessories	11.4[a]
4.	Blast furnaces and steel mill products	10.1
5.	Office machines, typewriters, etc.	9.4
6.	Radio and TV receiving sets	9.2[a]
7.	Semiconductors and related devices	7.2
8.	Paper mills, except building paper	4.6
9.	Children's outerwear, n.e.c.[b]	4.1[a]
10.	Radio and TV communication equipment	4.0
11.	Primary nonferrous metals	3.9
12.	Electronic components, n.e.c.	3.0
13.	Jeweler's mats and lapidary work	3.0[a]
14.	Photographic equipment and supplies	2.9[a]
15.	Sawmills and planing mills, general	2.9
16.	Industrial inorganic chemicals, n.e.c.	2.7
17.	Furniture and fixtures, n.e.c.	2.5[a]
18.	Men's and boy's shirts and nightwear	2.5[a]
19.	General industrial machinery, n.e.c.	2.4
20.	Miscellaneous plastic products	2.0[a]
21.	Construction machinery	2.0
22.	Women's footwear, except athletic	2.0[a]
23.	Pulp mill products	1.8
24.	Telephone and telegraph apparatus	1.8[a]
25.	Tires and inner tubes	1.8[a]

[a]All or substantially consumer goods.

[b]n.e.c.: not elsewhere classified.

SOURCE: Virgil Ketterling, "Industry Trends in International Trade," *U.S. Industrial Outlook 1986* (Washington, D.C.: DOC, 1986), 14–21.

Capital Goods

strong only in parts of Asia whose capital goods supplies are increasingly coming from Japan.

The implications of this transition for U.S. living standards are not complex. We cannot maintain a comparative advantage in our older, consumer-oriented manufacturing industries at the present national living standards. If we are to become an ordinary industrial power, we will be forced to live on ordinary industrial wages. The industrial structure and patterns of employment and profitability that suited us well in the 1950s—when automobiles were (relatively) high-tech and Korea, Yugoslavia and Spain were still peasant backwaters devastated by recent wars—can be sustained in the 1990s only at the price of a growing, and ultimately destructive, reliance on products designed and built with other nations' means of production. It is one thing to earn the monopoly rents that accrue to the owners of the most advanced techniques and another, less pleasant thing—requiring low wages, long hours and foregone social progress—to be obliged to pay them.

Nor did the Japanese (and to a lesser extent, the Germans) overlook the opportunity we have been providing. Production of Japanese automobiles is coming to the United States (as Volkswagen came earlier), to much shortsighted applause. U.S. domination of investment goods, in turn, is being lost to Japan. While Honda, Toyota and Nissan Americanize, Komatsu has been routing Caterpillar around the world and Hitachi and Fujitsu have been preparing their challenge to IBM. While we celebrate the U.S. revival of an auto industry in which even Korea and Yugoslavia are becoming world players, we should reflect on its displacement consequences, on the global picture. Effectively, such investments crowd us out of global markets where the future course of world technological development—and hence who will lead in living standards—is being decided. This is the long-term industrial consequence of the macroeconomic policy mix.

There are elements of cumulation and irreversibility in the deterioration that has already occurred. The process of economic development is not symmetric: leads build on leads, and leads once lost are not so easy to regain. Leadership in capital goods passed from the British a half-century ago, never to return. If it now passes from the United States to Japan or another country, it may not come back.

Yet leadership may not have passed; there may yet be time. And the Japanese and others may, for a saving transitory moment, repeat our own mistakes just long enough to allow us to rectify them in our own economy. Therefore I believe, and will argue in the chapters that follow, that a prompt and determined effort to reassert U.S. technological supremacy in a rapidly growing world economy would be worthwhile. Against the mainstream economists, I will argue that it can be done. Against the left-wing critics, I will argue that a fundamental transformation of American capitalism is not yet required.

CHAPTER 2

The Age of Contradictions

THE STRUCTURE OF international trade seems to have amply justified the neglect it received before 1965. Anyone who looked at the relationship between trade and macroeconomic policy in those years would have had little or nothing of interest or importance to relate. U.S. exports as a proportion of GNP, for example, fell in the early post–World War II years to about 5 percent in 1950, and fluctuated between that value and 6 percent for the next thirteen years (except for 1957, when it reached 6.3 percent). Imports as a proportion of GNP stayed at almost exactly 4.5 percent during this entire time. Neither fluctuated systematically with, for example, unemployment. If demand declined, the demand for imports fell with it, whereas when demand rose, the demand for imports returned, more or less exactly, to where it had been before. Under such circumstances, research on trade and research on macroeconomics hardly crossed paths—which is certainly not surprising.

In the first two decades since World War II, U.S. leadership brought peace, financial stability and rapid recovery and growth to the Western world. The preoccupying challenge had come not from Europe or Japan but from the Soviet Union. Yet despite public hysteria over Sputnik, there was no doubt that in the long run our technological genius and industrial flexibility would serve us well in meeting the Soviet challenge. The developing nations were still an international economic sideshow: the focus of aid and development efforts, but neither major markets for our goods nor major players on the industrial or financial scene. And so, economists felt secure in working within a closed analytical framework, in treating the problems of full employment and price stability as though they were almost wholly domestic, troubled occasionally by gold outflow but otherwise without serious reference to the external situation.

Thoughtful observers were aware that the preeminence and autonomy of the United States would not last. Industrially, Europe was emerging from the American shadow, creating the political framework for a permanent peace and the integrated economic community that would be required to erect an advanced manufacturing colossus on the American scale. Robert Triffin had warned (as early as 1960) that the dollar-based international monetary system was unstable.[1] Robert Mundell had developed modifications of the Keynesian framework to control the exchange rate and account for the effect of exchange rate fluctuations on the domestic price level.[2] Raymond Vernon had discovered the product cycle and its inherent dynamic of changing industrial structure.[3] Richard Cooper was starting to analyze the economics of interdependence.[4] The farsighted could also see, on the distant horizon, the consequences of the rapid expansion then underway (soon to be greatly stimulated by the Vietnam War) in still-backward Japan. But not one of these ideas penetrated to the core of the macroeconomic policy debate at the time.

The year 1965 may be said to mark the turning point. By that time, product cycle–based relocation of U.S. manufacturing investment to Europe was in full swing, prompting worries here about the loss of jobs and the publication there of Jean-Jacques Servan-Schreiber's 1967 book *The American Challenge,* on American dynamism and the extent of U.S. multinational penetration of European industrial life.[5] The nature of the product cycle was also changing. Europe was developing its own advanced capital goods–producing infrastructure, so that Europe too could begin to play the quasi-rent-producing game of originating technical advances. German chemicals and machine tools, French engineering, Anglo-French and Swedish aerospace, and armaments industries of all kinds threatened to find niches in world markets dominated up to that point by the United States. Moreover, the increasing scale of the European marketplace meant that such enterprises could develop with or without American sufferance. They could reach their full technical potential in European markets, without relying on the American high-income consumption base that had been necessary for the successful introduction of new products (and on which the export platform IMPs of East Asia still rely).

There was no reason to regret the emergence per se of multiple centers of technical development in the modern world. The issue from the standpoint of a single country, such as the United States, was whether the market for the fruits of technical development would expand along with the competition to supply it. And in principle, that expansion could be achieved. It could be done by extending the logic of capitalist development to peoples and nations not previously favored. High standards of consumption need not be the preserve of the existing rich; development could assure that they would not so remain. If this were done, strong worldwide demand would continue to foster innovation and industrial renewal in all of the developed nations, no matter how broad the base of advanced development eventually became. Sustained American growth was thus already coming to depend on accelerated world economic development.

As Triffin saw, U.S. global financial responsibilities were a barrier to the wholehearted pursuit of such acceleration of worldwide development by the United States.[6] We could not provide exports cheap enough for the Third World at prevailing fixed exchange rates without providing massive amounts of credit on very liberal terms. But the U.S. role as provider of the world's reserve currency required stabilization of the exchange value of the dollar. So long as the dollar remained the currency of international finance, credit creation on the scale required for rapid development would conflict with stable exchange rates. One or the other would have to give.

The parities in existence had been chosen at an earlier time. The yen, for example, at 360 to the dollar, was extremely cheap, deliberately so since Japan's recovery was dependent on exports to the United States. Dollar-valued goods were therefore enormously expensive in Japan, as they were in Europe. But European and Japanese recovery, and their purchases of American food and machinery, were made possible by massive infusions of capital and cheap credit. These were provided under the Marshall Plan for Europe and by the Korean war boom for Japan. Japan, in particular, fueled the rebuilding of its industrial sectors with enormous purchases of American equipment.[7]

As time went on, however, the overlying exchange rates had ceased to fit the underlying situation. European economies grew stronger in relation to the United States, while European markets for U.S. machinery shrank. So, sustained U.S. growth in the capital goods sector began increasingly to require large sales elsewhere in the world. However, official credits on the scale required by the recovery in Europe were not to be made available to countries such as Egypt, Mexico, Malaysia or Brazil. Private commercial financing for such countries did not, as yet, exist. And at the prevailing exchange rates, their demand for U.S. exports was too slight.

The value of the dollar was thus too high. Moreover, it grew even higher over the decade as European nations, particularly France and the United Kingdom, were hit by recurring currency crises and devaluation. Measures of overall U.S. trade competitiveness consistently show a deepening decline from the early 1960s on.[8] It was a period when the American tourist was still king in Europe, but that status no longer reflected the previously crushing advantages of the American industrial system. Solutions that would let the dollar fall, such as the substitution of the IMF's Special Drawing Right (the SDR, created in the early 1960s) for the dollar as an internationally created alternative reserve asset, would have implied the vesting of further major powers in the Bretton Woods institutions at the expense of financial powers then enjoyed by the United States. For this reason, such proposals were destined to go nowhere.

Left alone, the prospects were for a slow decline in the U.S. trading position and in the superiority of the American industrial system as the markets where we held our strongest trading advantages failed to develop rapidly enough to provide a large enough market for our advanced products. There would be, as this process continued, increasing penetration of U.S. markets by foreign manufactured goods. This would steadily increase the pressure on U.S. manufacturers to shave costs and keep up standards so as to compete with the Europeans in their own and third markets. Convergence of living standards with Europe and later with Japan would have ensued—a perfectly natural process, and one to which one cannot raise much objection, unless one believes that it embodies large opportunities unnecessarily foregone.

And as the mid-1960s came and went, the share of imports in the U.S. GNP began to rise, as figure 2–1 shows. For a decade and a half, imports had commanded a bare 4.5 percent of total U.S. spending. In 1964 their share began to creep up at a steady one-quarter of 1 percent each year. By 1966, the proportion of imports topped 5 percent. By 1968, it had reached 5.5 percent. By 1970, it was within a tiny fraction of 6 percent.

FIGURE 2–1
Exports and Imports in Real GNP

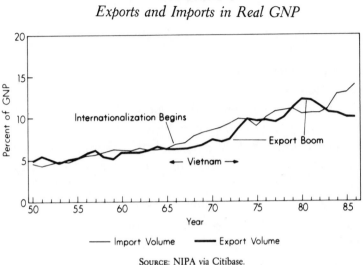

Source: NIPA via Citibase.

The increase over the half-decade was the equivalent, in relation to the GNP of the late 1980s, of around $60 billion 1987 dollars. At the time it was barely perceptible.

Over the same period, exports barely stirred. From a pre-Vietnam level of around 5.9 percent of GNP, exports nudged upward in the years 1965–69 to about 6.1 percent. The reasons for the stasis are clear. The U.S. exchange rate and high economic growth rate were fostering the growth of imports, given the increasing manufacturing capacity in the rest of the world, especially in those areas that already enjoyed a highly competitive exchange rate with the United States. Yet the shift of the most favorable markets for U.S. exports to countries that could neither afford U.S. prices nor gain access to large-scale international credits meant that the world's appetite for U.S. goods could not grow as rapidly as our appetite for theirs. In consequence the constant-dollar U.S. export surplus, a feature of the international scene since World War II, disappeared.

Still, internationalization and the U.S. competitive decline of the 1960s might have occurred in so leisurely, so imperceptible a way as not to have provoked a policy crisis for a long time. The Vietnam War, however, deepened U.S. trade difficulties and pushed the U.S. political economy toward an abrupt and dramatic adjustment.

The War Policy Crisis

By 1967, the rising inflation associated with the Vietnam War had become a severe political problem. How to fight that inflation became a key policy issue. Direct intervention in investment and pricing decisions was one way: mobilization of the production base and a direct freeze on prices. This had been the course taken during World War II and the Korean War. But Lyndon Johnson had steered clear of this method, and in 1969 the newly elected Republican president, Richard Nixon, presiding over an unpopular war, was not about to order the national mobilization that his predecessor had spurned. Moreover, Nixon, who moved in his first days in office to dismantle the Kennedy–Johnson system of wage-price guidelines, had made an ideological commitment to the opposite course: less rather than more direct government intervention in private pricing decisions.

Severe restrictions on demand achieved either by a sharp tax increase or a financial contraction or both would have been, of course, a second option. But in the early stages this would have revealed too sharply the contradiction between the war policy and the peacetime objectives of the Johnson administration. In 1969, President Nixon's shift away from wage-price guidelines implied a presumption of greater reliance on the restraint of demand. But this shift, too, was qualified. President Nixon was not prepared to shoulder immediately the responsibility for a deep recession.

As guidelines weakened in the late 1960s, the United States, in effect, came to rely on a third solution. The dollar, increasingly overvalued, came to aid in the control, however imperfect, of domestic inflation. Nominal foreign exchange parities (20 percent or more higher, on a trade-weighted basis, than at the peak values of the late 1970s) were maintained at a time when the U.S. international competitive position was deteriorating, and so circumstances called for devaluation. The result was to keep imported consumer goods artificially cheap. Substantially for this reason, American wages, though rising in response to the wartime boom, remained comparatively under control. And this was no small accomplishment at a time when, unaided by a similar commitment to discipline, commodity prices and foreign wages were exploding. It was perhaps the first important integration since World War II of international economic forces into the management of a domestic U.S. economic policy problem. It would by no means be the last.

The Age of Contradictions

Because of the high dollar and international cost pressure, U.S. inflation during the Vietnam War was substantially lower than it might otherwise have been given the growth rate and the very low rate of unemployment. This can be seen by comparing the U.S. domestic inflation rate with a price index capturing inflation in imported goods (when the latter's prices are measured in dollars). Figure 2-2 shows the gap between the two indices in the years 1968–69 and 1971, a small yet significant counterpoint to the dramatic import price shocks of the 1970s. The gap at this time indicates a rising real foreign exchange rate and shows that a rising volume of relatively cheap foreign products was keeping competitive pressure on U.S. producers. These conditions would arise again, with much greater force, in the 1980s.

American voters did not see or understand the additional inflation that they did not experience. Understandably, they continued to focus their ire and political discomfort on the rise in U.S. inflation that did in fact occur. But a significant feature of the time was not that inflation rose, but rather that the rise was not substantially greater.

American macroeconomists also, as a rule, did not see the inflation that was not there. There did not, indeed, seem to be any reason to take it into account. For U.S. labor markets in the late 1960s were breaking into new terrain as unemployment rates dropped below the 4 percent full-employment threshold for the first time since the Korean War. The econo-

FIGURE 2–2
Import Inflation and Total Inflation

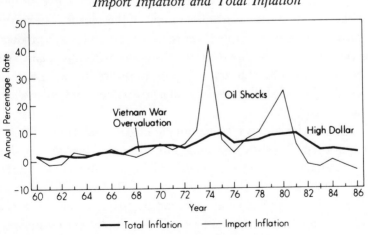

Source: NIPA via Citibase.

metricians, calibrating their Phillips curves, had no clear idea of how much inflation to expect. They merely absorbed what was there, and so charted the slope of the Phillips curve at the new low rates of unemployment.

Theory did not yet suggest making alternative estimates for alternative exchange rate regimes. Had such estimates been made, they would have shown by how much the econometricians were living in a fool's paradise. War-driven inflation was being repressed by rising levels of imports. Without this, the Phillips trade-off would have been worse, with higher inflation at the new low level of unemployment. And econometricians might have been able to sound a warning. They might have foreseen that if the pressure on costs from a high dollar was removed, a much higher unemployment rate would be necessary to restore customary and unproblematic rates of inflation.

That we were at the same time and for the same reason risking the accelerated sacrifice of whole advanced industrial spheres to the reemerging European powers was also not clearly seen. The United States was creating a competitive advantage for foreign suppliers of third markets, who also moved in to take advantage of the favorable conditions for imports that U.S. macroeconomic conditions were creating. And the war demand was working to make U.S. export sectors, already hobbled by the overvalued dollar, even less price competitive with the emerging competition. Over the long run, this situation threatened to erode the U.S. ability to continue to earn Schumpeterian quasi-rents as the world's primary generator of technological gains.

By the end of the 1960s, the U.S. economy was about 30 percent more open to imports than it had been at the middle of the decade. The relative price of those imports was sharply lower than the prices of goods produced in domestic markets. U.S. export prices, distorted by the Vietnam War, were uncompetitive. The U.S. trade surplus, in real terms, was gone. On the domestic scene, unemployment was at a postwar low and inflation was at a postwar high.

Phillips curve calculations relating inflation to unemployment revealed a clear need to cut domestic spending and demand. This would reduce inflation, it seemed, at a tolerable, predictable and reasonably low cost of lost output and somewhat higher unemployment. However, for reasons we will explore later, the Phillips curve was not destined to work in reverse. In a mild recession, unemployment would rise without curing inflation, and a nation accustomed to full employment would balk at the cost long before a climate of price stability had been reestablished.

The Age of Contradictions

Given that the foreign manufacturing capacity was new and efficient, as well as cheap, the rise in the American appetite for imports was now an established fact. To offset it without a recession, there would have to be a return to competitiveness in U.S. export firms and a vast expansion of their markets. But any adjustment that might restore U.S. exports to competitive pricing would have to tolerate a corresponding rise in import prices. This would mean a reduction of the gap between foreign and domestic prices of consumer goods, and, consequently, a sharp decrease in the competitive pressures that had been keeping U.S. domestic inflation down. The choice was, in effect, between an unexpectedly ineffective recession and an inflationary export boom.

The Nixon administration was due to learn first one lesson and then the other.

The Improvisations of Policy

In late 1969, Richard Nixon decided to take the easy way out, the way prescribed by the orthodox conservative opinion of the time. A domestic recession, brought on by the combination of new taxes, spending restraint, and tight money, could bring down inflation and clear the decks for a strong, noninflationary recovery and expansion in 1971 and 1972. Or so it seemed. A new group of conservative Keynesians (exemplified by Herbert Stein, who joined the Council of Economic Advisers in February 1969) had come to power. They were prepared to put the Keynesian tools to work in the service of conservative goals. And they hoped to ride back on the gentle trade-off that the liberal Keynesians had discovered.

The collapse of the Phillips curve quickly dispelled this illusion. From 1968 to 1970, real GNP growth fell by 4.4 percent, about 1.5 times as much as it had in the recession of 1958. Unemployment rose from 3.4 to 4.9 percent and continued rising to an average of 5.9 percent in 1971, the highest rate since 1961. Yet, inflation continued to rise: from 5.4 percent in 1969 to 6.1 percent in 1970, a postwar high (except for the price decontrol year of 1946). This was hardly what the models had predicted.[9]

An election year loomed, and in late 1970 President Nixon was trailing in the polls. The quick-recession strategy of 1970 had proved ineffective and a costly policy failure. It had to be abandoned. It was abandoned: by the beginning of 1971, economic expansion was resuming. But inflation remained, and now something new had to be done.

"Total war on all economic fronts"—so Treasury Secretary John B. Connally proposed to President Nixon in August 1971. Connally's strategy was simple: full recovery in the shortest time, including recovery of exports so that U.S. trade would be balanced at high employment. Spending increases and monetary expansion, dollar devaluation, a freeze on wages and prices and export controls came in a rush—more intervention than had existed under the previous eight years of Democratic rule. Later, in 1973, there came another devaluation and the end of official convertibility between the dollar and gold. The monetary structures of the Bretton Woods Agreement lay in ruins, and the willingness of the United States to exercise leadership in world monetary affairs lay under a cloud of doubt.

But were these actions the harbinger of a decade of decline, as most suppose? Or were they the opening shots in a technological and export war that could have restored—and nearly did—the world preeminence of the United States?

The results of Connally's opening shots were immediate and dramatic. Real U.S. growth accelerated from 2.8 percent in 1971 to 5.0 percent in 1972. Inflation fell to 3.3 percent in 1972, proof of the power of controls. Unemployment stabilized and then started to decline. The share of imports in GNP, which had stabilized near 6 percent in the slow-growth conditions of 1970 and 1971, jumped over 1 percent, to 7.2 percent, in 1972 and 1973. The first true trade-distorting business cycle expansion was underway, and internationalization of the U.S. economy was proceeding at a forced-draft pace.

But at the same time, a worldwide spending boom, touched off in part by rapid growth in the United States, was also underway. And for this, Connally's other measures—devaluation and price controls—were well suited. There resulted, in 1973, the first favorable effects of devaluation on U.S. exports. The share of exports in U.S. GNP rose from 6.7 to 8.4 percent, then a postwar record high, and U.S. trade went strongly into surplus despite full employment. Unfortunately, the worldwide boom was also producing a worldwide explosion of commodity prices and wages, from which the United States would not long remain immune.[10]

Accelerated inflation hit the United States in 1973—from domestic pressures, from the further devaluation of the dollar, and then in October from a quadrupling of the price of oil. By this time, domestic price controls were a spent political force. Impelled by price shocks beginning with wheat and ending with oil, inflation rose to nearly 9 percent between December 1972 and December 1973. Now inflation again threatened political crisis. And the first failure of the Phillips curve in 1970–71 had taught its lesson: a light dose of austerity would not be enough to put matters right. The Connally strategy of boom plus controls was abandoned, and the government got tough. In particular, interest rates were driven sharply higher, and the real money supply was forced to contract.

A new recession followed, which lasted for over a year. Unemployment rose to 9 percent in the spring of 1975, a rate not seen anywhere in the Western world since before World War II.

The external origins of the inflation and recession of the mid-1970s were exaggerated at the time for political effect and have been greatly exaggerated in modern cultural memory. The oil shock was neither so arbitrary an event nor so important in its macroeconomic effects as is commonly believed. All commodity prices and wages had been rising sharply since the late 1960s, and therefore the oil shock was in part a catch-up, though an abrupt one, to established trends. As to its effect on demand, the shock's direct macroeconomic impact was limited to the amount of real purchasing power taxed away from the United States by higher oil prices, or about 1.2 percent of GNP. In relation to the economic damage inflicted a little later on by policy, this was small. The recession of 1974–75 may have been foreshadowed by events in Teheran and Riyadh, but it happened as a result of actions taken on Constitution Avenue and Capitol Hill.

The mid-decade slump was much more profound in its consequences for national perceptions of our economic future than the 1970 recession had been. For all the crisis it provoked in macroeconomic theory, the 1970 recession could have been dismissed by the public as a postwar adjustment, made inevitable by the deceleration of our commitments in Vietnam. For the 1974–75 events no similar excuse could be made. The business cycle had been reestablished in the economic mind. If the 1970 recession shook our faith that the economy could be managed without a recession, the 1974–75 episode made those who continued to articulate such a faith seem archaic and out of touch.

Still, the policy of harsh austerity could not be long sustained. Along with Watergate, it brought political disaster to the Republicans in 1974. In 1975 Congress and the Federal Reserve reversed course to end the recession and bring back growth. Taxes were cut, countercyclical expenditure programs approved and interest rates eased sharply. Shortly afterward, the decade's second business cycle expansion got underway. But not soon enough for the Republicans: in 1976, the aftertaste of recession helped elect Democratic President Jimmy Carter, whose economic philosophy at first was entirely simple: steady growth at all costs.

The Export Boom

The oil shock, with its strong effect on the dollar value of imports in the recession year of 1974 (when the dollar value of imports as a share of GNP rose a full 2 percent while the real volume of imports fell), somewhat obscures the underlying trade picture. Nevertheless it is clear that the growth of oil imports was soon declining, while the volume of manufactured goods demanded by the American public rose sharply. By 1977, total imports were accounting for 9.5 percent of GNP. This rose to 9.9 percent in 1978 and 10.8 percent in 1979, before the data were again strongly affected by the second oil shock.

Three things in this period saved the U.S. economy from a trade crisis. First, a boom in investment and development occurred throughout the world, financed by private commercial bank recycling of petrodollars that could not find nearly so profitable employment in the comparatively depressed economies of the North. Second, the United States made resources available to its advanced sectors by pulling back from its military commitments. Third, the exchange value of the dollar fell, and U.S. exports could compete again with those from Europe.

As a result, U.S. exports surged: from 6.7 percent of GNP in 1972 to 8.4 percent in 1973, then to an average of about 10 percent from 1974 through 1977, and finally up to 11.6 percent in 1979 and 12.8 percent in 1980. In dollar terms, the growth of exports averaged 20.2 percent annually from 1972 through 1980; after adjusting for inflation, export growth was 9.4 percent per year. Thus, for a decade after 1972, dollar exports exceeded dollar imports, and the United States was running a

The Age of Contradictions

current account surplus despite high oil and commodity prices and despite an insatiable appetite for imports of manufactured goods.

Data on manufacturing shipments for U.S. military and nonmilitary uses have been published from 1968 on. They show that with the deceleration of the Indochina conflict, the share of U.S. resources devoted to the production of capital goods for national defense dropped by half: from over 3 percent of GNP in 1968 to less than 1.5 percent of GNP in 1974. Some of these resources were shifted to nondefense use, and nondefense capital goods consequently rose as a share of GNP, toward their recorded peak of 9.9 percent by 1980.

The same phenomenon is revealed by the data on industrial production, where the defense share fell from a wartime peak of 7.4 percent of all industrial production in 1967 to only 4.0 percent by 1973. Meanwhile, the share of business equipment in all industrial production rose, from a low of 12.5 percent in the recession and export doldrums of 1971 to a postwar high of 16.5 percent by 1980.

What Americans perceived as a "supply shock" thus became, in only a short time, an immense, favorable "demand shock" for many advanced U.S. industrial sectors. Internally, the shock first moved resources away from energy-intensive consumption activities. Externally, the shift was toward industries for export.[11]

As European governments also realized, faster adjustment and greater exports would mean faster recovery from the global recession. And so, the Germans and the French scrambled for export contracts in Saudi Arabia, Iran, Korea and Brazil, mainly selling the products of industries that had already been developed for the European markets: capital equipment, heavy engineering, nuclear power plants and armaments. No doubt, some aspects of national policy were helpful in securing large contracts from government buyers. For the Japanese, the adjustment was to a changed U.S. automobile and consumer goods market, something which did not require much prompting from the Japanese government.

The United States did not marshall any of the governmental export effort that the Europeans made haste to develop. U.S. export subsidies, such as through the Exim Bank, remained a minor factor in world trade. And yet, U.S. manufacturing for export went head-to-head with that of European competitors and beat them consistently. What was required was a competitive price, given by the exchange rate, and strong demand, given by the development boom in the Third World. Thus was the technical superiority of advanced U.S. industry up to 1980 conclusively established, and the basis laid for the profound sense of defeat that settled over Europe when their external markets collapsed at the beginning of the 1980s.

For this reason, the Ford–Carter expansion was typified by a dramatic increase in advanced-sector industrial production corresponding to the dramatic boom in high-value U.S. industrial exports. A small number of additional workers—total manufacturing employment grew by only about 1 million from 1969 to 1980—were earning enough on world markets to satisfy the increased demand for imported goods of a much larger number of consumers. There was no competitiveness problem in any meaningful sense; to the contrary, U.S. competitiveness was dramatically reestablished. Nevertheless, at the same time, twin crises were persuading many American economists, and through them much of the public, that the economy was heading toward disaster.

The Productivity "Crisis"

From 1973 on, measured productivity growth—that so-called ultimate determinant of living standards—began a mysterious decline. Productivity had grown at an average rate of 3 percent per year from 1950 through the end of the 1960s. Now productivity growth slowed to an average rate of 1 percent per year and fell toward zero by 1979.

Based on some of the evidence available at the time, it seemed plausible that a decline in gross capital formation was at fault. Measured shares of gross private domestic investment in GNP were falling. Some surmised that the energy shock had rendered obsolete a considerable amount of U.S. industrial capacity, reducing capital available per worker. For others, the fault lay with the diversion of resources to antipollution, health and safety, and other facets of a growing mass of government regulation. Whatever the cause, theorists of a "capital shortage" saw a gloomy future of declining living standards as the United States evolved toward a nebulous but assuredly disagreeable postindustrial age.

There came into being a view that linked together all the visible symptoms of economic instability in a unified vision of decay, which

The Age of Contradictions

came, in turn, to dominate the popular perception of the decade. Inflation could be traced to poor productivity performance; poor productivity performance to declining capital formation; declining capital formation to inadequate savings. And inadequate savings? Well, that was more conjectural. Perhaps families were responding to inflation and consuming ahead of their incomes. Perhaps savers were reacting to the low real rates of return in a general atmosphere of capitalist decline. Perhaps workers were setting aside less for retirement as Social Security made them ever more dependent on the state. Perhaps people were reacting to the decay itself— dancing in the graveyard in the plague year. Nobody knew. But that it was "the worst economic mess since the Depression," in Murray Weidenbaum's 1981 phrase, could, by the time conjecture had been linked to conjecture in a seemingly seamless web, hardly be doubted.

Bit by bit, the underlying factual record has since been corrected, undermining the theory of fundamental decay. There was, it develops, no systematic decline in gross investment shares in the 1970s. A declining share of investment in GNP, which had been reported, was revised out of the data in late 1980.[12] Initial figures had shown the share of investment in GNP falling from 15.7 percent in 1948–72 to 14.8 percent in 1973–77. Revised figures showed a rock-solid share at 16.0 percent in both periods and a rise in the investment share to 17.0 percent in 1978–79. The newly discovered increase was wholly in producers' durable equipment; it reflected among other things a prior undercounting of the output of new firms that had come into existence since the selection of the previous reporting sample. These new firms were, in great measure, producing for export. In fact, the growth of manufacturing investment, whether calculated as a total or per person employed, had actually accelerated in the 1970s.

The most prestigious econometric studies have found no evidence of a fall in capital available per employee in the civilian manufacturing sector.[13] And the best measures of capital scrapped after the energy shock or diverted to satisfy government regulations show that these influences account, at best, for a small fraction of the measured decline in output per person employed.[14] The supposed shortfall of savings has disappeared along with the supposed shortfall of investment. Since external accounts were balanced over the 1970s, it must be true that savings came from some internal source to finance the undiminished share of capital investment in all spending. This is true whether one believes that savings engenders investment or that investment, causing a rise in income, engenders savings. The two must have been equal—and so the savings, willy-nilly, were there.

Nor was the comparative record bad. U.S. manufacturing investment growth from 1972 to 1979 far exceeded that of every major Western industrial power, and Japan as well, as figure 2-3 shows. The great Japanese investment boom, geared to the U.S. market for imports, had come to an end before the 1970s began. And in relation to the United States, Europe never recovered its competitive position.

The net result of this unraveling has been to leave even serious analysis of the supply side—which was to provide policy-relevant solutions to the productivity "crisis"—at a loss. In the words of the most careful scholar, Edward F. Denison, "What happened, to be blunt, is a mystery."[15]

I do not propose to solve the productivity question here, but only to point to two matters that can be traced directly as effects of the trade-distorting business cycles with which the 1970s were afflicted.

Most published research on productivity growth rates relies on multi-year averages, which show that a marked deceleration occurred between 1968 and 1974. Precisely when this occurred remains a matter of dispute. But a look at the annual pattern of productivity growth rates leaves one most impressed with the degree to which *annual* shifts dominate the data, and with the degree to which those annual shifts coincide with the big movements of demand management policy. Pronounced declines in mea-

FIGURE 2–3
Manufacturing Investment

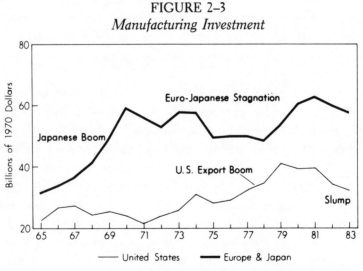

SOURCE: Oxford Institute of Economics and Statistics.

sured productivity growth occurred in 1970, 1974–75, 1980 and 1982. Every one of those episodes coincides with a recession. Outside of those years, annual growth rates of labor productivity are not incommensurate with the rates prevailing from 1951 to 1969. That is, the average is brought down mainly by a few bad years rather than by a multitude of mediocre ones, as figure 2–4 shows.

The slower productivity growth, on average, in the 1970s compared with the 1960s may therefore be largely a consequence of the greater frequency of recession years after 1970 than before. But this raises a question: why would recessions have this effect on productivity growth in the 1970s, but not in the 1950s, when cycles of boom and bust were just as pronounced?[16]

The effects of internationalization point to a possible answer. In the 1950s, recessions were short, abrupt and—most important—quickly reversed in the subsequent expansion. Productivity growth was cyclical, then as later: a fall in output overmatched immediate declines in employment. But in the recovery this was more than offset as output raced ahead, while employment growth lagged. Thus the sharp declines in productivity growth of 1954 and 1958 were followed immediately by years of productivity gain, in 1955 and 1959, more than twice the preceding average. This meant that cycles were washed out in multiyear data, and a greater or lesser frequency of recessions would have had no effect on average productivity growth rates in the 1950s.

The recessions of the 1970s were not deeper than those of the 1950s,

FIGURE 2–4
Productivity Growth Rates

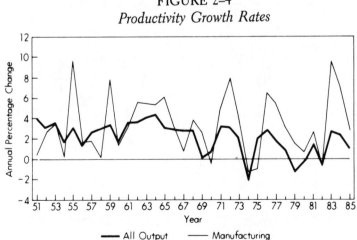

SOURCES: Citibase and *Economic Report of the President.*

but they were followed by a slower rebound of output growth. Thus, growth in industrial production reached only 10 percent in 1972 and 9 percent in 1976, compared with 13 percent in 1955 and 12 percent in 1959.

At the same time, employment growth rates, both inside and outside of the manufacturing sector, were comparable across recessions and recoveries in both periods. Thus, declines in total employment on the order of 1 to 1.8 percent (1954, 1958, 1975) were followed by years of employment growth in the range of 3 to 3.5 percent. A major difference was that expansions of employment in the 1970s lasted for a longer time. Employment grew, in particular, for six consecutive years from the 1975 trough until recession struck again in 1980.

The output/employment patterns of the 1950s, therefore, produced years of very high measured productivity growth in manufacturing and in the industrial sector generally—1955, 1959—that have no counterpart in the 1970s. Moreover, in the 1950s, the end-of-expansion productivity doldrums, when output was rising slowly while employment continued to rise unabated, were relatively short. By contrast, at the end of the 1970s, the end-of-expansion productivity doldrums continued for three full years. These two patterns appear to account for a significant part of the difference in the average rate of productivity growth between the two periods.

Plausible reasons now emerge. In the 1950s, output growth recovered

FIGURE 2–5
Components of Productivity Growth

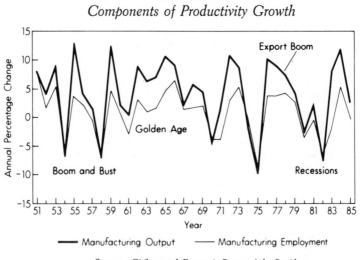

SOURCES: Citibase and *Economic Report of the President.*

sharply after each recession because recessions did not entail major structural dislocations of industry. The factories that went down in the slump came up in the boom, and technological change within them proceeded much as before. Demand generated by the recovery of spending was directed exactly where it had gone before the slump. This is the exact counterpart of the fact that the share of imports in total spending was completely unaffected by the phase of the business cycle.

In the 1970s, in sharp contrast, the demand that was revived by the recovery did not return idle consumer goods factories to work. Instead, it was directed significantly to imports. Since imports are a drain on GNP, the total early growth of GNP was slower in the recoveries of the 1970s, and the rebound of productivity growth was far less complete. Yet employment recovered with the recovery of spending power, just as before. The newly employed found themselves in service industries, where they obtained command over purchasing power sufficient to restore their living standards, but in occupations that did not entail capital formation sufficient to raise the real value of measured output at its former rates. The productivity slowdown was thus partly the work of internationalization, which had changed the structure of industry and the composition of employment in ways that traditional macroeconomic models were not equipped to see.

As the expansion of the 1970s proceeded, the other half of the trade-related distortion came into play. Export sectors producing, in the main, business equipment, began to grow with great speed, absorbing resources from the military and elsewhere. The growth of these sectors should have increased the measured rate of output growth, restoring measured productivity growth. But it did not do so as much as it could have. And this is because the national income accounts are constructed in a way that overstates the amount of true inflation occurring in these sectors and correspondingly understates the rate of output growth they enjoy.

The creation of new products is one of the great problems in the construction of index numbers, such as measures of aggregate output or average price change. To provide accounting continuity in the construction of such index numbers, the quantity of output of new or radically changed products is not measured directly. Instead, quantity changes are deduced from the quantity of the factor inputs that produce them. New products are then linked to the index and assigned shares in total output that reflect the resources they absorb. This can, and commonly does, result in temporary anomalies. For example, if a microchip-based wrist-watch is linked to the index as a new product and then drives out the spring-driven variety, which costs ten times as much, the index may show a drop in quantity of 90 percent.[17]

Price changes are equally hard to capture under these conditions. Often, as in our wristwatch example, a new product will enter the market at a price that reflects its resource costs. When this happens, the price index does not change at all, even though the "price of wrist-based timekeeping" has fallen tenfold. Moreover, technical change does not stop at that point. In later years, new features and design elements are added almost continually as a stopwatch, a calendar, an alarm, and so on are added to the chip. Yet, by common practice, the price of the product does not change significantly. In effect, the real price is falling as capabilities are being added, and in some sense the "quantity of timekeeping" is being increased. It is impossible for national income accountants to keep track of all of this development for thousands of science-based products, particularly in the industrial sphere.

In the late 1970s, the dollar volume of advanced-technology exports was rising sharply. Dollar exports just about doubled, from $178 to $351 billion, from 1976 to 1980. But when one brought down this increase by the official export price deflator, one found that the measured output of the export sectors rose only 42 percent. The official deflator for exports shows an inflation rate in this sector about as great as that of the economy as a whole. But it is extremely unlikely that this was really the case. For in that event, would an export boom have occurred? It seems hardly plausible that capital goods sales would have surged as much as they did unless buyers perceived quality improvements—increases in an effective but unmeasured quantity of output—that more than offset the rising prices they were being asked to pay.

In December 1985, the Bureau of Economic Analysis of the Department of Commerce published for the first time a special price index for computers.[18] Working from data supplied from IBM, the bureau calculated that the price of computers had fallen about six-fold from 1969 to 1974 and about nine-fold through 1984.[19] When this finding was substituted for the previous assumption that computer prices had been stable, a large, hitherto unmeasured increase in the "real output" of computers emerged in the data. By 1984, the newly measured real quantity was estimated at *$102.4 billion* 1972 dollars above the previous estimate, enough so that real growth in the computer sector would have made a sizable difference to *aggregate* productivity growth in the late 1970s had it been measured at the time.[20]

Similar though less dramatic considerations apply to a range of capital goods, indeed to all products that are in an accelerated phase of product change and declining prices due to technological advance. In a 1985 estimate by Fred Block, if the unreported price declines for 1973–1979 in just two sectors, communications equipment and instruments, were only as large as 5 percent per year, GNP in 1979 would have been $15 billion higher than reported. Taking various industrial estimates together, Block concedes, "the numbers are so large that there can be no question of their impact on levels of aggregate output."[21]

If so, then distortions in the patterns of trade deprived the economy of growth in the consumer goods sector of manufacturing, where measured productivity growth (but not technical change itself) has always been strongest. Employment grew instead in the service sector, to which displaced consumer goods workers and their families increasingly repaired. This was one element in the measured decline of labor productivity growth. The other element has to do, as we have seen, with the difficulties of measuring output in sectors producing advanced, rapidly changing capital goods where measurement anomalies understated the growth of real output. A shift from established consumer goods sectors to advanced-technology capital goods may, ironically, have the effect of lowering the measured rate of output growth, and hence of average productivity growth relative to what it would otherwise be.

The Inflation Crisis

Inflation was the second crisis of the expansion of the late 1970s, generating a corresponding intense pressure for policy change. As in the mid-decade, this crisis would lead to a consensus for recession among virtually all professional economists and, most powerfully, among spokesmen for financial orthodoxy. As in the mid-decade, the policy change would be spearheaded by a massive shift to tight money and high interest rates by the Federal Reserve. As before, this would cause within months an unprecedented increase in unemployment. And as before, there would be assurances that the pain had a purpose: after inflation had been beaten, conditions not otherwise present for the restoration of stable, noninflationary growth would return.

The inflation crisis began in early 1978, when, after three years of noninflationary economic expansion, the price indices began to jump up. Inflation leaped from under 7 percent to 9 percent that year, and then was kicked powerfully up again, to 13 percent, by the doubling of oil prices in 1979. Consumer price increases then continued in double digits in 1980 as workers tried to offset the prior fall in their cost of living. By that time, financial orthodoxy in the form of Paul Volcker had taken over at the Federal Reserve, and an already defeated administration (for practical purposes) was prepared to give him free rein. On October 6, 1979, Volcker announced changes in the procedures of monetary policy that gave a clear signal of his intent: to use tight money and high interest rates to bring inflation to an end.

An important difference between the episodes of 1974–75 and 1979–81 lies in the evolution of economic theory between the two. By 1979, the *theoretical* mechanism whereby recession and unemployment would create conditions for a sustained resumption of noninflationary growth afterward was much more clearly specified than it had been before. This had to do with the effect of rising unemployment on *expectations of inflation.* If economic agents—workers setting wage demands, resource suppliers setting the supply schedule for commodities, and lenders of capital setting interest rates—came to believe that a change of policy promised a permanently lower rate of money growth and therefore of inflation, then, it was said, they would adjust their behavior accordingly. Specifically, they would stop demanding compensation in present agreements for inflation that was expected to occur in the future. And this, in turn, would permit a resumption of steady real economic growth without inflation, a growth that could now continue indefinitely so long as expectations of price stability were not disturbed. Following this line of argument, Harvard's Martin Feldstein, who later became chairman of the Council of Economic Advisers under Reagan, could argue that recession itself was worthwhile: the loss of output was only temporary, but the gain in price stability, once the new policy was understood, would be permanent.

In practice, exactly the opposite was true. Recession would indeed, if sufficiently severe, provide a check to inflation. But this would prove, by the very nature of the economic process, to be only temporary (unless it was prolonged, as in the 1980s, by unbalanced trade). Meanwhile the loss of output and the structural change brought on by recession would be permanent and, in some measure, irreversible.

In fact, and for good reason, Volcker's early efforts to whip inflation with strong words and weak action failed: the short recession of 1980 had no such effect. It took, instead, a record setter from early 1981 through the end of 1982 to deliver the desired (even if, in the end, temporary) knockout punch. It is worth examining in detail why this was so and how inflation was eventually reduced.

The Phillips curve had accustomed economists to consider inflation in relation to unemployment. And using a conventional model, in which prices rise at the rate by which wages exceed measured productivity growth, one can indeed theorize that there is a relationship between the rate of unemployment and the rate of wage increases. This relationship is based on *threat:* workers are thought to demand higher wage increases when they do not fear unemployment. And they fear unemployment when there is a long line of workers at the gate. So long (and this is the crucial point) as the unemployment rate in society at large measures reasonably well the probability that any particular worker may become unemployed, the Phillips curve relation may "work" in the sense that the unemployment rate may serve as a good predictor of changes in the rate of wage increases and of price inflation.

In the open economy of the 1970s, however, the key assumption that unemployed workers could be considered good substitutes for those already holding jobs, and particularly for those holding jobs in the wage-leading manufacturing sectors, was no longer valid. In 1970, the unemployment rate had doubled—but not from *net* job losses. Instead, the mild recession, while costing few manufacturing jobs, had unleashed a flood of new workers into the labor force. Many of them were secondary income earners in their families who suddenly realized that a second income might be useful auxiliary income insurance. These people did not compete with manufacturing sector workers for manufacturing jobs. They were, by and large, housewives and school leavers, without the skills and experience of the seasoned factory employee, and often still subject to discrimination in finding such employment. They sought, and in most cases eventually found, jobs in the service sector. They did, in the interim, increase the measured unemployment rate. But they did not deter manufacturing sector workers from demanding higher wages. And this experience of the 1970 recession was largely recapitulated, for the same reason, a decade later. The 1980 recession raised unemployment, but without greatly endangering existing jobs or bringing relief from inflation.

A better measure of the threat that employed workers feel to their own jobs, and hence of the power of a recession to bring down wage increases and the rate of inflation, is the change in the total volume of existing employment. Only if a recession is deep enough to reduce employment is job loss an imminent threat to most employed workers. Only then, arguably, will wage demands in the wage-leading manufacturing sectors slack off, and with them, price inflation. And this is what the record shows. In the light, short recessions of 1970 and 1980, total employment did not fall, and neither did the rate of inflation. It took the deeper and longer recessions of 1974–75 and 1981–82, when manufacturing employment fell sharply, to change the behavior of workers and so to "whip inflation."

One might ask, however, why it is that even in a deep, job-threatening recession rational workers make pay concessions. It is not obvious that they should do so. After all, all recessions end, and when they do, demand and employment return. Workers who refuse to make concessions might endure a longer spell of unemployment, but they will be better off in the long run than those who cave in. Why not accept a temporary layoff without compromising one's wages and benefits?

The answer is that in an economy open to international trade, which by 1980 the United States was, the deep recession threatens much more than a temporary plant closing. The threat is of a *permanent* loss: of the factory itself, its jobs, and its surrounding community. Workers offer pay concessions not simply to avert a temporary layoff but to save their entire way of life. For if the factory closes, it will not return in its old location and with its former employees. Korea, not Zanesville, is the likely new place of business.

One can in fact name at least five ways, all distinctly different from the conventional argument about expectations, in which a deep recession reduces manufacturing costs, and so prices and inflation. First, there is the obvious effect of wage concessions themselves, passed on to prices through markup pricing rules. Second, there is a corresponding effect of slack demand and unexpected inventory accumulation on commodity prices. Third, there is the fact that recessions are managed by manufacturing firms so as to *rationalize* capacity: the oldest, least efficient, highest-unit-cost facilities are invariably scrapped first, so as to concentrate resources on preserving newer and better plants. This reduces the price required to earn profits on the last equipment kept in use. Fourth, in the recovery the old plants are not reopened. Instead, the gaps in capacity as demand returns are filled with newer, more efficient, and, above all, cheaper technologies: the Korean plant provides the best practice, whereas the Zanesville one did not. Fifth and finally, there is the fact the mechanisms of recession itself, especially high interest rates, tend to attract foreign capital and raise the foreign exchange value of the dollar. This depresses import prices and enhances the attractiveness of building new plants overseas rather than at home, thus expanding the employment of inexpensive foreign labor.

The striking and inescapable fact is that *none* of these influences can survive the revival of demand from the recession itself (so long as the recovery is conducted with free collective bargaining and in a balanced way). Once scrapping ceases and employment stops falling, the pressure on workers for new wage concessions is off. With new demand, commodity prices recover. Further, as soon as the transition to new plants and technologies is complete, wage pressures can emerge among these new, and disproportionately profitable, centers of production. Finally, if internationalization has occurred in the recession, balanced recovery demands the growth of exports. And so, the temporarily overvalued exchange rate cannot be sustained.

A further effect occurs a little later on in trade between an LTP and an IMP. For as manufacturing in the IMP for the LTP market (as well as its own) expands, so must the IMP's demand for goods in which the LTP retains a comparative advantage. These, we have seen, are the advanced capital goods. But, as we know, advanced capital goods are produced by relatively few, extremely well-paid workers. And as their share in total employment grows, so do pressures on wages in the LTP. It pays to hire the best in the capital goods lottery, since the returns for winning are astronomical, while the rewards for finishing second are nil. But the auto workers, relying on past patterns of relative wage determination, will want what the airplane mechanics are getting. Thus, asymmetric trade distorts previous wage and income patterns in the advanced country in ways that further exacerbate inflation.

In short, even if both inflation and inflationary expectations are whipped in the slump, the mechanics of balanced recovery in the open economy will bring them back. In the absence of a strong incomes policy from 1973 on, this is what happened. The recession of 1974–75 worked powerfully to bring the inflation of the first oil crisis to an end. But it failed completely to establish the promised climate of sustained, noninflationary growth, even though a slow-recovery macroeconomic policy was pursued with precisely the objective of making sustained, noninflationary expansion possible. The requirements of balanced trade in the asymmetric expansion of the late 1970s—a falling dollar, rising import prices, and rising wages in the growing advanced sectors—precluded price stabilization over the cycle.

Thus, in the 1970s there was no systemwide crisis on the supply side. Rather, there were, above all, vast and difficult-to-reverse changes in the international conditions of domestic demand management. These altered the investment behavior of businesses selling into the U.S. market and the productivity performance of the economy as a whole, but without compromising, through 1980, the technological and competitive resources, and the capability for flexible adjustment, that had made the United States a superior performer on the world stage in the first place. In the external market, where demand conditions remained strong from 1973 to 1980, neither did any crisis of production occur.

Yet the political consequences of the misunderstanding were far-reaching. "Malaise"—the effort to blame the public generally for the perception of poor performance—served the purposes of a president who sought to depict his troubles as beyond the reach of his own power. As things happened, it also served the purposes of that president's eventual opponent. Ronald Reagan set himself up as a miracle worker; it is obvious that, to a miracle worker, an exaggerated picture of the miracle to be worked is an asset.

And the economics profession, ideologically divided and trapped in the intellectual cul-de-sac of expectations models, provided no effective barrier to the spread of alarmism by the politicians and the press. Thus was the new administration freed to apply its own more effective but far more costly solution to the productivity crisis and the inflation dilemma. This would be recession followed by unbalanced recovery, imports without exports, growing international debt, and the wholesale sacrifice of those troublesome advanced export sectors that seemed to be the source of so many awkward problems.

CHAPTER 3

What Reagan Did

—

I T IS AN irony of recent history that in the election campaign of 1980, the high inflation of the previous year and a half played almost no role. Ronald Reagan's candidacy advanced on a program whose economic centerpiece was large phased tax cuts, together with large increases in military procurement. It had no spending cut and no monetary component. Such a program had nothing credible whatever to say about inflation. Candidate Reagan did not go beyond Paul Volcker's gradualist monetarism, in force since October 1979 with no demonstrable effect as of the fall of 1980. Perhaps Reagan believed, not unreasonably, and not unlike the Carter administration he sought to oust, that with enough time inflation would diminish on its own as the oil shock of 1979 worked its way through the system.

Only *after* the election did circumstances force a change of focus. These circumstances are not difficult to discern. Inflation, against all predictions, spiked in the last quarter of 1980 and into early 1981 (figure 3–1). Interest rates surged, reaching 20 percent in December 1980 for the first time in postwar history. These developments were wholly unexpected. They seem to have shocked the incoming administration (and certainly made an impression on their rhetoric in the presidential campaign four years later). And, as in the inflation crises of 1974 and 1978–80,

FIGURE 3–1
Inflation and the Prime Rate

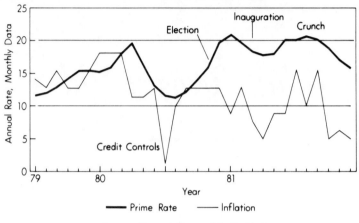

SOURCE: *Economic Report of the President.*

a collapse of policy imagination followed. There was, it seemed, only one thing to do.

The Crunch

This was a crisis. It was immediately obvious that Congress would enact no tax cut nearly as large as the one the new administration sought so long as inflation remained a crisis. Without the tax cut, the new administration would have no economic program at all. Credibility, even political survival, were at stake. And so, to the vindication of the monetarists and conservative Keynesians and to the provisional grief of the supply-siders, the tough job of fighting inflation came to the fore.

The first departure from the plan—as announced in the campaign and reaffirmed later in the administration's famous white paper, "A Program for Economic Recovery" (published on February 18, 1981)—was a tactical retreat on tax strategy. The personal income tax plan of Congressman Jack Kemp and Senator William Roth, adopted by Reagan late in the summer of 1980, had called for the first of three 10 percent reductions in marginal income tax rates to take effect on January 1, 1981. This was changed within weeks after the inauguration to a 5 percent reduction for mid-1981, ultimately made effective on October 1, 1981, to be followed by the first 10 percent reduction only on July 1, 1982. Later in the summer, new business tax cuts were added to the tax cut bill in the famous "bidding war" with the Democratic leadership in Congress over who would control the final legislation. But, with notable exceptions like "safe harbor leasing" and unlimited Individual Retirement Accounts, these tax cuts promised their largest revenue losses in 1982 or later. The net effect of the tax-drafting debacle was to reduce the effective tax cuts in 1981 and early 1982 to small, indeed nearly negligible, proportions.[1]

Much more important immediately, monetary policy also became much tighter. The president's original monetary program implied a track of gradual deceleration of money growth, and a similar strategy had been spelled out in the annual targets for money presented by the Federal Reserve to Congress in early 1981.[2] Because of the higher than expected inflation (and thus of income growth, measured in dollars), the stock of money in the first months of 1981 had begun to surge far above this track. The overage was particularly grave in the case of M1, the most narrowly defined and best-known measure of the money stock.[3] This development threatened the monetary pillar of the Reagan program and the credibility of its (up to that point, purely rhetorical) anti-inflation commitment. The administration seems to have decided by March 1981—not sooner—that it could not afford to be soft on inflation or on the Federal Reserve.

Action came in April, following intense pressure from the administration, and particularly from the Treasury Department, on the Federal Reserve.[4] It took the form of a determined effort to stop the growth of the money stock. This effort was immediately successful. Monthly money growth dropped to zero and the prime interest rate rose, for the second time, to over 20 percent. This time, the money growth rate stayed down, and interest rates remained at those levels—German Chancellor Helmut Schmidt called them "the highest since Jesus Christ"—for six months. By the time the Federal Reserve let up, in September 1981 (and then only a little), the recession of 1981–82 was well underway.

For reasons that did not become clear until later, fiscal policy was substantially *more* restrictive at this early stage than either policymakers or the public understood. High inflation itself was adding an unmeasured drag to the economy. The reason is that inflation acts like a tax, taking away real value from the stock of government notes, bills and bonds held by the public, and therefore depressing the public's real spending power.

This point, which was not pressed with vigor until the publication of the work of Robert Eisner in 1984 and 1986,[5] had not yet been understood by policymakers or the press. Yet the inflation tax was the most important single factor affecting the true fiscal policy posture from 1979 to 1981. Fiscal policy had grown tight and the budget had gone into surplus, in real or after-inflation terms, by the end of 1976. In 1979 and 1980, the real surplus in the federal budget was running between 1 and 2 percent of GNP. And when inflation surged in late 1980 and early 1981, so did the hidden collections of the inflation tax. Figure 3–2 shows how the official deficit would have looked had it been adjusted to correct for inflation.

The 1981–82 recession was, in fact, largely unpredicted. (Murray Weidenbaum's Council of Economic Advisers made a private prediction in the early spring of 1981 that there would be a recession in the second and third quarters of the year. This prediction—correct on sign, way off on magnitude and duration, was kept secret until mid-1982.[6]) Still, with hindsight, one can explain the recession well and in terms that do not depend on mysterious "inevitable forces" (other than the inflation tax) left over from the Carter administration.

To begin, the recession of 1980 had been too short and too weak to break the rising inflation of that year. In this respect, 1980 recapitulated 1970: a weak recession after a long expansion failed to halt the growth of employment, and so failed to produce the requisite scrapping or to make

FIGURE 3–2
Official and Real Federal Deficits

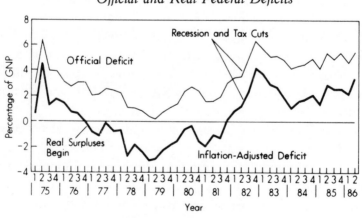

SOURCES: NIPA and author's calculations.

56

a sufficient impression on the psychology of the workforce. Unemployment jumped sharply, but as in 1970, the cause was new entry into the labor market, not job loss. With no check to inflation, the 1980 recession did not relieve either the effects of bracket creep on nominal tax collections or the larger and more important hidden collections of the inflation tax on the stock of government debt. Thus it failed in several distinct ways to clear the air for a recovery.

Second, the change in tax strategy in early 1981 deprived the economy of demand stimulus for a critical year. Third, and most important, the attempt to force the money stock back down, building on but going far beyond the October 1979 tightening, created an environment of exceptionally tight credit conditions. These factors interacted to produce a sharp drop in business confidence and a fall in investment—the usual opening bars of the recessionary chorus. But then there were secondary effects: a rise in the dollar, a fall in world commodity prices and the beginnings of depression and debt crisis in the most rapidly growing U.S. export markets. All of these can be traced to the sharp rise in real U.S. interest rates, given the increasing integration of U.S. and world financial markets and the rising role in world development of private debts denominated in dollars that had been going on since 1973. They led to a fall in export production and investment in export industries, which deepened and prolonged the recession far beyond what purely domestic influences would have done.

The recession served the purposes for which it was intended. Total employment dropped by nearly a million, delivering a sharp check to real incomes and the aspirations of labor. Export trades where wages had been rising most strongly were strongly affected, as were import-competing consumer goods manufacturers, who scrapped with abandon. The check to wages then amplified the drop in inflation which would have occurred anyway as the price shocks of the late 1970s worked their way through the system. As the dollar rose and commodity prices started to collapse, imported goods of all kinds suddenly became cheap. Inflation fell below 4 percent and disappeared, for practical and policy purposes, by 1982.

Full Throttle Forward

By the summer of 1982, the anti-inflation campaign was clearly successful ad interim, but its costs were growing by leaps and bounds. There were fears, shared at the Federal Reserve that summer, of an accelerating collapse of production and employment in the United States.[7] Congress was nearing the end of its toleration of high interest rates. And the world debt crisis was on the verge of breaking out into the open.

For all of these reasons, policy in mid-1982 moved radically in the other direction. First, the scheduled personal income tax cuts of the Economic Recovery Tax Act (ERTA) took effect. Second, total spending rose. Third, monetary policy eased.

The full-employment budget deficit increased by about 2.4 percent of GNP from the second to the fourth quarter of 1982. This was the largest two-quarter shift and the largest in value since before 1970, with the exception of the one-quarter shift from the first to the second quarter of 1975. The actual budget deficit nearly doubled, from 3.6 to 6.8 percent of GNP, comparable to 6.5 percent of GNP in the second quarter of 1975. At the same time, inflation fell. Thus inflation-induced depreciation on the debt fell from about 1.5 percent of GNP in 1980–81 to a mere 0.4 percent of GNP by the fourth quarter of 1982. The full-employment deficit adjusted for inflation rose from −0.9 percent of GNP (a surplus) in the second quarter of 1982 to 1.9 percent of (full employment) GNP by the fourth quarter.

At the same time, the Federal Reserve abandoned its efforts to keep money growth down.

Economic theory teaches that the influence of monetary policy on economic activity acts through two distinct channels, both of which must be measured in real terms, net of the effects of inflation. First, an expansion of money affects real wealth, represented by holdings of money in relation to the level of prices. If the real money stock grows, so will real wealth and consequently real spending.[8] Second, an expansion of money increases liquidity, drives down the real rate of interest and encourages an increase in physical investment.

Now, when the Federal Reserve abandoned monetarism in July 1982, it did so with real vigor, as figure 3–3 shows. Over the following year, the real value of the narrow money stock (M1) rose by 7 percent, more than in any year since 1960. The real value of M2, a more broadly defined and

FIGURE 3–3
Growth of Real Money

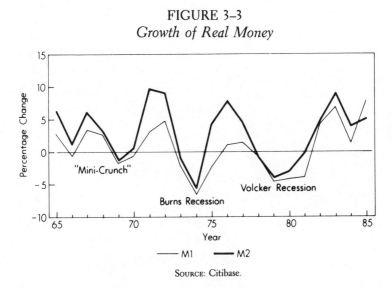

Source: Citibase.

probably more reliable concept, rose by 8.9 percent, a performance matched only in 1971 and 1972.[9] This was enough to raise the real size of the money stock, which had been falling since 1978, to its level of that year.[10]

Nominal interest rates, long and short, began to drop, as Keynesians would have predicted and as monetarists, who had argued that inflationary expectations would drive rates up as soon as monetary policy eased, had denied. However, we now come to a curious event. *Real short-term interest rates,* measured by subtracting the contemporaneous rate of inflation from the rate of interest on a short-term instrument like the 90-day Treasury bill, did not drop at all. The real short-term rate on Treasury bills remained just where Paul Volcker had put it in 1981, at about 5 percent— a factor we shall reconsider when examining the continued rise of the exchange value of the dollar. But how, then, could investment have been stimulated, as it undoubtedly was?

The answer is probably that *long-run* inflationary expectations proved more inertial than inflation itself. Investors were willing to accept the fact that inflation had been checked, but not to believe that it had been defeated. Thus the pertinent measure of the real interest rate over a normal investment period—the long-run real interest rate—from early 1983 on must take into account an *expected rate of inflation* that was higher than actual inflation happened to be. Since undiminished long-run expected inflation was meeting a falling nominal long-term interest rate,

FIGURE 3-4
Long-Term and Short-Term Interest Rates

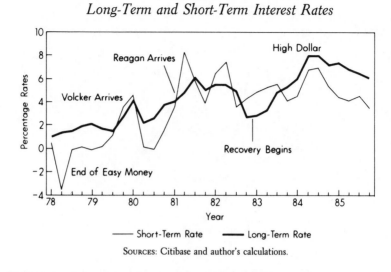

SOURCES: Citibase and author's calculations.

a fall in real long-term interest rates occurred even though none was evident in real short-term rates. Improvements in construction and auto-mobile sales quickly reflected this change in perceived medium to long-run conditions. Figure 3-4 provides some real interest rate estimates, based on a projection that might have been made by typical economic agents in the summer of 1982.

Did these swings "cause" the recovery? Once again, it makes a persua-

FIGURE 3-5
Investment, Savings and Profits

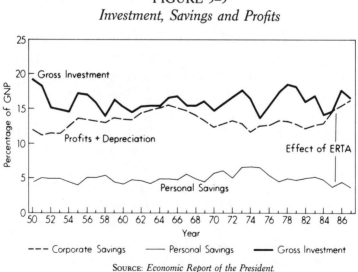

SOURCE: *Economic Report of the President.*

sive story. In any event, if one accepts the belief that policy had a role in the events of early 1981, one is compelled to agree that a countervailing policy had a countervailing effect about fifteen months later. And this demand-side explanation is far more plausible than efforts to attribute the recovery to the original Reagan recovery plan. The "Program for Economic Recovery" had called for a surge of savings to drive investment (and of work effort to drive production). Elementary examination of the data (figure 3-5) reveals that no such surge occurred.

Effects on Trade

The combination of fiscal stimulus, growth of the real money stock and the peculiar structure of real interest rate changes in 1982 and early 1983 began to give the Reagan recovery its characteristic effect on the structure of U.S. industry and the U.S. position in world trade. The first two influences raised real domestic purchasing power, pure and simple. This restored real demand for consumer goods, just as the recession had gone far to reduce domestic capacity to produce them. Consumers turned to foreign suppliers, and imports made cheap by the rising dollar again surged. Measured in 1982 prices, the share of imports in GNP rose over six-tenths of 1 percent in 1983 alone. It then jumped a full 1.76 percentage points in 1984, the largest such one-year increase on record.

The high dollar and world depression also deeply damaged, in short order, the competitiveness of U.S. export industry. Whether measured in volume terms or by value, the share of exports in GNP began the steepest fall since the end of World War II: from 12.8 percent in 1980, the dollar value of exports in GNP fell to 10.4 percent by 1983. This decline continued through 1986, with recovery beginning only as the dollar fell in 1987.

Thus the Reagan recovery was marked by a deepening depression of exports and a vast flow of imported consumer manufactured goods. One might ask whether there was any recovery of domestic production, and if so, what accounts for it. The answer is that, of course, there was. It came, above all, in the large third sector, the sector that neither exports nor competes directly with imported goods.

There was a vast expansion in building, evidenced in every city by new office towers and upscale suburban residential tracts. Total construction activity rose by 29 percent from 1982 to 1985 in dollar terms, while new housing starts jumped over 60 percent, from under 1.1 to over 1.7 million, in the single year from 1982 to 1983. There was a vast expansion of service-producing employment too. For every new job in manufacturing created in the Reagan expansion, eleven new service jobs emerged. Manufacturing employment by 1986 was some 700,000 higher than in the trough year of 1982, but still below what it had been in 1980. Service employment had risen by nearly 10 million. Indeed, the rise in service-producing employment from 1982 to 1986, from about 65 to about 75 million, equals more than half of all manufacturing employment in existence in 1986.

Finally, the change in the composition of government spending must be noted. Here, expenditures supporting sectors that do not participate directly in foreign trade declined as the administration cut sharply into public capital investment. However, the effect of this on the aggregate performance of the economy in the short run was slight. The deficit/exchange rate mix was creating private sector jobs of precisely the same general sort—construction trades and services—as the government was abandoning.

On the other hand, government spending increased sharply on purchases of advanced equipment, mainly weapons. Military purchases rose 56 percent in real terms from 1981 to 1986. Government spending thus helped to sustain employment in those sectors where, with the export collapse, employment would otherwise have fallen even more than it did. Bright graduates in advanced engineering continued to find jobs—but now on the Strategic Defense Initiative rather than in advanced civilian aerospace or computer design. Manufacturing shipments in the defense sector rose by 0.5 percent of GNP from 1981 to 1985, and so partly offset a fall of 1.8 percent of GNP in nondefense shipments, much of which would have been destined for export.

What Reagan Did

The Third Phase

In the second quarter of 1983, real GNP passed its previous peak, and afterward the Reagan economic policy may be said to have entered its third phase. The features of this phase included high but stable deficits, continued economic growth at rates between 4 and 5 percent, high but stable real interest rates (by the standards of the 1970s), a very high dollar and a stable or declining rate of inflation.

The third phase differed from the second in two important ways. First, there arose an immense preoccupation with the budget deficit, which was running, in nominal terms, at between 4.5 and 5.0 percent of GNP or, in full-employment terms, at between 2.0 and 3.0 percent of full-employment GNP, depending on which concept of full-employment GNP one uses and whether measured in nominal or real terms. The concern that the deficit evoked reflected two departures from historical practice: (1) it was not declining as the economy continued to expand and (2) it was actually expected to rise under existing law in future years even if economic growth remained strong. In consequence, the nominal value of the national debt was rising at an annual rate of 15 to 20 percent. These departures meant that budget plans to at least stabilize the deficit through the end of the decade came to dominate the legislative agenda, culminating in the enactment of the Gramm–Rudman–Hollings legislation in late 1985.

The third phase also brought with it the return of the Federal Reserve, after the brief and exhilarating liberation of July 1982 through April 1983, to its usual and now highly untimely preoccupation with fighting inflation. This led to a stabilization of short-term real interest rates at very high levels and the consequent reinforcement of the high value of the dollar.

The most distinguishing features of the third phase were the failure of inflation to accelerate, despite falling unemployment rates, strong growth of demand and the Reagan administration's abolition of the formal incomes policy structures, such as the Council on Wage and Price Stability, which had limped along in the later years of the Carter administration. There are two possible explanations for this. The first follows the orthodox line: as inflationary expectations were said to have kept inflation up, so their collapse in consequence of an implacable policy could account for a new low-inflation equilibrium. The second and more plausible hypothesis is that the continuing and enormous press of imports intervened to maintain strong downward pressures on U.S. costs and prices.

If an explanation based on falling inflationary expectations were true, the same theory would predict that (nominal) interest rates, long and short, would also have fallen far more quickly than they did. Once inflationary expectations were down, high nominal interest rates would not have been necessary. Yet the monetary authorities seemed to think that they were necessary. Overnight, thirty- and sixty-day real interest rates were kept extremely high. And yet, as we have seen, over the longer three- to five-year term, real interest rates must have fallen; otherwise, investment and the sales of homes and automobiles would not have revived. The only thing that can plausibly reconcile these phenomena is the persistence of substantial long-run inflationary expectations despite the decline in the actual rate of inflation.

The Federal Reserve's continued support of high short-term *real* interest rates and of high long-term *nominal* interest rates therefore betrayed an insecurity in conflict with the official posture, and indeed with the whole announced strategy of conquering inflation. Evidently, the economists who had laid such stress on changing long-term price expectations had failed to persuade those actually in charge of policy, and perhaps themselves as well, that inflationary expectations had actually fallen.

The Dollar as Incomes Policy

So, with inflationary expectations unvanquished, why did inflation stay low? One answer is that the Reagan administration did not abolish incomes policies after all. They continued to exist, but now they took the destructive form of supporting the high dollar exchange rate.

Standard econometric studies are constructed in a way that does not lead directly to this conclusion. Instead, such studies tend to show that the decline in price inflation from 1980 to 1985 can be explained without direct reference to low import prices generally. Far more important is the fact that wages lagged far behind measured productivity growth after 1981; after wages, only the falling price of oil (measured in dollars, and therefore not directly an exchange rate matter) is needed to complete the statistical picture. When these two factors are taken into account in a statistical analysis, the exchange rate does not emerge as an independent determinant of prices.[11]

This is, however, not decisive. For what explains labor's continuing, extraordinary, unprecedented wage restraint? Measured labor productivity growth from 1981 to 1985 came to 4 percent per year. Yet average weekly earnings, after adjustment for inflation, *fell*. Why?

High unemployment is clearly part, but only part, of the answer. Wage militancy took a severe check in the recession of 1981–82. But during the five years after the recession ended, the unemployment rate fell from 11 to 6 percent, and over 11 million net new jobs were created. By 1987, labor markets were no longer slack. Certain U.S. industries that have been traditional wage leaders (automobiles, for instance) were nearing full capacity. It is the continued restraint of workers' demands in spite of this that must be explained.

Increased internal competition in the wider economy may have played a role. New entry to two unionized industries, airlines and trucking, was deregulated under the Carter administration. In one of the ironies of the decade, the Reagan administration acted against free-market principle to delay effective deregulation in both cases. A pro-competition acting chairman of the Interstate Commerce Commission was replaced, in early 1981, by a public utilities lawyer from Nevada who brought trucking deregulation to an abrupt halt.[12] Airline deregulation was slowed for a different ostensible reason: flight restrictions imposed in 1981, when the president destroyed the professional air traffic controllers association. Then the recession of 1981–82 slowed the growth in demand for air travel, so that major market changes as a result of deregulation were delayed until 1984.[13]

Deregulation, and cutthroat wage competition throughout the rising service sector, has no doubt lowered average wages in the affected industries. This is a one-time effect, however, not a durable bar to wage inflation. While the transition is in progress it will depress the rate at which all wages are rising, but in theory, once a new equilibrium wage is reached, wages in the competitive sectors should be more prone to rise in booms as well as to fall in recessions, and they should therefore have started going back up as labor markets tightened. Yet, despite strong growth for five years after 1982, no wage surge has yet occurred.

There are cultural explanations, often offered but unpersuasive. How much can rest on such unobservables as a tougher management attitude inspired by the new era? What is the force of the alleged respect of workers (not shared, we have seen, by bond buyers!) for Paul Volcker's determination? How long can the president's treatment—many years ago—of the air traffic controllers reverberate in the consciousness of industrial workers in the private sector? These are not satisfactory explanations.

It was the exchange rate: a pervasive, comprehensive, multiple-channel anti-inflationary force. The situation in automobiles may be taken as representative of how the exchange rate can affect wages in an industry despite strong recovery of demand and employment and good profits. The high dollar could even, in this case, force workers to overlook the provocation of extravagant and highly publicized executive bonus awards in 1984.

There are five distinct channels for the exchange rate's effect.

First, there is direct price competition from economical foreign cars. Despite the so-called voluntary quotas, Japanese-made cars were made cheap to Americans, on a dollar-for-quality basis, by the high dollar. And Hyundai and Yugo showed that with IMP labor a $6,000 vehicle that meets U.S. standards is possible in the late 1980s. Their ability, and that of other potential new entrants of the same class, to expand their U.S. market share in the event that U.S. wage discipline breaks down has become and will remain a large latent threat.

Second, the high dollar held down nonwage costs to American automobile manufacturers. U.S. auto companies are heavy buyers of components from other countries: Canadian parts, Mexican castings, Brazilian engines, Korean steel, Malaysian rubber. The high dollar made these external purchases relatively inexpensive, and so eroded the "back end" of the automobile manufacturing chain in the United States. That which is partly gone today can be gone completely tomorrow.

Third, the exchange rate directly depressed the demand for and profits of U.S. export industries. The United States does not, of course, export many new automobiles. But it does export trucks, motor vehicle parts, farm equipment, and other related products. When sales in these high-wage industries are soft, automobile workers take notice.

Fourth, the high dollar directly raised the real value of the wage of auto workers. When the dollar is rising, the cost of the consumption basket for affluent workers must fall: such items as Japanese VCRs and Canadian beers become available more cheaply. If imports comprise 15 percent of consumption, a 50 percent rise in the dollar exchange rate over two years or so (1981–83) cuts the direct cost of maintaining a constant living standard by about 2.5 percent per year. This could be taken out of the dollar wage gains that would otherwise have occurred.

Fifth and finally, the high dollar raised the ratio of U.S. average industry pay to Japanese (or Canadian, or Korean) pay valued in dollars. It thereby made American workers appear to be more highly paid on the international scale than they had been in 1979 or 1980. And this provided management with an additional "competitiveness" argument at the bargaining table—an argument whose force grew stronger as the share of imports in U.S. consumption grew ever larger.

The automotive industry is a traditional wage-leading, traded-goods industry. Its wage settlements have national importance. When they are low, restraint is transmitted to wage-following and service sectors through interdependencies in the collective bargaining system, and they reverberate throughout the entire structure of U.S. costs. Even sectors unaffected by direct pressures of imports on costs (for example, housing construction) feel the climate of low wage norms that currency overvaluation fosters.[14]

Nor was U.S. officialdom unaware of these effects. Studies over the years at the Federal Reserve had proposed that, as a rule of thumb, every ten percent change in the exchange value of the dollar would be followed, over two years, by a 1.5 to 1.75 percent change in the price level.[15] By this guideline, the rise in the value of the dollar from 1980 to 1984 accounts for at least half of the decline in the rate of inflation. And this estimate is, in turn, reasonably consistent with the decline in inflation that cannot be explained by purely internal factors, such as a slower cumulative rate of employment growth.

Oil is a wild card in the inflation process. Because oil is priced in dollars, many assume that its price to the United States is unaffected by the value of the dollar. But this is clearly false; one must consider how the dollar's value affects the dollar price of oil.

Because oil is priced in dollars, its real price to countries outside the United States varies with the value of the dollar, as well as with the vicissitudes of the oil market. When the dollar rose in 1981–82, European and Japanese oil importers experienced a third oil price shock in terms of their own balance of trade. Their import bills went up at a time when tight financial conditions were causing their export markets to collapse. It was a supply shock, in other words, that did not transfer net new dollar income to the suppliers. This import shock contributed in no small measure to the restrictive policies that conservative European governments, afraid of deficits, then felt obliged to pursue. And the fall in demand that resulted contributed heavily to the subsequent decline in the dollar price of oil.

One need not believe that the high dollar was planned in advance to achieve these inflation-depressing effects, only that once events unfolded, the effects were recognized, if not by all econometricians, then at least by the more intuitive thinkers in the upper reaches of the administration and the Federal Reserve. There is ample evidence in the business press that—given the deficits—a further sharp reduction in the dollar's international value would indeed be seen by top policymakers as courting the risk of returning inflation. Chairman Volcker made such fears explicit in congressional testimony in April 1987.[16] Such fears can be overruled if the dollar goes too high—as it did in early 1985—or if the stability of U.S. banking or of the economy itself is threatened, as it was by the stock market crash of October 1987. But in normal times, the fear of inflation accounts for a strong aversion to allowing the dollar slide.

Thus, *in effect, the high dollar—achieved mainly by monetary policy— has been the incomes policy that the Reagan administration forswore on ideological grounds in 1981.* Like an incomes policy, it helped to reconcile, but only temporarily, high consumption standards with low rates of price and wage increases. As such, it was a politically necessary complement to the huge deficit, and together the two framed the macroeconomic posture of the Reagan administration's first six years.

The Undeclining Dollar

Publicity surrounding the Plaza Hotel Accords of September 1985, and the coordinated reduction in the value of the dollar effected thereafter, created a largely false impression of events in currency markets as they affect the structure of U.S. trade. News reports spoke of a reduction in the dollar's value of 30 percent in two years after the peak. It was then a matter of surprise, puzzlement and disillusion that the U.S. trade and current account deficits continued to rise. Analysts began to wonder whether venerable rules about the price responsiveness of trading patterns were suddenly being broken.

But until October 1987 at least, the dollar's decline was still largely a statistical illusion. Newspapers spoke of dramatic movement in the dollar/ yen and dollar/mark exchange rates: West Germany and Japan account together for 30 percent of U.S. imports. And even the common references to "trade-weighted exchange rates" are misleading. The terms of reference for such figures include the currencies only of industrial countries (such as Canada), weighted by their U.S. trade share. They do not include the currencies of those IMPs and RBEs with which the United States now conducts a large and growing fraction of its trade. For example, in 1985, imports from East Asia outside Japan and from Latin America accounted for just under a quarter of U.S. imports. Yet the currencies of Korea, Singapore, Hong Kong, Brazil and Mexico are not included in the most commonly used trade-weighted exchange rate index.[17]

Measured against a basket of currencies including those of Mexico and the East Asian IMPs at their proper trade weights, a 1986 Federal Reserve study found that the true rise in the real value of the dollar had been 43 percent from 1980 to 1985—while the fall after the Plaza accords amounted to only 14 percent.[18] Figure 3-6 shows how the dollar's value rose against Latin American currencies and held firm against the Canadian dollar after 1985, even while falling against Japanese and European currencies. Meanwhile, even as the yen rose, Japanese exporters to the United States held the line on their dollar prices, absorbing cuts in profit margins instead of risking the loss of market share. Thus U.S. imports did not become either more expensive or more scarce, threatening in any immediate way the success of the anti-inflation strategy reliant on the high dollar.

FIGURE 3–6

The Real Value of the Dollar by Region

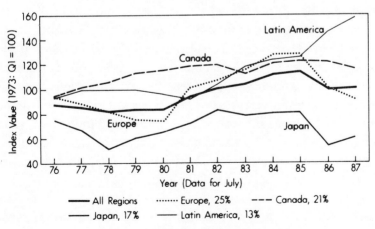

SOURCE: Dallas Federal Reserve Bank.

And even in the post-crash uncertainty of late 1987, when the dollar was again falling sharply, U.S. authorities could not let the dollar go low enough to hope to reestablish equilibrium in the U.S. current account.

Toward the Crash

As Jeffrey Sachs has noted, the Reagan economic program in its third phase lost the Keynesian touch that had guided it through 1981 and 1982, and acquired instead the patina of Columbia economist Robert Mundell, who had argued for just such a policy mix—tight money, large deficits—in response to the not dissimilar conditions of 1971.[19] High interest rates and a high dollar assured low inflation; the budget deficit supported demand and assured growth. And foreign borrowing, at high interest rates commensurate with the large need, provided the finance.

The strategy worked, but because of its effects on trade, it could not be sustained. A high-demand/high-currency policy means, inevitably, a large and rising trade deficit. The current account, in near-balance as recently as 1982, fell into a pattern of deficit that exceeded $100 billion per year within two years. By early 1985, these deficits had accumulated to the point where the official net creditor position of the United States had been erased. The country was a net debtor to the rest of the world for the first time since World War I.[20]

Ultimately, rising trade deficits act as a drag on growth. To sustain growth as time passes, either fiscal or monetary policy must ease. But with the deficit already so huge, a deliberately bigger deficit is a political impossibility. Easier money is feasible, but it must necessarily threaten to sacrifice the high currency, and thereby to restart inflation.

Nevertheless, given certain recession as against the risk of inflation, easier money becomes the only course. From September 1985 on, the Mundell shift gave way to a fourth phase of effective fiscal tightening and intermittent monetary expansion. As a share of GNP, the budget deficit declined, from 5.0 to about 3.3 percent in 1987,[21] as figure 3-7 shows.

The new strategy aimed to sustain growth by restoring U.S. industrial competitiveness in advanced markets, and so stimulating exports to major trading partners in Europe, Canada and Japan. In this, by 1987, there

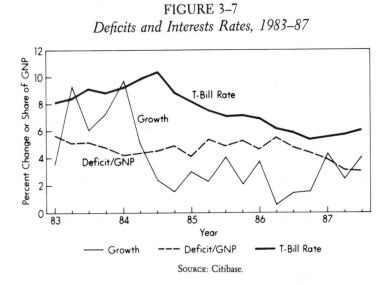

FIGURE 3–7

Deficits and Interests Rates, 1983–87

Source: Citibase.

were signs of success: U.S. exports rose sharply, and growth at a modest pace was indeed sustained. But so long as the markets of the developing countries failed to recover, this strategy also faced severe limits. And the price of those limits was a continuing problem of the cumulative effect on U.S. industry, in effect the reduction of the United States from its commanding position on world technological frontiers.

It is one thing for a country such as Brazil, which imports capital goods and exports manufactures, to maintain, for a brief period of rapid investment, the overvalued exchange rate combined with rapid internal demand growth generated by a Mundell shift. Such a policy cheapens vital imports, and so makes possible accelerated investment in exportable manufactures. And it can be reversed when the new export sectors come on line, making effective the necessary competitive access to the international markets that they require.

But it is quite another matter for a capital goods exporter, such as the United States, to do the same thing. When the United States maintains an overvalued exchange rate, potential consumers of U.S. advanced goods seek an alternative source of supply. In present conditions, the Japanese and others are more than willing to provide the choice. To induce a depression in the capital goods sector while stimulating the demand for consumer goods, whether produced at home or imported, is therefore progressively to abandon one's technological advantage in capital goods altogether. Ultimately, for the United States to become an importer of capital goods means to become primarily an exporter of consumer manufactures, or even of basic resources. No country that must export consumer goods to pay for its capital equipment can hope to enjoy the living standards of a country in the converse position.

At the same time, the battle waged against inflation by means of imports and debt is inherently a futile battle. Sooner or later, there must come a dramatic change. The dollar must fall and exports must cheapen sufficiently to restore their competitiveness; the country cannot run large international deficits forever. And because the fact that one cannot fight inflation with debt over the long run is widely known, as incomes policy the high dollar must have *perverse* effects on price expectations. Since the dollar must eventually come down, it follows that the victory over inflation will prove temporary rather than permanent. Rational economic agents will prepare for the worst.

The real questions are whether the turn will come sooner, so that the exports in question will consist of advanced goods; whether it will come later, when one's competitive advantage had deteriorated so that only mundane goods are wanted and available for export; and whether the incomes of the workers producing them will be high or low by the international standards of that time. U.S. policy at the end of the Reagan years has, in short, found itself in the impossible position of fighting a lost war against inflation with the real blood and treasure of its advanced industrial structure.

After the Crash

The stock market crash of October 19, 1987, when the Dow-Jones Industrial Average fell 508 points in a single day, was widely said to reflect the unwillingness of foreigners to hold American debt. In fact, it signaled an altogether different sort of crisis: a crisis of expected profitability in worldwide business, and so the limits of a tight-money, high-real-interest monetary order in the developed world.

After five years, domestic economic expansion in the United States had run its course. Major industries such as housing and automobiles had reabsorbed as much labor as they were going to do, and were producing at close to domestic capacity limits. Measured unemployment had fallen to near what conservative economists considered full-employment rates. Measured productivity growth was slowing in the now familiar end-of-expansion pattern.

Within the Reagan administration, there was an evident dilemma. The election year of 1988 loomed ahead. A new engine of growth was needed. Exports could provide such growth, but only if the dollar fell even further than the Plaza accords had contemplated. On the other hand, if that happened, the anti-inflation strategy of the Reagan expansion would have to be abandoned.

As early as February 1987, tension over this dilemma was being felt in world financial markets. Private Japanese investors and others foresaw the changes ahead and reacted in short-term speculative anticipation of a fall in the dollar. They stopped buying U.S. assets, and so virtually the entire U.S. trade imbalance for the rest of the year would have to be offset by increased dollar holdings at central banks.

In July, Paul Volcker announced his departure. Treasury Secretary James Baker, adrift, had agreed with the Germans to stabilize the dollar. This was, in effect, a commitment to coordinate U.S. interest rate policies with those of the Germans. Effectively, it would have put the Bundesbank, and the world's foremost *rentier* economy, in place of Volcker's Federal Reserve in charge of global monetary policy. The Germans almost immediately began to test their power by raising short-term interest rates in slow steps from July to October. For a while, the United States followed suit.

As the summer ended, however, conflict between U.S. policy imperatives and German monetary leadership became inescapable. Currency stabilization under German hegemony could be purchased only at the price of rising worldwide interest rates. In the United States, this raised a threat of domestic recession. The debt stalemate, to which American but not German banks were vulnerable, could have unraveled. A default crisis would have precipitated a regulatory crisis in the administration of the American banking system, with terrible political results for a Republican administration. Most important, the necessary growth of U.S. exports could now be achieved only by dollar realignment.

Possibly the threat of a competitive currency defense, and so an upward spiral in interest rates around the world, provoked the stock selloff. Clearly, the cause did not lie solely in domestic U.S. problems, for the crash occurred not just in New York but around the world. As the Dow-Jones Industrial Average fell by 508 points, or 22 percent, on October 19, London declined 10 percent, Paris 6 percent, Frankfurt 7 percent, Singapore 15 percent, and Toronto 9 percent. On October 20, the Tokyo exchange lost 15 percent of its value. In Hong Kong, exchanges closed and mutual funds were frozen.

The stock crash broke U.S. monetary policy free, at least momentarily, of the post-Volcker ascendancy of the Germans. For several weeks caution was discarded, and the Federal Reserve committed itself to supporting financial values by the policy once advocated for such situations by Keynes: monetary expansion *à outrance*. Within a month, the policy seemed to have succeeded: stocks and interest rates stabilized for the time being. Meanwhile the dollar had again fallen sharply against the yen. At this point, uncertainty once again set in. A fallen dollar, we have seen, raises inflation risks even as it improves the prospects for exports. How much of one, how much of the other? Policymakers in the United States were feeling their way, alert to the political minefields on either side of a path that seemed extremely narrow, even if it was not altogether blocked off.

There were three possibilities. The administration could have decided to protect price stability at the expense of growth and the 1988 election; the stock crash and its aftermath showed that it would not do so. Second, inflation could rise sharply before export growth revived, provoking yet another domestic political crisis. Third, in the reverse case, exports might come before inflation. It remained unclear which of the last two possibilities would transpire. But as the U.S. government stumbled forward in the darkness, gambling on the third outcome, it was evident that caution was once again playing its role. Whatever the allocation between growth and inflation, the gradual approach assured that, for a time, the best (and worst) one could expect was small doses of either.

In the upshot, the Reagan expansion could yet turn into the post-Reagan stagnation, which could continue for quite a while. In this scenario, falling deficits remain just large enough to forestall recession, but at very low rates of real economic growth. With the dollar remaining high in relation to those currencies that are supplying our major manufactured imports (increasingly the IMPs of East Asia, Canada and the middle-income Latin American nations), imports, trade deficits and competitive pressures against U.S. wages and costs can remain strong. The recent

What Reagan Did

Japanese flirtation with a high-yen strategy will probably not last. When the yen again falls, Japanese gains, to our cost, will continue in the supply of equipment to all third country markets. Increasingly, the Japanese will come to be the suppliers of capital goods to manufacturing industries in the United States itself.

As a policy strategy, a post-Reagan stagnation would avoid the alternative political suicides of outright recession and uncontrolled inflation. But this does not come free of other risks. The adjustment out of advanced industries is no easier than the transition into those industries proved to be in the first place. First among the costs is the certain long-term decline in basic consumption standards that they entail. The rising dangers of bank failures and financial crisis, both at the level of the vast Latin American sovereign debts and in certain American domestic sectors, such as energy and farming, compound the political and economic risks. Regional patterns of dependence on exports within the United States threaten to change the political map. Certainly an atmosphere of apprehension, bordering on fear, about the political consequences of stagnation in the Sunbelt existed in Washington as the Reagan years drew to a close.

In the final analysis, therefore, the only real question is one of timing. Sooner or later, the forces pushing strongly for a lower dollar, coordinated world monetary expansion, and reduction in the real burden of U.S. external debts are bound to prevail. This can take either of two forms: further decline in the dollar, or joint monetary expansion by the major industrial powers at exchange parities not too different from those of the present. The effects, either way, will include some revival (depending on the strength of the expansion and the steps to resolve the debt crisis) of U.S. advanced technology exports, a decrease in our consumer imports, and a profit squeeze on external suppliers to the U.S. consumer market. Perhaps the domestic growth rate of the United States will rise, as almost certainly will that of the debt-ridden developing countries and of the Europeans and Japanese. These forces will all, in their turn, work to loosen the vise of competitive pressures holding down prices and, above all, industrial wages in the United States.

Thus, if and when full-fledged monetary expansion takes hold, even under the most benign configuration of policies, the price consequences will follow. For the strategy of world monetary expansion amounts to nothing more than a return to Carterism in macroeconomic management: global monetary expansion with no provision for the management of supply prices. This will be beneficial for the leading sectors of industry, as Carter's policies were. And they will be inflationary, as Carter's policies were. The only real difference is that the time elapsed after the recession and before the monetary expansion began has been far longer in the Reagan period than it was under Ford and Carter, so that the international competitive position of U.S. industry has suffered more, and the damage will require a longer and stronger dose of global monetary stimulus if it is to be reversed.

Established opinion clearly prefers to delay inflation as long as it can be delayed. And established opinion, which cannot defend a tight policy before inflation becomes an actual problem, will clamor for recession as soon as the inflation hits.[22] There will be more talk of the need to reestablish a "noninflationary growth path." But this is a will-o'-the-wisp. Recession cannot cure inflation permanently in a world where the United States must recover its international price advantages and export competitiveness in advanced industrial sectors. To use recession as a tool for this purpose merely strengthens the dollar, induces new trade distortions and makes more difficult—nearer to impossible—the ultimate adjustment task.

Established opinion must therefore be resisted at the outset, and the task of wise policy is twofold. First, it must recognize that there are worse things than cutting one's losses. If the repressed inflation of the Reagan years must come, better sooner than later. A farsighted central banker is needed, one who recognizes the real, accumulating costs of delay in the adjustment of U.S. prices relative to those faced in the rest of the world.

Second, international adjustment and a return to competitiveness can proceed from a high original living standard or a lower one. The second path, in the climate fostered after long decay and by recession, is the path of facile governance. High unemployment and the destruction of productive industrial capacity are great motivators of industrial transition. But the first path is superior from the standpoint of the public, since it permits a continued accumulation of real wealth and softens the brutal edges of the business cycle. What it requires is prompt action to restore competitive pricing and clever action to avert recession while this is done.

Of course, success will depend entirely on what alternatives to recession and to the high dollar for coping with inflation may exist. The Connally program of 1971 cannot be repeated. And so, to the task of creating feasible alternatives and placing them in the larger context of a newly re-created macroeconomic strategy we now turn.

CHAPTER 4

The Nature of the Case for Price Stabilization

————

WE HAVE SEEN that world recovery, on which a restored competitive position for U.S. industry depends, cannot be accomplished without generating several distinct types of inflationary pressure. First, dollar devaluation implies higher dollar prices of imported goods and a reduction of competitive pressure against the price increases of home goods that compete with imports. Second, lower interest rates imply higher stock demand for commodities, and so higher commodity prices. Third, the recovery of advanced sectors will be accompanied by rising wages in those sectors, and the pressure of these wages on the general wage structure will impart an inflationary bias to labor costs throughout the system.

The question is what to do about it, and for this we need a more subtle understanding of why price stabilization is a desirable public goal.

Arguments Against Inflation

There are, broadly speaking, three reasons to oppose inflation. The first is an antitransfer motive: creditors do not like the erosion of the real value of financial instruments that inflation brings. The second is an efficiency motive: opposition to inflation's effects on production and on the smooth functioning of markets. The third motive is political: distaste for inflation's debilitating effects on the organizational stability of civil society. I shall argue that the first motive is not a proper concern of public policy, that the second is practically unimportant in our economy, and that legitimate attention should focus on the third. This will lead us to consider price stabilization policies of a special form, which can, happily, be made compatible with a strategy of global growth.

The antitransfer argument against inflation is surely the most often cited, but it is also the most vacuous and most easily dismissed. One is told of the widow and the orphan, of the pensioner "living on a fixed income," for whom inflation erodes the bare means of an already meager standard of living. But the image is a Victorian one, appropriate to an age of fixed annuities and thirty-year, 3 percent bonds, of landless bourgeoises in London flats.

Inflation brings many changes to economic life, but a systematic redistribution of income across social classes, at least in the United States, is not among them.[1] Membership in a social class in our society is defined by the aggregate of one's wealth, not by the form in which it is held. The forms are almost indefinitely various: from real property to real business assets to corporate equities to bonds to cash. And they respond with great variety to the onset of price inflation. There may be a flight from cash and bonds, and the latter, if not indexed, may lose capital value. Land prices may soar, keeping holders of land well ahead of the game. And there will be waves of financial innovation producing new types of variable-rate debt instruments, as those issuing bonds seek markets from inflation-shy investors, while speculating on the possibility that the inflation and interest rates will fall.

This financial turbulence is certainly real, and among those with assets to lose there is a wide range of outcomes. A landlord may move up and a bondholder may crash. But this is not enough to effect a transfer across social classes. Great landholders and great bondholders belong to the same social class; they may well be the same person. And the same is true of middling holders of residential housing, money market funds and corporate stock. The United States today is not late-nineteenth-century England, whose middle classes could hold bonds but had no access to the land. Nor is it interwar Germany, with vast cash savings to be wiped out by hyperinflation. Inflation in our time does not seem greatly to change the social positions of large groups. And the churning of portfolios and the churning of people do not have the same consequences for society at large.

As it happens, the holding of bonds (particularly of tax-exempt bonds) is a form of wealth highly concentrated in the upper reaches of the income and wealth distribution in the United States: in 1976 the richest 1 percent of the population held about 31 percent of all such bonds.[2] So it may be true that among a small class of the truly prosperous, real wealth losses from (unanticipated) inflation are especially likely to occur.[3] That this stratum provides the most vocal and effective political opposition to inflation, and the strongest support for tight fiscal and monetary policies to fight inflation, is scarcely a surprise.

But what are we to think of this type of redistribution? For every bondholder who loses on the real value of his holdings, there is a corporation (and its stockholders) or a government (and its taxpayers) that gains. Economics teaches that inflationary redistribution is a zero-sum game— every loss in value is offset somewhere by a gain. Nor is there any ethical doctrine that fixes the right of particular persons to their wealth as measured at any particular time. We all speculate on financial matters of all kinds all the time. Those who choose to concentrate their wealth in long bonds are merely speculating that the government will firmly resist any changes whatever in the general price level. Or perhaps they are gambling on their own political influence and ability to bring this outcome about. But that being so, there is nothing wrong in economics or ethics about placing one's bets the other way.

Thus the social costs of inflation do not include the commonly cited losses for creditors, bondholders, and "people on fixed incomes." For such losses are always and everywhere exactly offset by gains—to borrowers, owners of corporate equity and "people on variable incomes." These transfers may or may not, in themselves, harm social welfare: that depends on a social judgment of the merit of the winners compared with that of the losers. In actual practice, most sensible people of means have diversified investments, and a portfolio of stocks, bonds and real property need not be affected at all, on average, by inflation.

The economist, when pressed, adverts to the efficiency costs of inflation, to the losses of real current production and smooth market function that inflation is said to entail. These, unlike transfers, are indisputably losses to society at large, as they reduce for all time the consumption possibilities of the public. The issue is whether they are quantitatively important in real life.

Some efficiency costs are said to stem from the effects of inflation on relative prices. One common argument is that inflation raises the variability of prices, making any particular future price-ratio harder than otherwise to predict. This is said to mean that the cost of price discovery rises: it becomes more difficult to know what prices are and what they will be. There is then an efficiency loss as businesses devote a larger share of resources to search for the best deals.

A related story holds, in a more general way, that inflation increases the uncertainty surrounding the real rate of return on prospective investments. People are risk averse: they dislike a rising variance even if the average rate of return is unchanged. If this is true, utility is lessened. Inflation may then depress business confidence, more or less directly, and undermine investment.

Yet, confirmation of these conjectures is hard to find. There is no direct evidence that in practice moderate inflation causes an increase in aimless search activity by business. Nor is there any showing that investment falls during moderate inflation. To the contrary, there is some evidence that investment shares may rise in inflationary periods. Theory relates the rate of investment to the prospective real (after-inflation) rate of return in relation to the real (after-inflation) rate of interest. If nominal interest rates are sticky (which in practice they sometimes are), an unanticipated rise in inflation tends to cause temporarily low real interest rates. This may well stimulate investment, in spite of the more uncertain relative price climate. Considering the data, there is reason to think this optimistic story more plausible than the conventional pessimistic one.[4]

A second efficiency issue concerns the effects of inflation on the management of financial resources. In inflations money is a wasting asset and economies in the holding of money become profitable. Resources are therefore devoted to ways of making necessary money holdings smaller. The results include the invention of new financial instruments, which may be indexed against inflation, and the development of faster means of getting money to and from the bank (including more bank branches, electronic funds transfer, automatic cash machines, and so on). These effects, without doubt, do exist. In hyperinflation, they become important.[5] But in relation to the size of the U.S. economy, given the moderate rates of inflation that have been at issue in the United States, they are quite small, to the point where no one could justify even a minor rise in unemployment and loss of real production in order to fight inflation if this were the only factor at issue.[6]

Where financial instruments indexed to the inflation rate are not available, inflation may produce excess holding of stocks of real materiel. Inventories, commodities, work-in-progress and the like increase. Such stocks hedge against inflation in ways that directly reduce real production, at least for a transitional period while stocks are rising. In extreme situations, as in Germany and Japan toward the end of World War II, manufacturers may hold inventories rather than deliver on orders for real goods, since to do so would merely add to cash balances which are rapidly becoming worthless. However, this behavior can be profitable on a large scale only in anticipation of wholesale economic and currency collapse, which have not been at issue in the postwar United States.

Some economists find the upshot disconcerting. The economic costs of inflation appear to be small. Worse, they are largely defined in terms of market imperfections: uncertainty about the future, transactions costs, imperfect financial markets, and nonmarket-clearing behavior. It is especially difficult to model the real effects of inflation in the purely theoretical context, where these imperfections typically do not exist. Thus, the closer one's model comes to approximating the perfectly competitive, perfect-information, free-market economy of the neoclassical ideal, the *less* one can say with formal certitude about why any constant rate of inflation— not involving large shocks or surprises to economic agents—should be thought a problem.

This has led rigorous theoreticians to attack inflation on another ground. The ground is aesthetic. Let us admit, the argument goes, that money is dynamically neutral: inflation at any sustainable constant rate is harmless. We can have any rate of inflation that we like, so long as we refrain from attempting to drive the unemployment rate above or below its "natural" rate. So why not, the final argument goes, shoot for zero inflation? "You may have wondered why God," economist John Rutledge once testified before Congress, "put zero in the middle of the numbers. That's because that's the optimal rate of inflation."[7]

This final argument is clear and simple. But it hardly explains the loathing that the experience of inflation, anticipated or not, seems to inspire in public life. Political leaders, journalists and others, faced with guidance of this order, are understandably at a loss. They persist in the deviant thought that nominal events have real effects. As Professor Frank Hahn of Cambridge University summarized:

> The government's inconsistent beliefs are widely shared: ". . . reduction in inflation is needed to lay the basis of sustainable growth" (*Times Leader*, 10 May 1980). Presumably this sort of belief explains why governments all over the world are busy engineering recessions. All this should not stop one from pointing out that the belief has no foundation in general theory and certainly no foundation in any version of the Monetarist theory which these advocates typically embrace.[8]

The Public's View

Can this be right? Can inflation aversion rest entirely on money illusion or, worse, on theoretical error? And why do some countries with inflation (the United States, the United Kingdom, West Germany) have an "inflation problem" (producing domestic political trauma), while others (France, Japan, Italy) seem not to? The hypothesized costlessness of *anticipated* inflation clearly fails to explain this. Inflation rates in countries inured to inflation are characteristically not only higher but also more variable—and therefore presumably less well anticipated—than in those whose populations are highly inflation averse. Conversely, in countries with low and stable inflation, pressures to fight inflation grow stronger as time passes and inflation continues, even though, as it continues, inflation presumably becomes easier to anticipate and therefore, from a theoretical perspective, less costly.

As with the international competitive challenge, the economists may equivocate but ordinary Americans hold a firm view. They loathe inflation. In overwhelming numbers, they prefer a stable dollar and a stable price level. Many, moreover, seem prepared to support politicians who deliver this result even at a gigantic cost to real income.

The transfer costs of inflation to the public are small on average. The efficiency losses from inflation are indefinite or negligible. This suggests

The Nature of the Case for Price Stabilization

that political and constitutional reasons for opposing inflation may be the compelling ones to most people.

Inflation is a public evil. Its private costs may be small, but its effect on faith in public institutions inspires public citizens to oppose it with an energy and perseverance devoted to few other tasks. Inflation control becomes, in a word, a matter of defending the constitutional order.

We may now ask what special implications for policy the political perspective may have.

In the first place, constitutional issues override economic concerns. A threat to the constitutional order cannot be evaded. The appropriate question cannot be, as some would have it, "How much inflation are we willing to put up with to achieve a given reduction in unemployment?" Rather, it must be "How little inflation must we have, irrespective of all other considerations, so that we pose no significant threat to the constitutional order?"

This means that in the design of anti-inflation policy, all policies that keep inflation below the threshold level are appropriate. None that fail to do so are tolerable. The public is prepared to support extraordinarily costly means of reducing inflation to tolerable levels, so long as they are persuaded that no credible, effective, less costly alternative means of achieving the same objective exists.

Categorical inflation aversion has a practical corollary in the politics of macroeconomic policy. Normally, we might like advocates of particular policies to justify them on cost-benefit grounds, to show that the social benefits of what they propose outweigh the social burdens they plan to impose. But with inflation this type of justification is unnecessary. The argument that inflation must be fought at all costs can be made, is widely respected, and will often carry the day. Those who oppose particular anti-inflation policies on the ground that they are "too costly" (indeed, the typical liberal position of the late 1970s) find that their arguments carry virtually no weight in the political system.

Advocates of particular means for controlling inflation can therefore win their point solely and simply by discrediting proposed alternatives. In particular, so long as the public remains persuaded, as it is today, that the Federal Reserve constitutes "the only anti-inflation game in town," no serious challenge can be raised to the periodic use of restrictive monetary policy to force inflation down to an acceptable rate. Proponents of one (highly costly) approach defend their position by accusing their adversaries of advocating the intolerable. This powerful rhetorical advantage is not entirely rooted, as some suppose, in reactionary cant.[9] Rather, it is based on an exploitable understanding of how the social welfare question is viewed by the public.

Political Costs of Inflation

What is the precise nature of the political/constitutional problem? As Keynes wrote, it is that inflation breeds arbitrary transfers *between persons,* and so distributive conflicts, and *these destroy the legitimacy accorded in more normal times to market outcomes.* Destruction of political legitimacy occurs when the conflicts thus displaced from the market enter the political arena and come to absorb the energies of the state. For Keynes, inflation was not far removed from revolution:

> The sight of this arbitrary rearrangement of riches strikes not only at the security, but at the confidence in the equity of the existing distribution of wealth. . . . Lenin was certainly right. There is no subtler, no surer means of overturning the existing basis of society than to debauch the currency. The process engages all the hidden forces of economic law on the side of destruction, and does it in a manner which not one man in a million is able to diagnose.[10]

The state is a limited instrument. It comprises, at its high decision-making level, only a few thousand people engaged in a vast variety of tasks. They cannot assume the functions of the market and still maintain their effectiveness in other missions. If national defense, or social welfare, or the administration of justice, or economic planning, or any other public purpose requires the attention, planning, commitment and resources of the state, then the state mechanism must be available. It cannot be distracted and absorbed by the resolution of distributive conflicts between powerful economic interests that are thrown before it by inflation. It is the preemption of the ability to act, the threat to the independence or maneuverability of the state, that constitutes inflation's grave effect on the political order.

Keynes, of course, understood this in 1919: the threat is not economic but political instability, not redistribution across class lines but the increas-

The Nature of the Case for Price Stabilization

ingly speculative character of individual changes in status within the existing class structure, not massive wealth transfers to debtors per se but the disruption of financial relations *in general*. Moreover, it is the political order, not the productive process, that is threatened: "All permanent relations between debtors and creditors, which form the ultimate foundation of capitalism, become so utterly disordered as to be almost meaningless, and the process of wealth-getting degenerates into a gamble and a lottery."[11] Keynes spoke from European experience of his time, and it is obvious that his comments are not invariant to political and financial structures. Countries with strong political orders are more predisposed to fight, and less likely to accept chronic inflation. That is, the degree of national inflation aversion varies with national institutions; some governmental structures are better suited to managing the resulting conflicts than others.

Democratic systems, indeed all governments with the ability to do so and claims to legitimacy in the modern world, develop ways and means of buffering their populations, reducing and adjudicating distributive conflicts and protecting organized constituencies among them from extreme changes in economic condition, including the increase in the level of undesired uncertainty about prices and capital values, of the speculative element in business life, that inflationary times produce. But they do so with differing degrees of ability and skill. Democracies in the West either have relatively open political systems with a high degree of party competition and viable alternative governments (such as the United States, the United Kingdom and West Germany), or they have coalition systems dominated for long periods by a single party (France before 1981, Japan, Italy). Where the political system is competitive, the forces seeking protection turn to the political arena, and inflation tends to produce political crisis. Where the political system is less competitive, the cooperation between state and business is less politicized, and the buffering function may be institutionalized away from the parliament and the political process. In Japan this is done through private banks linked to the large industrial groupings, which assume long-range financial responsibility for the companies to which they lend.[12] In France, it is done through state control of the financial sector, equally effective before and after the nationalizations of 1981.[13] In either case, inflation may come and go, but social relations are not disordered and the political crisis does not occur.

In the late 1970s, as domestic inflation rose, structural shifts in comparative advantage and patterns of trade created a large, amorphous class of economic losers in the United States. Among them were industrial corporations—steel and autos were the trite examples—for which international economic transitions were going badly. It was easy, in the circumstances of a loose and ill-informed political debate, to attribute their losses to the inflation that was incidental to this process of transition.

Given a pattern of chronic losses, losers grow frustrated and angry. And they mobilize. This was true of the German middle classes of the 1920s, of U.S. heavy industry in the 1970s, and of certain upper-income taxpayers at the same time.[14] The first group had lost their cash savings. The second had too much capital and too little debt, and so lost out in the great depreciation sweepstakes. The third faced rising marginal tax rates due to the U.S. habit of slow and imperfect periodic income tax indexation.

The American losers turned to Congress, demanding protection, tax relief, subsidies and adjustment assistance. Among their demands was reform of the depreciation provisions of the tax code, and their battle cry was the removal of "distortions" said to have been induced by the interaction of inflation and historic cost inventory accounting. Economists could, and did in this instance, argue that reform on these grounds made little sense. There was a readily available private remedy: the corporation could leverage itself so that the depreciation of its debts would offset the overstatement of its profits. That some had failed to do so was the consequence of their own failure of foresight, for which the tax code, the government, and ultimately taxpayers and alternate claimants to government spending were hardly to blame. However this was an *ex ante* argument; the real debate was over *ex post* public restitution for private inflation-related losses that had, in fact, occurred.

Once caught up in a gargantuan struggle over the distribution of wealth among the already wealthy, lasting roughly from 1978 to 1982, the political system could devote attention to few other issues. Social reform and economic initiative disappeared from legislative calendars. Tax-relief lobbies for heavy industry and for upper-income families, whose share of total income was not actually falling but who had a complaint of their own about bracket creep induced by inflation, displaced other constituency groups from the national political agenda. Inflation fostered the rise of the New Right, a cadre of public officials and private hucksters dedicated to meeting the demands of every available propertied interest.[15]

The inflation of the late 1970s thus tied together numerous diverse business and individual concerns for a brief period in a powerful political coalition. There was a unity of purpose that lobbies for the powerful have not, in the absence of inflation, succeeded in replicating. And inflation legitimized their turning to the political system, despite their own religious aversion to public welfare, by widely discrediting the legitimacy normally attributed to the market outcome.

From this the core of the argument for average price stabilization easily follows, and it does not, after all, depend on money illusion or other forms of irrational behavior. Reasonably stable prices are a necessary precondition to calm political consideration of increasing real income, of increasing productivity, of maintaining comparative advantage, of social justice and welfare, and even of national defense. The United States, as a two-party democracy with a tradition of alternating power, does not have the French or Japanese option of buffering inflation outside the political process. It must seek satisfactory price stabilization through the political process and risk disruption of the political process if it fails.

The Nature of Price Stabilization

We can now see why the precise nature of price stabilization for this purpose differs from ordinary inflation fighting. The dimension of time enters in a critical way. Political crises are not dangerous if they pass quickly; to the contrary, demonstrated ability to surmount crises is the classic test of competence in American political culture. Instead, it is the chronic crisis that paralyzes political minds. In other words, it takes time for expectations to crystallize into an intractable political/economic problem. If time can be denied to this process, victory itself will have been achieved.

The time distribution of a given amount of price level change is a separate variable, a separate policy dimension. It is independent of the amount of price-level change that occurs. Or, to put it another way, we must now distinguish between the inflation rate per se and *the popular attitude toward what the inflation rate is expected to be* as matters of policy. For it is the second, and not the first, that determines whether any particular shift in the general price level will come to be seen as a political/constitutional threat.

Popular reporting of inflation tends to concentrate on the rate of price change in a given unit of time: this month, this quarter or this year. Economic analysis of the costs of inflation relies on the same concept. This is sensible for the given purpose, which includes a lot of attempted micromanagement of gains and losses through transfers. If I am stuck for a year of unexpected inflation with a long bond which I might otherwise have disposed of, my losses depend on, and only on, the amount of price change over the year.

In particular, the bondholder does not care *when* inflation occurs within the year. Suppose 20 percent inflation occurs in either of two alternative hypothetical cases. In one situation, the entire price change occurs in July, while in the other, inflation is spread evenly over each month. So long as behavior is the same (the next month's inflation is repeatedly unanticipated, and the bond is not sold before year's end), the bondholder's losses are the same either way. The fact that in the former situation there were actually eleven months of price stability and only one of inflation is of no special interest to the bondholder. Nor is it of interest to the issuer of the bond, who has received, either way, a 20 percent diminution of the real value of his debt.

Confusing this type of transfer loss with social losses from inflation, designers of anti-inflation policy have sought policies that reduce the total change in the price level from the beginning of an arbitrarily defined period to the end. They have focused, in a word, on *suppressing* inflation, even when, as following an oil-price shock, eventual price-level adjustments are virtually inevitable. And so, policy designers have, in such cases, sought to transform what might have been short, sharp inflations into prolonged, slow inflations.

In this way, policy design acts in the service of those creditors with good information, those who see that a small, partly repressed inflation today means another small, partly repressed inflation tomorrow. Such creditors can sell bonds, buy real estate and ride out the storm. Thus, to the extent that policy contains information, it serves the purposes of those groups—a privileged class—who can use information best. In the twelve-month inflation example given above, sharp bondholders will sell early to the naive, who will then suffer the capital loss.

Rational public policy, however, regards such capital losses as a purely private matter; each such loss is offset by another's purely private gain. The pattern of rewards raises no deep questions about the worthiness or unworthiness of the gainers and the losers. Ethical questions arise only if

The Nature of the Case for Price Stabilization

the distribution of gains and losses has a defined social pattern, changing the distribution of income and wealth across groups, which the evidence fairly clearly shows it does not. Under any capitalist system, large and arbitrary rewards for successful speculation are a fact of life. There is no social reason to separate speculation on the future of the inflation rate from other types of speculative endeavor.

Yet rational policy is rightly concerned, on the other hand, with the political fights that develop during prolonged inflation. When groups of losers band together and threaten to force the taxpayers to make restitution through the government for what the financial markets have wrought, then there is trouble.

If this political theory of the costs of inflation is correct, the length of the inflationary episode must become a critical factor. It may make all the difference whether the shock is massive but transient, or smaller but chronic.

That this is plausible is easily argued. Is it large but perfunctory external shocks that damage the constitutional order of democratic nations? Or is it instead the chronic, insidious ailment, the sense of impotence in the face of a prolonged challenge that poses the greater harm? Which caused more lasting political trauma, the Depression from 1929 through 1933 or the Japanese attack on Pearl Harbor? The answer seems clear. Wars of attrition are worse than wars of movement; the Iran hostage crisis did more political damage to Jimmy Carter than even the Beirut massacres did to Ronald Reagan; the persistence of poverty is more insidious than periodic recessions; cancer as a public health threat and a source of suffering is more widely feared than heart attacks.

And sustained inflation is more corrupting than a massive but transitory price shock. Thus, if what would otherwise be a chronic and insidious ailment can be converted into a large but transitory event, there may be a political and social welfare gain even though the transfer effects occur just as they did before.

Long periods of reasonable price stability, when inflation is below the threshold at which it is thought to be a problem, breed the self-assurance, confidence in government and sense of resilience that healthy political institutions require. It is such periods that policy should seek to extend and to return to when they are interrupted. The plain may be subject to occasional flooding, but whether the floods are large or small, people will live on the plain if the floods are sufficiently infrequent. What matters for the residents is how long the plain can be expected to remain dry, much more than the depth of the water in the rare deluge.

The political/constitutional perspective tells us that we have designed anti-inflation policy in a way that is nearly the reciprocal of how we should have designed it. In the past we have sought to minimize the price change in a given unit of time. We should, in addition, seek to maximize those periods of time when prices do not change. Obviously, these are not always incompatible goals. But policy measures that would not be relevant to the former may become relevant when both objectives are considered in tandem. And in a conflict, when an external shock or necessary adjustment to external conditions requires a change in the general price level, which course is chosen may determine whether a stable political order can survive.

In such times, anti-inflation policy will succeed, and be perceived as having succeeded, if it concentrates a given amount of price level change into a short period of time. This permits a rapid return to price stability following an external shock. It will fail, as it has failed under Reagan, if even a long period of price stability strengthens the rational conviction that renewed inflation is eventually certain. In short, means of policy should be devised that enable us to pack unavoidable inflation into the shortest possible period of time, and so to enjoy longer periods when the political system can turn to other questions.

The tragedy of inflation, in a word, lies in its destructive effects on the political capacity of democratic systems. Yet, these effects are in no way essential. They are, rather, mere artifacts of institutions, of outdated (or perhaps ill-designed), habitual modes of behavior. Institutions can be changed in such a way that inflation could cease to form the barrier to material progress that it has become in recent decades. We shall return in later chapters to specific ways and means for accomplishing this objective.

In the next two chapters, however, we shall examine two of those other questions that the political system ought explicitly to consider. The first of these is *employment:* what is the nature, distribution and quality of job opportunities in an advanced society that is doing its part to promote growth and development around the world? The second is *distribution and accumulation:* what is the relation between wages and profits in such a society, and how can the disposition of profits in productive investments best be arranged?

CHAPTER 5

The Obsolescence of
Full Employment

—————

$\mathbf{F}$ULL EMPLOYMENT REMAINS an icon of liberal social thinking, an emblem of virtuous aspiration that is both remote from reality and not too closely or too often reexamined. It has been for a decade the chief statutory objective of economic policy in the United States. It has not been an actual goal of policy, in any meaningful sense, under Reagan, nor has it ever been except perhaps for brief periods in the late 1960s. What is of interest about the full employment goal is therefore not its direct consequences for the economy but perhaps its more serious implications for thinking about social policy. Does the full employment goal serve a purpose? Is its implicit emphasis on the *number of jobs* the right emphasis? Or does it tend to obstruct clear-headed consideration of more basic questions of public and social welfare?

A persistent objection to having any full employment goal arises from conventional macroeconomics. Here a thirty-year debate has been waged over reactionary ground, over the nature of the inflation–unemployment trade-off and over the appropriate attitude of policy toward it.[1] Optimists once argued that a high employment policy can be effective and that it is worth an inflationary price. Pessimists have argued that expansionary policy cannot achieve its employment objective and would be hyperinflationary into the bargain. Both sides have agreed that to change the terms of the trade-off would require structural reform: changes in institutions, in the organization and behavior of government, corporations and markets. But for both sides the design of such changes has been very much a secondary matter. Keynesians like tax-based incomes policies and profit-sharing schemes,[2] while rational expectations theorists push for money growth rules and constitutional amendments to balance the budget; neither devotes much energy to either one. Only a few holdouts on the leftward edges of economics and public life—Robert Eisner and the late Leon Keyserling come to mind—have insisted steadfastly over the years that the task of policy is to reconcile high employment with price stability, not to acquiesce in unacceptable choices between them.

The optimistic Keynesian position suffered an immense loss of prestige when the high inflation of the 1970s failed to yield full employment.[3] Yet, ironically, the apparent Keynesian successes of the Reagan administration have restored the credibility of that position. We may declare, as of 1988, the provisional triumph of the view that government policy can and does influence the level of employment, at least in the short and medium term. The evidence of the senses on this point is overwhelming. Still, and sadly enough, the evidence also suggests that absent structural reform, the Phillips curve continues to exist: policies that raise employment also tend to generate pressures for inflation. There is no equilibrium of full employment with price stability *and balanced trade* under the current structure of markets.

A new criterion for price stabilization, as outlined in the preceding chapter, would ease the tension between anti-inflation policies and the goal of full employment under the circumstances commonly encountered. In a supply shock, we could learn to absorb a blow to costs without generating a catch-up wages spiral, and so avoid the otherwise inevitable political pressures to bring on a recession and reestablish price stability at the expense of workers. Thus a major cause of trade-distorting business cycles and the unemployment they generate could be removed. Excess demand inflation and overfull employment would remain as recession-inducing risks. Still, these forces have not been at the root of any U.S. inflation/recession cycle since 1970. One may conclude from this that the problem they represent, if it is a problem, is demonstrably manageable with the instruments of policy we already have.

The Obsolescence of Full Employment

Redefinition of the price goal alone does not resolve all the problems of a coherent strategy for employment. Its virtue lies in its ability to allow us to look beyond the surface questions, on which the debate has turned for years, to the more fundamental ones. Now we must consider what types of employment opportunities we as a society want to have. What mix of jobs and incomes do we desire? What degree of equality of wages and of family incomes? We need specifically to consider how changes in our labor force, and in the character of employment opportunities, have resulted from the persistent efforts of American families to maintain their living standards and relative positions when two decades of trade-distorting business cycles have brought an increasingly hostile work environment into being. We need to consider, in short, whether there is a trade-off between the quality of work our economy offers and the raw number of jobs.

To place this issue in perspective, it is helpful to think back over the fifty-year change in intellectual and political attitudes about full employment.

The Rise

Full employment as a national policy became a conceptual possibility only when the Keynesian revolution overturned the classical belief in the impossibility of involuntary unemployment. However, an intellectual revolution at that time (as ever) was not enough, by itself, to effect political change. Keynes made intellectually respectable the visceral response of humanitarian politicians to mass suffering since at least the time of the Irish famine: the provision of public jobs and public relief. He did not give those politicians the parliamentary majorities and sheer nerve required to bring about full employment on a mass scale.

"Sad to record," as Axel Leijonhufvud has written, "Schickelgruber did it."[4] Recovery from the Depression required World War II; full employment in peacetime became a matter of serious political dialogue only during and immediately after the war. Three further conditions at that time, beside the rise to intellectual hegemony of Keynes and his followers, made the establishment of full employment as a permanent peacetime policy goal seem newly coherent. Of these, two reflected intellectual and political changes, while the third reflected a shared sense of what the words *full employment* ought to imply.

First, there was the actual achievement of full employment along with price stability as part of the war effort. This was a monumental achievement in Great Britain and the United States, much celebrated by its authors and attributed by them, in some ways with exaggeration, to the power of Keynes's ideas.[5] It inspired a general technical confidence in the manageability of the postwar macroeconomy, not unaided, it may be said, by the intellectual self-confidence of its promoters. Goals could be set and reached. Keynes, safely dead by 1946, ceased to be a brilliant and hectoring dissenter. He became the founding father of a permanent economic management system, little trace of which can be found in his own writing.

Second, there was the rise in the power of the state and of labor within the state. Workers and returning soldiers went socialist in Great Britain, and in the United States they went union. Trade union membership in the United States reached its all-time high of 24 percent of the labor force in 1948, compared to only 7 percent at the trough of the Depression in 1934.[6] Never had labor's power been so great or its social role so well accepted.

Alongside this, there was the Depression-born and war-bred disesteem of business values that made the tycoon, the captain of industry and the financier seem inept, archaic—figures of fun and captives of dogma. No one in the late 1940s and the 1950s would have dreamed of aligning political power overtly, as a public relations matter, with corporate and financial interests. To preserve their very existence, Conservatives in Britain and Republicans in the United States had to rely on war leaders; thus Churchill and Eisenhower hung on in the 1950s. The first report of the Joint Economic Committee (then the Joint Committee on the Economic Report) of the U.S. Congress, endorsing the achievement of the goals of the Employment Act of 1946 that had brought the committee into existence, was unanimous. The instruments for attaining full employment had been placed in hands that seemed prepared to use them.

The Obsolescence of Full Employment

The Decline

Four decades have evidently changed this situation. Whether well or poorly founded in the first place, today managerial Keynesianism has collapsed, and a diminished sense of technical possibility in macromanagement is the political norm. No alternative paradigm has won sufficient adherents to form a long-standing basis for policy decisions, let alone proved capable of achieving the original Keynesian and post-Keynesian goals. Politicians have hardly been won over by rational expectations, but they do approach macroeconomic events with a wary passivity that would have been foreign to the outlook of the early postwar era.

The reversal of political fortunes between business, labor and the state is also no secret. Organized labor's share in the workforce has fallen below 10 percent and is still falling. Labor's political sway within the Democratic Party experienced a last hurrah in the 1984 campaign, and the reach of the trade-union movement's ideas is next to nil. In the meantime, a new generation of celebrants has taken up the age-old and deeply enjoyable task of telling a business culture what it wants to hear. Our Kristols, Wanniskis and Gilders have restored for a time the self-esteem that, as businessmen over the decades have discovered, money only sometimes buys. Robert Reich, Lester Thurow, Charles Sabel and others have made the discussion interesting by providing an argument, the gist of which is that corporate and managerial failures are the source of declining productivity growth rates. But in raising questions about the competence of business, these scholars reaffirm the centrality of the businessman in relation to economic welfare.[7] We live again in an age whose intellectuals are under the sway of the capitalist class.

To that extent, the desire to achieve full employment with public means has receded. This, of course, was as predicted in the 1948 comments of the Polish economist Michal Kalecki, a man whose analytical work in the early 1930s is widely regarded as having paralleled that of Keynes: "The assumption that a Government will maintain full employment in a capitalist economy if only it knows how to do so is fallacious. In this connection the misgivings of big business . . . are of paramount importance."[8] Kalecki's dissection of business opposition to the use of high government spending (other than for defense) to sustain full employment foreshadows in a marvelous way the mood and the official rhetoric of the 1980s:

The attitude is not easy to explain. Clearly higher output and employment benefits not only workers, but businessmen as well, because their profits rise. And the policy of full employment based on loan financed Government spending does not encroach upon profits because it does not involve any additional taxation. The businessmen in the slump are longing for a boom; why do not they accept gladly the "synthetic" boom which the Government is able to offer them?

. . . We may expect the opposition of the "leaders of industry" on three planes: (i) the opposition on principle against Government spending based on a budget deficit; (ii) the opposition against this spending being directed either towards public investment—which may foreshadow the intrusion of the state into the new spheres of economic activity—or towards subsidising mass consumption; (iii) the opposition against maintaining full employment and not merely preventing deep and prolonged slumps. . . .

In the current discussions of these problems there emerges time and again the conception of counteracting the slump by stimulating *private* investment. This may be done by lowering the rate of interest, by the reduction of the income tax, or by subsidising private investment directly in this or another form. That such a scheme should be attractive to "business" is not surprising. The businessman remains the medium through which the intervention is conducted. If he does not feel confidence in the political situation he will not be bribed into investment.[9]

A Late Revival?

Yet, though the wheels of theory and politics have turned, their turning is possibly transitory. It is not safe to regard the fashions of theory or the fortunes of politics as permanent matters; having turned once, the wheels can turn again.

We may yet see a revival of confidence in the technical possibility of full employment. There is certainly residual and continuing sympathy for the idea. In 1987, meetings of the American Economics Association in Chicago were organized around the theme of "Achieving Full Employment" by that association's president-elect, the aforementioned Professor Robert Eisner of Northwestern University. Macroeconomic theory, after flirting for a decade with the policy nihilism of rational expectations, has veered toward accepting the arguments of an MIT-based school that restore an axiomatic basis for the belief that a full employment policy can be effective.[10] Eisner's own 1986 book, *How Real Is the Federal Deficit?*, has helped to restore some of the empirical grounds for believing that expansionary macroeconomic policies work.[11] Much more has been achieved by the simple evidence of the senses in the Reagan years: it takes a hardened ideologue not to recognize the connection between Reagan's tax cuts and deficits and the economic recovery and expansion that almost immediately followed.

The revival of a popular political base for a federal full-employment policy and a restoration of the will of government to pursue full employment seem further off. Certainly no serious revival of the 1940s political coalition for full employment has yet occurred. Yet a spreading disenchantment with the behavior of big business in the Reagan period—evidenced by the popularity of calls for controls on corporate mergers, acquisitions and plunder generally—has restarted the cycle of disesteem that could, in some years, foster a new search for policy alternatives. One Democratic presidential aspirant in early 1987, Senator Paul Simon of Illinois, was bold enough to make a government jobs program the foundation of his campaign; the eventual nominee, Governor Michael Dukakis, played on sentiment in a more general way by describing himself as a "full-employment Democrat." These are straws in the wind; tomorrow's unforeseen events have their way of effecting rapid changes in the popular mood and will.

The Female Factor

Let us turn now to the third circumstance that made peacetime full employment seem plausible in 1945. This was of a different type, reflecting the prevailing social conception of full employment rather than the conditions for its achievement. To be blunt: for most people full employment meant employment of male workers in industrial jobs. Note the conscious wording of the most famous definition of full employment at that time, offered in *Full Employment in a Free Society*, the 1944 Beveridge Report: "having always more vacant jobs than unemployed men, not slightly fewer jobs. It means that the jobs are at fair wages, of such a kind and so located that the unemployed men can reasonably be expected to take them."[12] It is evident from the context that the use of the male noun is not unintended. There was, safe to say, little discussion in Britain (and none, specifically, in the Beveridge Report) of what might happen if this comfortable limit on the necessary achievement were lifted.

Herbert Stein recently commented on the American debate that changed *full* to *maximum* employment in the statement of objectives of the Employment Act of 1946: "In the discussion of the bill, which was originally called 'The Full Employment Act,' the point was made that if the word 'full' was taken literally all the women and children would be required to take jobs. Of course, that was not the objective of the bill."[13] Evidently here was a reason for changing the wording to which no one in a position to influence policy could object.

Although during wartime women extensively staffed the industrial workforce, women workers were all but invisible to designers of the postwar economic world. It was assumed they would return to the home. The task, as it was seen, was to employ heads of households in order to avoid regressing to the appalling social conditions of the Depression. The task was assuredly not to perpetuate the full change in social conditions occasioned as a temporary matter by the war. To the contrary, there was a common policy presumption that social relations would return to prewar (and even pre-Depression) normality.

In this normality, single women would work until marriage. Married women would withdraw from the workforce. And so, in 1950, 86 percent of the men of working age were in the labor force, compared with 34 percent of the women. Seventy-one percent of all jobs were held by men. Moreover, one-third of all nonagricultural jobs were in the manufacturing sector, and this was a male preserve. The single-income family was the social norm, and perhaps a majority of all jobs had the purpose of supporting, through a man's income, an entire family.

All of this has changed completely. In 1986, 44 percent of all jobs were held by women, and 53 percent of all women of working age were in the labor force. Male participation had dropped, to 76 percent, due mainly to an increase in early retirement. Of all jobs, those in manufacturing now comprise only 19 percent. The two-income family is the social norm, along with an increasing number of unattached individuals. In general, a single job can no longer support family life. As noted in the *Economic Report of the President* for 1987, the largest rates of increase in labor force participation were for married women, and "the sharpest increases have been for wives with very young children."[14]

The Obsolescence of Full Employment

In 1978 *full* finally displaced *maximum* as the qualifier describing the declared goal for employment in the Employment Act. This reflected, in part, a symbolic drive by those associated with the original bill to complete their victory of 1946. But even more strongly, it was a recognition that the desire of women and children (and, importantly also, of blacks) for jobs could no longer be disregarded in the grand symbolic design.

Here we run into difficulties that are far more fundamental than the matters of theory and politics discussed above. The collapse of the sociological stereotype of the male industrial worker is, one might reasonably say, the single most pervasive social fact of the late postwar era. Women and young people, but especially married women, have moved into the labor force in a vast and undiminishing stream. If one allows the possibility that active pursuit of full employment might again become politically attractive, attention must focus on what this broadening of labor force participation means for that objective.

What does it mean that we now have women and children, in unprecedented numbers, deserting hearth and higher education and crowding into the workforce? Does this make the problem of creating jobs any more urgent? Does it make the problem more difficult? Should policy accept the drift to universal workforce participation or resist it? To approach these questions, we need some understanding of why the phenomenon has occurred and what it entails for social life.

At the most fundamental level, economists believe that individuals make the decision to work for a wage by comparing the utility that would be lost by working with the purchasing power that a cash income will bring. Thus, in principle, a decision *not* to work can change due to any of four distinct reasons. The wage may rise, overcoming the temptations of leisure or housework or community life. The quality of work may improve, making the disutility of labor less onerous than it had been. The quality of nonwork life may decline, again making wage work more attractive than it had been. Or, finally, preferences may change, either because the individuals in question change or because they change their minds. Thus the identical decision made one way at one time is made a different way, by the same or different persons, at a later time.

The explanations of rising female labor force participation rates that still prevail in most discussions today originated before 1973 and are still rooted in the improving labor market conditions of that time—and thus are covered by the first two of the above explanations. Real wages for women were then rising, both absolutely and relatively to those of men.

Married women especially were therefore presumed to be substituting market work for home work for the first reason. Higher-valued work, taking advantage of education and ability previously run to waste, was supposedly taking over from lower-valued (and unpaid) home work, which in theory was being taken over by the household appliance. Moreover, as occupational discrimination broke down, women were entering the upper ranks of the professions—a fact that was not numerically important but that no doubt influenced the outlook of professionals studying the question and perhaps also, by example, of women workers at large. All of this seemed to explain well the rise in the civilian labor force participation rate for women over the first twenty years after World War II, which changed from 27 to 36 percent for all women and from 15 to 34 percent for married women.[15]

There was a corresponding higher unemployment experience for women. But that evidently reflected a larger frictional element in their work lives, the transitional oversupply of their relatively undifferentiated skills, discrimination, smaller endowments of search experience and ability. Surely unemployment rates would converge as time erased these disadvantages. Hence, higher total or average unemployment, known to conservative economists as a shifting *natural rate of unemployment*, might be expected at each phase of the business cycle for a time, but should be regarded as an epiphenomenon of a deeper social change and not a matter with which macroeconomic policy should be concerned.

Fluctuations in the raw unemployment rate attributable to rising female or teenage labor force participation were therefore seen as independent of the underlying state of demand. They would distort the standard, and hitherto stable, measured relationship between the inflation and unemployment rates, but these distortions were predictable and not a social problem; rising female participation and unemployment did not require a macropolicy response. To help keep the measured Phillips curve stable, researchers calculated adjusted unemployment rates that removed from the measured rates effects attributable to changes in the composition of the workforce.[16] In so doing, they made a critical implicit assumption: that the rise in female workers had nothing to do with, and did not reflect, any change in the quality and social primacy of the jobs held by prime-age male heads of households.

Since 1973, the optimistic judgment behind this consensus has lost its foundation. Real and relative wages for women have ceased to rise. It is

The Obsolescence of Full Employment

no longer plausible to assume that women and children are substituting higher-valued paid work for low-valued home work and leisure in response to a rising wage. But participation rates keep going up. It therefore seems that women are now taking jobs that under earlier conditions they would have rejected.

Imagine an economist working in 1973 with the accepted theory of female labor market participation in the 1960s, suddenly confronted with a projection of economic conditions for "secondary" laborers in the 1970s and 1980s. Imagine telling him that the real wages available to women would fall, while at the same time the improvement in their labor market opportunities relative to those of men would slow or stop. Such an economist would have made an unequivocal prediction. He would have said that, as women were clearly substituting into the labor market in response to rising wages and improved conditions of work, a reversal of these incentives would lead to a reversal of behavior. Given the adverse assumptions, women would respond by substituting out.

The conditionals came to pass, but the hypothetical prediction did not. Average real wages have fallen since 1972 and now stand below their value in 1968.[17] This means that the purchasing power of a week's work has declined: one cannot buy as comfortable a standard of living for forty hours on the job as one could have a decade and a half ago.

The quality of work for women is also not getting better. Before 1973, labor economists celebrated the improving quality of work available to women. But a rising desirability of available jobs, either absolutely or relative to those held by men, though still clearly true in some cases, does not characterize most modern stenographic, retail trades and other service employment. And this is where the vast bulk of incremental employment occurred in the expansions of the 1970s and 1980s. Women are now accepting jobs that are, in terms of pay, prestige, potential promotion and the conditions of work itself, increasingly bad.

Yet despite the deterioration in the attractiveness of work, despite the fall in the remuneration of labor, the labor force participation rate for women has continued to rise sharply. It reached 55 percent in 1986 compared with 46 percent as recently as 1975. The actual rise may be contrasted with a 1976 projection by the Bureau of Labor Statistics, still based on the older causal presumptions, of a 46 percent participation rate for all females by 1990.[18] Women are defying the previously accepted explanations of their behavior. Why?

From this question, mainstream economics takes refuge in the fourth possible answer. Preferences have changed. Women did not want to work before, but now they do. Sociological pressures can be cited, at least by economists who need not claim mastery of any sociological literature that may exist. In taking this path, economists remove the issue of rising female labor force participation from the roster of researchable topics in economics.

No doubt, changing preferences *are* a factor. But the changing dynamics of the household seem to be a factor of even more fundamental importance. This is the third hypothetical explanation: the quality of nonwork has declined. This hypothesis has been relatively neglected. Yet of all the alternatives given, this one has the strongest implications for social policy—while the changing preferences explanation has the weakest.

Traditional explanations of labor market participation do not, of course, wholly neglect the marginal utility of leisure, and they recognize, in passing, the effect of total family income on it. Statistically, the relation between family income and the labor force participation of auxiliary workers is long established: families with low-income heads have more workers. Perhaps, though, the relationship is now stronger than it was when average real wages were rising. At heart, the old theory rested on a primary connection between individual labor force participation and the individual wage. It did not sufficiently recognize that while earnings are individual, consumption is ineluctably a family matter.

Now suppose that households also conceive their need for income in relative terms—that they measure their well-being in terms of living *standards* absorbed from the community in which they live. This is a most banal fact of common observation. From it, it follows that households are likely to have stable notions of satisfactory and unsatisfactory consumption possibility growth rates. That is, families measure their well-being by observing their own consumption patterns in relation to those of their neighbors. If they keep pace, fine; otherwise, not so fine.

Right after World War II, consumption standards were highly unsettled. No one really knew what the economy was capable of producing under postwar economic conditions, or what macroeconomic management could bring by way of effective full employment. Initial consumption standards were set as social facts about employment and productivity emerged, and these were largely according to the real earnings capabilities

The Obsolescence of Full Employment

of the male worker. This meant, in turn, that so long as women stayed out of the workforce, most households could enjoy rising real consumption at just the rate at which the real productivity of the existing workforce would grow.

So long as economic growth remained steady at predicted rates, consumption expectations of families were largely satisfied and the erosion of the immediate postwar employment arrangements was slow. Community consumption standards did not rise above the levels attainable within traditional family employment patterns, and so families did not feel compelled to challenge those arrangements and patterns. Nor, if they had, was success likely. A small penetration of women into the world of work met diminished opportunities and seemingly insuperable barriers to sustained progress. Opportunities for supernormal advance, even if they existed, were checked by routines of community life and occupational discrimination. Married women did not work because the leisure and home work available to them were more highly valued by them, under the circumstances, than the work opportunities that existed.

Nevertheless, over the years, the separation of women from work did diminish. The sustained growth of real incomes and employment opportunities through 1973, together with the demographic, social and cultural changes of the 1960s, accelerated this process. Married women slowly reintegrated themselves into the labor force. Discriminatory barriers, such as access to the upper reaches of higher education, began to crumble. The Vietnam War no doubt speeded things up to some degree, partly by taking some men out of the labor force and reopening some job opportunities in industrial work for women, and partly by fostering a social climate more sensitive to demands for change. Indeed, the modern surge in women's labor force participation seemed to start in 1966, after a decade's stagnation, with a 1 percent jump that brought over 40 percent of women into the labor force for the first time since World War II.

There was no strong reason, at first, why these events should have disrupted the normal rise in consumption expectations and achievement. That is, at this point, women were joining the labor force because the reward for work was rising above the marginal valuation of home work and leisure. And more machines, made cheaper in labor terms by technological change and rising productivity, were moving into the home, supposedly to reduce further the time demands of unpaid domestic labor.

Work as Insurance

So it is to the 1970s, with its recessions and external shocks, that we must look, once again, as the cause of dramatic change. Suddenly, the normal rise of living standards could not reliably be maintained by normal, or even normally increasing, labor force involvement. Those unemployed outright faced the most immediate threat. But others, though holding their jobs and their wages, and so unaffected in direct material terms, were nevertheless worse off. They worried. They fretted. The *risk* of unemployment in the family—a wholly new thing for many people in 1970—came into their lives.

The proportion of males in the population who were employed had remained virtually constant over the 1960s, scarcely varying between 77 and 78 percent. In 1970 this figure took a sharp jolt, falling to just over 76 percent, from which it has never recovered. Suddenly, there was a new trend: falling male employment and a sharply rising rate of male unemployment. The unemployment rate for all males rose from 2.8 to 4.4 percent in 1970, and continued rising to 5.3 percent in 1971. It would jump again, from 4.9 to 7.9 percent, in 1975. Male employment at that time took another hard and permanent hit, falling from 75 to below 72 percent of the male population. Neither male employment nor male unemployment rates have ever returned to the values that existed constantly from 1965 to 1969, and male unemployment rates have been kept below double digits in the 1980s only because of a 3 percent drop since 1970 in the male labor force participation rate. Figure 5–1 illustrates the trend of labor-force participation for the two sexes—the male rate always falling, that for women always rising—against the backdrop of the unemployment rate for adult male workers.

If the actual experience of unemployment was a shock, the risk of unemployment no doubt cast a wider net over the working population, affecting families threatened by unemployment as well as those actually hit. It induced a rational, risk-minimizing reaction, namely, the diversification of employment experience within the household. It would be safer for two (or more, if available) members of the family unit to hold a job. Of course, in the recession, new jobs were not available. But when they became available, women flocked in increasing numbers to demand them. Female labor force participation jumped 2.3 percent in the recovery of 1972–74, and double that, 4.6 percent, in the recovery of 1975–79.

The Obsolescence of Full Employment

FIGURE 5–1

Labor Force Participation

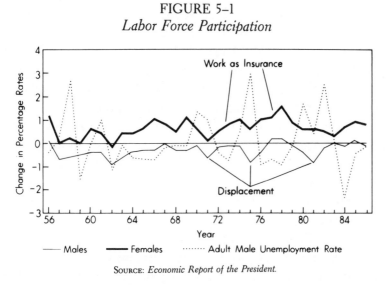

Year

—— Males   —— Females   ·········· Adult Male Unemployment Rate

SOURCE: *Economic Report of the President.*

Moreover, women did not flee the labor market in recessions, as theory might have predicted. Women's labor force participation now rose in good times and bad.

Thus a new cause of rising participation in paid work by women began to be felt. And this was not a response to improved opportunities, but rather to a demand for a degree of household security that, under prevailing economic conditions, a single income could no longer provide. The marginal utility of leisure had fallen for the precise reason that leisure—nonwork—no longer felt secure.

Now a chain reaction followed. The women were competing for, and receiving, nonmanufacturing jobs. Supply and demand dictate that the relative wage outside the manufacturing sector must fall as competition for nonmanufacturing jobs grows more intense. This indeed happened. Also, as the recessions struck at manufacturing employment opportunities, and these did not recover, primary (male) workers were also displaced downward into services at the same time as low-grade opportunities for women opened up. For those who had formerly lived well on no longer available factory employment, the two-income household became the *only* means to maintain household consumption growth near its previous rate. Each wave of disruption impelled more auxiliary workers from previously comfortable but newly insecure families into the labor market.

It is highly probable, as well, that some of the overall downturn in productivity growth observed by macroeconomists at this same time set in for much the same reason. An investment sector of a given size could not provide all the new labor market entrants with employment in the manufacturing sector. They found their jobs, instead, in the relatively low-paid and uncapitalized services sector, and in so doing shifted the mix of all employment away from sectors of relatively high productivity growth. As a result, total measured productivity growth slowed down.

The process, once started, had developed its own momentum by this decade even though recessions did not recur after 1982. As more families acquired second earners, the barriers that previously existed for female labor force participation eroded even more quickly. Some households whose material living standards were not directly reduced in the recession now perceived an opportunity for relative advance that had not previously been open. For them, dual labor force participation was a way to move up on the distribution of income. This intensified the competition for certain kinds of inherently limited goods, such as housing in the better neighborhoods and education at the better schools. In consequence, families previously satisfied with one earner's income found their consumption standards involuntarily displaced downward. Their reaction—which follows a "tipping" pattern as described by economist Thomas Schelling[19]— would, in turn, create a powerful incentive for more householders to join the labor pool. Of course, *all* households cannot simultaneously improve their relative standing by adding additional workers and incomes. But this changes nothing with regard to incentives: failure to do so must mean a relative decline.

In 1979, 50.9 percent of all women were in the workforce and 47.5 percent were working. By 1986, participation was over 55 percent, and employment stood at 51.4 percent. The share of women working rose in every year of the 1980s, while the share of men working dropped to an all-time low of 68.8 percent in 1983 before recovering to 71 percent by 1986. This value remains lower than in any year before 1981.

The labor market is flexible: people adjust their labor supply to sustained conditions. Risk spreading within the household, a desire to maintain consumption standards, and neighborhood effects on asset markets may have together accounted for the phenomenon we observe even without any change in underlying preferences for work and income. Over time, the previously typical family supported solely by the affluent male worker diminishes in number, and the multiearner family achieving comparable consumption standards, but at a higher level of group marketplace effort, takes its place.

The Obsolescence of Full Employment

Consequences for Policy

The meaning of the conventional unemployment rate as an index of welfare across such changes is increasingly murky. In 1986, as in 1980, the overall unemployment rate was about 7 percent. In 1986, 10 million more people were working, including 3.5 million more men and 5.5 million more women. There were more unemployed, too, in 1986 than in 1980: 263,000 more men and 337,000 more women. Was the welfare of the working population entirely unchanged by these shifts, as the unchanged unemployment rate would seem to tell us? The traditional perspective, which allows the use of the raw unemployment rate as an index of changes in social welfare in the short run, while in the longer run adjusting the numbers to filter out the adverse experience of women and teenagers, might lead to an argument that things were at least no worse, and possibly even better, in 1986 than in 1980. The unemployment rate in 1986 would be lower than in 1980—if it weren't, that is, for all those additional women.

My argument leads to an entirely opposite inference: the women (and teenagers) are telling us something about a secular decline in the quality of all available jobs. The men can find work—but it is often not good work, compared with past norms. If it were, fewer married women and fewer women with young children would be in the labor market. Employment was up by 10 percent in 1986 over 1980. But the growth of wages and salaries, which had averaged 1.6 percent annually in real terms from 1960 to 1973, was now falling at an average annual rate, from 1978 to 1986, of 0.7 percent.

The unemployment rate is therefore a misleading guide to the labor market, not because it is an inaccurately pessimistic measure of some true state, but because it misses altogether a central ingredient of labor market experience. This is the declining quality of employment for those who do work. Over time higher total employment, and even greater equality both across job types and across households as highly paid manufacturing employment declines in proportion to the total, can be fully consistent with declining social welfare.

As policy generates an ever-increasing demand for employment in non-traded goods and services, it is no doubt true that the labor market is becoming more competitive. Service jobs designed to accommodate new market entrants and high rates of turnover must be less differentiated, less skill specific, and more intersubstitutable than manufacturing jobs. This can be seen directly in the data, which indicate a declining share of union membership and a persistently low and steady average nominal wage. The new cadre of service workers do not enjoy the job protection, the cost of living adjustments, or the prospects of moving up a seniority or career ladder that their industrial predecessors had established.

This means that labor market transmission of inflationary pressures is likely to be reduced as time passes. A given rise in import prices, for example, will be less offset by effective demands for a compensating increase in wages. Correspondingly, any decline in aggregate demand and any rise in nonservice unemployment, such as would follow a reduction in investment or exports, will translate more rapidly into wage reductions as service workers struggle to keep their jobs. The labor market, long a source of inflationary bias, may now be harboring powerful new forces that pull just the opposite way.

Yet, while this seems reassuring, it should not be considered as such. Recall that the service workers are not selling their wares on the world market. How, then, are we and they to pay for the imported goods they consume? In 1985, U.S. merchandise imports exceeded exports by $125 billion. Consumption standards were, to this extent, maintained on credit. If, to take an extreme hypothesis, the credit were withdrawn and the United States were then forced to cut imports down to the level of exports in the mid-1980s, and if it chose to do so exclusively by curtailing consumption, *U.S. purchases of consumer durable and nondurable goods would have to fall by approximately 10 percent.* Purchases of durables would fall by 17 percent through a reduction of automotive imports alone. This would entail a drop in living standards comparable in severity to the Latin American crisis. This is not a prediction: the decline will not, in all likelihood, occur as a matter of crisis. But it will occur over time, so long as the U.S. economy remains unable to generate jobs that can pay for goods purchased on the world market.

The Need for Good Jobs

The policy message of these reflections is straightforward: we must look beyond grossly conceived full employment to the composition and quality of employment. Employment policymakers and full employment strategists should concede that employment as such is not an unmitigated good. Some—much—employment is a burden, the need for which can and should be avoided. Such employment can be sacrificed for the sake of improving the incomes and the welfare of the whole population. Employment generated by hardship and risk will tend to diminish unlamented if policy works effectively toward the primary goal of the reduction of hardship and risk.

Public resources therefore should not be directed toward the provision of universal employment. They should instead aim at the creation of a large central core of good jobs. These should be jobs that pay America's way in the world, so that our consumption standards need not fall when our credit runs out. It is essential that such jobs be open and accessible equally to men and women and to all racial groups. Nevertheless, it is a reasonable presumption that the return in number of such jobs would restore the marginal utility of nonpaid labor time in the family units to which the jobs become attached. It would thus slow and perhaps ultimately reduce the compulsion to work that is driving people into employment and away from activities they would otherwise prefer.

And such a slowdown should indeed be a major social goal. We do not need a culture of idle suburban housewives or, worse yet, of women again subordinated to the management of household consumption. But our national community life suffers immensely when all talents and time (of both sexes) are devoted to paid work of an increasingly menial and powerless sort. We need community organization, voluntary artistic and charity effort, political regrouping, educational and environmental activism and the option of full-time parenthood. All of these are values and elements of a vibrant social life. They are values endangered by universal work. They can be substantially restored by increasing on a sex-blind basis the share of high-income, empowering jobs in the total employment mix. This should be our employment goal.

The next step is to integrate a strategy for good employment into the larger macroeconomic and international context with which we must be centrally concerned.

CHAPTER 6

Profits and

Productive Investment

A CCORDING TO classical economists from Adam Smith to Karl Marx, economic surplus is generated in production and realized through sale at prices higher than costs. One of David Ricardo's accomplishments was to show how surplus accrued, as rent, to the fixed factor of production. Joseph Schumpeter's vision is of surplus created and destroyed in waves of technological change, an extension of Ricardo in which the fixed factor, now technological advantage rather than land, could be brought into existence, survive momentarily and disappear. John Maynard Keynes saw the accumulation of surplus, the profits boom, at work in French and British development after the Spanish discovery of gold in the Americas. And Michal Kalecki and Nicholas Kaldor, in formal models, developed a macrodynamics of income distribution that shows the links between profits, demand, investment and growth. Here again surplus is a key concept, and so has survived into the modern age.

In the Marxian vision, surplus is the basal evil of capitalism. Its very existence is due to property relations that are unique to capitalist systems, in which the means of production are held in private hands. For under

Profits and Productive Investment

capitalism, in order to work at all and earn his keep, the worker must work for the capitalist part of the day and for free. His "unpaid labor," then, is the source of goods for luxury consumption by a class that does not itself work, as well as the fount of capital accumulation on which expansion of the production process depends. In the postcapitalist world, surplus will disappear, not because there will be no accumulation, but simply because the workers will come to own, through the state, the totality of their own product: "Solution of the contradictions. The proletariat seizes the public power, and by means of this transforms the socialised means of production . . . into public property. By this act, the proletariat frees the means of production from the character of capital they have thus far borne."[1]

Schumpeter and Keynes both shared, in common with Marx, the analytical insight that *profit,* extracted in the first instance at the expense of wages, is the source of accumulation. Their difference—and it is profound—lay in their appreciation of the normative (or welfare) implications of profit. For Keynes and Schumpeter, accumulation meant, above all, social progress. In visionary moments, Keynes foresaw a world in which enough accumulation had occurred, particularly in the form of housing and public capital investment ("railways from London to York"), so that labor would be at its ease. Schumpeter had fewer illusions about stability, for he appreciated, uniquely among economists in the mid-twentieth century, the role of technical change in forcing the continual turnover of the capital stock. Yet Schumpeter also saw clearly the benefits of technically progressive accumulation, even under private capital, and its superiority over technologically conservative state socialism in this regard: "The capitalist achievement does not typically consist in providing more silk stockings for queens but in bringing them within the reach of factory girls in return for steadily decreasing amounts of effort."[2]

The odd fact is that for a well-trained modern or neoclassical economist, educated in the traditions prevailing in the United States since World War II, this debate over the social function of surplus, profit and accumulation has disappeared. The concepts of surplus and even of profit itself in mainstream economics are peripheral, at most a distraction. The big question of how capital accumulates is answered in another way.

In the neoclassical vision, accumulation arises not from profit but from *saving.* And saving is not creation, but abstinence; it is a set-aside out of present production that would otherwise be consumed. This is more than a semantic shift, for saving can occur equally from wages and from profits.

Under the assumption that markets are efficient (a key but highly questionable assumption), resources do not go unused, and that which is saved will be invested. Investment is therefore independent of profit: it can occur equally in low-profit and in high-profit economies (so long as there is high saving). And so, the neoclassical synthesis effectively separates the accumulation of capital from what classical economists perceived to be its social context.

The neoclassical theory of profit, then, is equally separated from the theory of investment. Profit is indeed not surplus, but an earned return to the factor of production called *capital*. This return is earned in the market; it is an attribute of technical relations, of marginal productivities and of the capital-intensity nature of production. It is therefore homologous to, of the same form as, wage income earned in the labor market by workers, which also rests on technical relations and marginal productivities and so on. And profit income is also nothing special: like wages, it can be either saved or consumed. Such profit has nothing to do with "exploitation" or "macrodynamics." "Quasi-rents" and "monopoly profits" exist in the neoclassical world, but as addenda; they play no essential role in the central neoclassical vision of production, accumulation and the distribution of income.

Oddly, it has been at just this point that American Keynesians, though following Keynes in other respects (such as a rejection of the assumption that free labor markets automatically tend to full employment), have absorbed the neoclassical vision. American Keynesians and pure neoclassicists (of, say, the Chicago view) differ vigorously on numerous matters, such as the relation of money to prices, how interest rates are set and whether expectations are rational. Yet they agree on the distributional essential, on deriving investment from a savings function and profits from production, rather than both from an integrated model of macroeconomic flows. And so, American Keynesians have sought to avoid the conflict over distributional vision, with its ideological implications, that have linked economic theory to politics in other places and earlier times.

Nevertheless, the idea of economic surplus keeps reappearing in economics, and for a reason. Rent-seeking behavior, for example, has lately become a fashionable topic in the economics of public choice.[3] Increasing returns to scale, a technological fact that is inconsistent with the neoclassical view of profits, has been established at the heart of a new neoclassical trade theory by Paul Krugman.[4] A crisis of exploitation of labor has been

Profits and Productive Investment

proposed by Sam Bowles and his colleagues to explain the productivity slowdown.[5] Closer to the topic here, the concept of profits as part of macroeconomics remains at the core of the post-Keynesian tradition. Perhaps, therefore, the linkage of the classical economists between profits, investment and accumulation really has enduring merit.

I argue here that capitalism must be swallowed whole. Capitalism is a system of social as well as technical relations. In this system, profit emerges in ways that are integrally linked to investment, to capital formation, and to technical progress, and the former cannot be divorced from the latter without losing sight of the engine that drives the machine. Moreover, accepting Keynes and Schumpeter over Marx, accumulation need not lead to impoverishment and misery. To the contrary, it can (though it will not necessarily do so) lead to relative enrichment, and must do so as a practical matter if the system itself is to survive. Therefore a main goal of progressive macroeconomics must be (in an extreme irony) the profits boom—provided that profits are used for effective accumulation, or what may be termed *productive investment.*

To achieve this goal, furthermore, is not a matter, as the neoclassical paradigm leads one to suppose, of incentives and behavior, of parsimony, austerity, sacrifice, efficiency and thrift. It is instead a matter of achieving the right speed and structure of economic growth. It is a macrodynamic problem. This makes it far easier as a technical matter to accomplish, once the framework is understood. The difficulties are political, not economic: they stem from the displacement of older forms of capital, the creation and redistribution of wealth and the rearrangement of power that occur uniquely in capitalism under conditions of rapid change. Such dislocations are not costless, but the essence of a progressive vision is to recognize the degree to which they can, in fact, be liberating.

In what follows, I will present the macrodynamic vision of profits and productive investment as it bears specifically on the present structure of the world economy and the position within it of the United States. The key figure in the articulation of this vision is again Michal Kalecki, whose trenchant observations on political economy we have already encountered.[6] I ask the reader's indulgence for what is (so I'm told) a dense and difficult excursion. I hope it will be worth the effort.

Sources of Profit

Kalecki's worldview turns on the basic proposition that money profits are determined by macroeconomic conditions, and not, as neoclassical economics supposes, by the technical conditions of production. In an initial simplified version of the model, it can be shown that *current gross investment,* one of the great streams of aggregate spending, exactly determines *current gross profits.* Gross investment is a matter of the decisions of capitalists and entrepreneurs taken with regard to resources available and to the prospects for future profit. Thus, in this view, the most basic issues in economics—prices, profits and the direction of investment—are determined not by technical relations but fundamentally by human behavior. And it is not human behavior in general but that of a particular social class, of the capitalists or, to use less charged language, of businessmen and entrepreneurs. Business plays the central role in this view of economic life.

The analysis begins with a simple accounting framework and a few propositions about behavior. Consider a model economy divided into two sectors: the production of capital goods for industry and the production of consumer goods to supply workers with the necessities and conveniences of life. There are two types of agents: *capitalists,* who receive and invest profits, and *workers,* who receive and spend wages. These classes need not be entirely distinct: some capitalists may receive some wages, and some workers may earn some dividends and interest. What is important, at first, is not class identity but a clear association between the *source* of income and the *uses* to which income is put. There is no government or foreign trade in this simple model.

Assume, as a first approximation, that capitalists do not consume out of profits and that workers do not save from their wages. (This seemingly unreasonable condition is, in the aggregate, not too far wrong in the real world. It serves the critical purpose in the model of linking the value of wages to the value of output of consumer goods, and so matching the value of profits with the production of machines that are set aside for investment.) Assume further that the consumer goods market clears: producers adjust prices so that the value of consumer goods offered just matches the wage incomes available for their purchase. Wage earnings in both sectors, capital and consumer goods together, must now necessarily equal the value of consumer goods produced. From this the basic proposi-

Profits and Productive Investment

tion follows: profit earnings on the one hand and the value of investment goods on the other must complete the circular flow. Total expenditure on the production of capital goods (investment) must now necessarily just equal the total profit revenue earned in both sectors.

So much is necessarily true as a matter of accounting. But which comes first, investment or profits? Investment must come first! Rational capitalists make decisions to invest on the basis of *expected future* profits, not on the basis of cash they happen to have in hand. If they need more capital for their investment programs, they *raise it*—through the mechanisms of finance which are explored below. By their investment actions as a group, it is therefore capitalists who decide how much current profit will be earned. If large investments are made, large profits will be earned, and if investments falter, profits will slump. All this can be summed up as follows: "Capitalists get what they spend."

Capitalists Get What They Spend

When simplifying assumptions are relaxed, several important qualifications appear, and we move toward the ability to describe real events. First, we may introduce government. When we do, we find that a government deficit *raises* business profits, practically dollar for dollar. This reflects a basic fact of accounting: that financial surpluses and deficits throughout the economy (for the moment, closed to foreign trade), when taken together, must exactly offset each other and sum to zero. Yet working families, still by assumption, maintain a net financial balance at zero; they do not borrow to consume, and they do not save out of wage incomes. Therefore a rise in the government deficit must be just offset by a rise in business surplus or profits. This is true even if the deficit is brought on by a rise in government spending (instead of, say, a corporate tax cut directly affecting profit income) and so happens also to increase directly the total dollar sum paid out to workers as wages or in transfers. So long as workers do not save, their respending of new government transfer and wage income will raise business profits by just the amount of the rise in the government's deficit.

Incidentally, that this corresponds well to the U.S. experience can be demonstrated from national income data. In particular, business profits rise sharply in the immediate aftermath of recessions because the government's deficit has risen. Robert Eisner's recent work shows some interesting correlations between this phenomenon and the fluctuations of the stock market.[7] There is some variation in workers' savings in real life, but not enough to invalidate the usefulness of the generalization that fluctuations in government deficits mainly affect the flow of business profits. Figure 6-1 shows the pattern of budget deficits and business profits for the United States in the 1980s.

Now we may say that there is also some capitalists' consumption, some *spending* out of profit income for consumer goods. This might be thought to reduce money profits, since ostensibly such spending is diverted from investment. In fact, it is easily shown that consumption *out of profits* is (as Keynes observed) a "widow's cruse": such spending raises current profits dollar for dollar. It need have no effect whatever on capital formation.

In the initial position, wages entirely absorb the value of consumer goods production. Additional spending by nonworkers for the same goods may therefore drive up their price (and must, if goods markets are to clear). Wages remain unchanged. And so, higher prices must raise the profits earned in the consumer goods sector by exactly the amount of the new spending. Now, of course, total profit income is larger than total investment (which hasn't changed at all), and workers' real wages have

FIGURE 6–1
Profits and Deficits

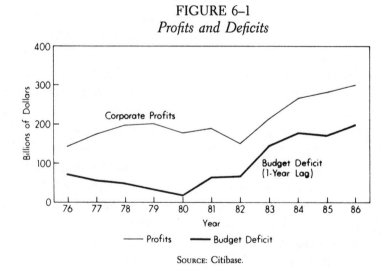

SOURCE: Citibase.

Profits and Productive Investment

fallen (because prices are up and money wages are not). There has been a change in the distribution of income, experienced by workers as price inflation and by business as a profits boom. But all the markets have cleared, and so businessmen will see no need for new investment beyond what they were planning to do to replace depreciated capital or embody recent technical change in their production process in the first place. That is, no more units can be sold than were in fact sold even at the new inflated price; to add new capacity would only drive the price back down. High living by capitalists, under these assumptions, has a tendency only to raise the share of profits in income, to bid real consumer goods away from the workers who would otherwise enjoy them. Again, "capitalists get what they spend." Investment in this case does not change.

Short-run market clearing in consumer goods, achieved by adjusting prices, is, however, something of a Chicago myth. It is not the characteristic case; certainly it is not for manufactured goods. Instead, the usual response of real business firms to a rise in spending from profit income is to hold prices reasonably steady and to seek to increase the supply. A typical pattern is that when demand rises, consumer goods distributors initially back-order their customers and place new orders for more product with their suppliers. The consumer goods producers, in turn, send out as necessary the call for new capital goods. A rise in investment over and above what was required to replace existing equipment, and therefore in the size of the capital goods industry, is now necessary to meet the demand for goods. When the goods arrive, they are made available to all consumers at or near the original prices. Thus, in practice, capitalist consumption (or any increment to demand) stimulates production; price inflexibility promotes quantity expansion over time.[8]

But now, the investing units wish to spend on plant and equipment ahead of final sales. The goods that are on order have not actually been sold. Since sales have not been made, the intended increase in total consumption has not occurred, and the profits this would generate have not yet been earned. The goods producers have cash on hand to pay for new factors of production in the capital goods sector, but only to the extent of the previous period's (retained) profits. For increased investment to occur, someone must bridge the gap between hypothetical future incomes and current cash needs. This is the fundamental function of the financial system, and it is the weak link of all capitalist relations.

Financing Investment

The link is forged in the following way. The expectation that a rise in consumption will occur, because the intention to increase consumption exists and has been signaled by back orders, motivates a shared expectation of increased dollar profits. Prices in asset markets, markets that deal in claims to ownership of capital, reflect the net present value of expected future earnings. Such prices, as in the stock market and commodity futures markets, now rise in anticipation of price and profit rises that will be realized when the rise in consumption actually occurs. Asset price rises can happen independently of (and with little or no increase in) actual transactions in such markets if buyers and sellers share the same perception about what the stocks and options are worth (analogously, the value of my house can rise even though I do not actually attempt to sell it).

Such increases in asset prices affect realizable gross profits. In fact, it is almost exactly as if consumption out of profits had actually increased. The increased asset price is experienced as a rise in the wealth of the investor; for practical purposes, it is equivalent to a rise in profit income even though there is as yet no new production. Such a wealth increase— the stock boom that starts at the trough of the recession—solves the investment financing problem. The new paper wealth can be lent out and converted into spending on capital goods. This is the sense in which, as Kalecki argued, a rise in investment is financed by itself.

Business debt, then, is a transfer of spending power within the capitalist class, not a transfer out of past savings but a capitalization of expected future earnings—a loan, as it were, from the expected future to the present. Whenever the investing unit and the recipient of rising profit incomes are not actually the same corporate entity, the legal act of debt creation must occur before the investment spending can happen. A rise in the value of previously issued corporate stock does not directly release funds for new investment. Instead, it gives the company whose stock goes up borrowing power at the bank, which is almost as good (so long, that is, as the central bank stands ready to accommodate the rising demand for bank credit). And so long as the boom continues, debt creation is a self-validating process—the debts incurred to finance investment are serviced out of the rising profit income that occurs when the investment spending goes forward.

It is worth noting that the legal situation, and hence the extent to which new investment requires the creation of new business debt, is quite different for firms at different stages of the corporate life cycle. A new firm is financed with equity: personal at first and then by going public on the stock market. In this way, access to the spending power created by rising asset values is transferred directly to the firm; new debt is not created. But an older, established firm faces a barrier to financing in this manner; for such a firm, to issue new equity would risk the dilution of shares already on the market. The older firm must instead generally use the rise in its value (reflected in the stock market) to secure the acquisition of new debt. Thus business debt creation (as opposed to new equity) is a matter of increased investment spending concentrated in older firms.

Effects of Saving and Dissaving

The same logic holds that when *workers* increase their saving out of wages, realized profits *fall*. The price of consumer goods must be lowered below the wage bill to clear the market or else the quantity produced must be cut. Either can only mean a sacrifice of profits. Profits now fall below investment. In principle, workers' savings may be reloaned to the capitalists to finance investment. But this is ineffective: with lower demand, the investment is no longer wanted. The expectation that consumption will fall destroys the link between confidence and credit; capitalization to finance investment no longer occurs. A rise in workers' saving is therefore no inducement to invest; it is instead the mechanism of recession and the harbinger of crisis.

Where workers have the opportunity to *dissave* by borrowing, the effects are the same as for an increase in investment or capitalists' consumption. That is, workers' borrowing raises current profit, which is offset on the balance sheet by workers' debt. Here the connection between borrowing and profits is direct: the credit is taken out by the worker at the time of his profit-increasing purchase. In this case, workers are acting as quasi-investors, spending out of income they have not yet earned. To this extent, future wages must rise so as to permit servicing of the debts, or else future living standards, demand and production will be squeezed. Workers' dissaving can thus be a dangerous phenomenon in the medium to long term, whose validation depends either on later inflation or on extremely rapid future rates of productivity and money wage growth. It is easy to construct scenarios in which the inability to pay interest generates a crisis in the household sector. But all of this is immaterial in the short run, in which, once again contrary to neoclassical intuition, workers' dissaving stimulates profits and investment.

In another counterintuitive result, taxation of profits by government *raises* money profits and induces the creation of private debt.[9] For now government is absorbing profit income and transferring it to expenditure on capital and (mainly) consumer goods. This must raise realized profits, and will do so by just enough to replace the profit income taxed. So now, total (before-tax) profits are greater than total investment, while after-tax profits again just equal investment. If, again, prices do not rise to clear the goods market, investment must again rise to meet the higher real demand for goods. But until the investments are made, the profits to finance them will not be created. And so, the investing agents must again incur debts to carry out their plans.

The government deficit, on the other hand, reduces the need of business to issue debt by raising current after-tax profits in advance of the need to spend for investment. When the government cuts taxes on private wage incomes, spending for a given volume of goods increases and money profits rise. The government's debt now substitutes perfectly for private debt in bridging the financial gap for new investment.

The acrobatics of this description of the financial relations of capitalism may seem daunting to those raised on the simpler verities of the neoclassical world view. Nevertheless, the logical links are tight, and readers can easily see that the description of events has many correlates in real life. A search for the purely logical sources for the departure from this vision of the neoclassical orthodoxy reveals two critical junctures. The first is the principled insistence on *expected profitability*, rather than available (saved) resources, as the source of the motivation for investment. It does not matter, in this view, whether resources have already been set aside for investment; indeed, the attempt to do so, by depressing demand, is counterproductive. Instead, investment proceeds at just the rate at which capitalists choose for it to proceed, using resources that were either otherwise idle or that have been diverted from other forms of current *production*. The second departure is the failure, in the real world, of consumer goods markets to clear by raising prices. This is the behavioral fact that leads to unsatisfied demands for goods and thus to the rise of expected profitability of *new* investment.

Profits and Productive Investment

Seeds of Crisis

In the full model of the closed economy, then, it is the sum of private investment and the government deficit, plus consumption out of profits (and workers' borrowings) and minus workers' savings that determine the flow of (after-tax) money profits to the private business sector. There is obviously a large potential for instability in this process, as changes in policy, outside shocks and financial disruptions can all disrupt the flow. Most fundamentally, everything hinges on distinct investment actions triggered by business profit expectations. Of course such expectations are volatile.

If, for any reason, consumer goods producers lose confidence in the prospects for continued expansion of demand, they will cut their demands for new investment goods. Immediately profits will fall, and capital goods workers will be laid off. However, the capital goods sector has a *higher* share of wages in total costs than does the consumer goods sector. This is because producers of capital goods are themselves less intensive in physical capital than producers of consumer goods. Capital goods producers traffic in human capital: scientists, engineers, craftsmen and skilled production talent. Workers in capital goods industries are being paid not for undifferentiated labor hours but for the application of special skills, which is a return (or quasi-rent) accruing to human capital but which is measured as an ordinary wage. Therefore, when capital goods workers lose their jobs, the *share* of measured profits in total income, ironically, may rise. This is because wages and total income are now falling even more rapidly than profits are.

The depressive process, once in motion, continues in its own way. Capital goods workers will now curtail consumption in order to raise their savings so as to continue to service their debts. Sales and profits in the consumer goods will now join the fall. Consumer goods companies, too, must now lay off workers to preserve their cash flow so as to finance debt. As profit income falls, the crisis may spread to sectors accustomed to consumption out of profits. There is now a further deflation of profits, accompanied by bankruptcies and the liquidation of debts. This is the mechanism of debt deflation, which can be stopped before the final liquidation of all debts only by the intervention of a profit-restoring force, such as a rise in the government deficit.

Depressions are, therefore, an endemic risk of capitalist finance, forestalled in modern times only by the genius of a government financing mechanism that does indeed drive up deficits and restore profits before the natural bottom is reached. Still, in the expansion, so long as confidence holds up and the economy grows and the size of the capital goods-producing sector expands, depression need not occur, and the debts incurred by business and by workers will be serviced. So too, then, will the flows of profits continue.

Exports and Imports

Introducing foreign trade allows the possibility that incomes earned as wages or profits will be spent outside the domestic producing sectors, and that incomes earned outside the economy under study will be spent within it. Naturally, a trade surplus must then flow into domestic profits, and a trade deficit must reduce them.

The relationship between the sizes of the sectors producing capital goods and consumer goods must determine the capacity of a closed economy to grow and the trading needs of an open one. When the capital goods produced are just sufficient to offset depreciation (in both sectors), there is a steady state: neither capital goods nor consumer goods production will expand. When capital goods are produced in excess of replacement needs, there is a potential for expanded domestic investment or for export, which will be offset by a wages bill and a corresponding demand for consumer goods to be met by import. This is the pattern of an advanced country in a developing world. Where capital goods are in shortage, either the consumer goods industries must shrink or a source of capital goods for import found, and domestic wages must be squeezed so that consumer goods can be exported to pay the freight. This is the pattern of a developing country pursuing export-led growth into a rich country's market—and of a former leader overtaken by a rising rival.

The relation between the cost and demand environments and the profitability of a firm depends on how the production processes and the markets of the firm happen to be situated with respect to national boundaries. We can define, for any country such as the United States, two cases: *inward-looking firms* and *outward-looking firms*.

Profits and Productive Investment

Inward-lookingness for a firm with respect to the United States may be defined by the ratio of a pair of shares. The first is the share of imports to the United States in all costs incurred in production. For a foreign firm selling only a final product to the United States, this first ratio is unity: all costs are incurred abroad. For a firm conducting assembly operations in the United States with imported components, this ratio can vary widely, depending on the dollar value added that comes over the border. Thus to establish a *maquiladora* on the Mexican frontier, substituting Mexican labor for American in the assembly stage of electronics manufacture raises the share of imports in costs.

The second share of interest is that of exports from the United States in all sales. This is zero for the wholly foreign firm. For a domestic producer, it can again vary widely: the United States exports only a tiny fraction of the finished automobiles it produces, but a very substantial share of its jet aircraft.

Now consider the ratio of imports-to-costs over exports-in-sales. Where this ratio exceeds one, the firm is inward-looking. Such a firm is relatively more concerned with cost conditions outside the United States and with demand conditions inside the United States. The firm in the converse position (ratio less than one) is outward-looking. Such a firm is relatively more concerned with U.S. costs and with the conditions of worldwide demand. General Motors, with its substantial use of Canadian labor for the U.S. market, is inward-looking. Boeing, which applies American know-how to a market that is nearly 50 percent foreign, is quintessentially outward-looking.

It is clear that (except for cases of exact balance) all firms are either inward- or outward-looking. And it is equally clear—as will be seen—that this method of classification captures the big difference in the cost and demand climate of the 1970s as opposed to the 1980s.

The Uses of Profit

The generation of profits and investments is one problem, and the uses to which they are put is another. It is the gross volume of investment that *inter alia* determines profits. But it is the disposition of retained profits and new borrowings for particular investment projects that determine the capacity of the economy to grow. There is no grand, infallible blueprint for the course of technology any more for a nation than for a business. Profits can be spent shrewdly on machinery of the right kind, increasing current wages and future productive capacity. Or they can be spent poorly on investments that are ill-considered or unlucky and that do not pay off, increasing current wages but not future production. Or they can be spent directly on consumer goods rather than on investment at all. All of these courses return an equal flow of current profits to business. But not all of them generate the same capacity to produce and reproduce productive capacity in later periods. Hence the problem of accumulation has physical aspects that go beyond the macrodynamics of profit generation. Poor investments do not immediately reduce profits. What they reduce is the real quantity of potential future consumption.

We may now usefully make another distinction of a kind that neoclassical economics does not like. This is between productive uses of profits, on the one hand, and expenditures that are counted as investment but do not add to productivity, on the other. The distinction is unmeasurable in principle, and certainly not before the fact. Nevertheless, it defies common sense and perception, in an age of commercial office overbuilding and golden parachutes, to deny its existence. Clearly, some portion of expenditures, where total costs are not determined wholly or perhaps even primarily by considerations of technology, engineering and the bottom line, should be considered as managerial consumption out of profit income or as an absorption of surplus.[10]

Corporate expenditure may therefore be divided (as a conceptual exercise) between productive investment on the one hand and absorbed surplus on the other. Productive investment is an abstraction. It can be found nowhere in the national income accounts data, and no official estimates for it exist.[11] Yet its meaning and economic importance are readily appreciated, and one can reflect with some confidence on what has been happening to it under the macroeconomic conditions of real life.

The late 1970s were a time of (comparatively) low government deficits, but of balanced trade and strong investment spending. Thus corporate profits rose sharply, doubling in nominal terms from 1974 to 1979, with, as one would expect, the strongest growth coming, along with the largest deficits, in the early part of this period.

The type of investment spending was dictated by a cost and demand environment that strongly favored outward-looking firms, and especially so as the expansion wore on. The dollar floated sharply downward, raising the relative price of imports to the United States and lowering the relative price of U.S.–produced components on world markets. At the same time, reflecting the rise of international lending, demand grew more rapidly outside the United States than within it, especially in Latin America toward the end of the decade. These elements meant that the strongest growth of profits occurred in firms favored by cost structures weighted toward the domestic economy and demand structures weighted toward the outside world. Their response is seen in the rising share of investment in GNP and the rapid growth of exports at the same time.

Let us now briefly review the experience of the Reagan years in terms of its likely effects on the generation and disposition of investable resources.

As soon as recovery began, it is clear, the policies of the administration were designed to raise gross business profits powerfully. The ground for this was laid in the recession in three separate ways. First, by forcing the liquidation of past debts (of businesses and of households), the recession of 1981–82 improved the balance sheet of the private economy as a whole, setting the stage for recovery. Second, the federal deficit injected a large and continuing stream of payments into the economy, which showed up nearly exactly, as one would expect, in a rise of business profits. Third, the recession damped sharply the rise of wages and other business costs by creating unemployment and excess supply in resource and commodity markets, and thus improved the cash flow of businesses that buy resources and hire labor to produce manufactured goods. Since the United States is a net resource importer, this had the effect of improving U.S. manufacturing profits at the expense of foreign and foreign-based resource and commodity producers.

Then, the sharp rise in the value of the dollar continued the squeeze on workers' wages that the recession had begun. As demand for product recovered, first because of government and military demand, credit-financed housing and automobile purchases, and then because of investment demand from consumer goods producers, a massive rise in imports made wage militancy extremely imprudent. And essentially there was none. Meanwhile the high dollar and persistent excess supply kept the dollar prices of commodities low, while high real interest rates discouraged commodity restocking. So, cost pressures from that source remained at bay. Thus, for a time, demand expansion and cost repression produced a sharp recovery of profits and an expansion that was led by investment spending. The net effect of this was a doubling of measured corporate profits from 1982 to 1986, from $150 to $300 billion, with most of the rise occurring in 1983 and 1984.[12]

This, however, could not last, for it contained an internal contradiction. The high dollar made manufactured imports too cheap. Consequently, from 1984 on, the trade deficit exploded, rising almost $100 billion in two years. And this, along with a rising surplus of state and local governments that helped to stop the rise in total government deficits, killed the profits boom. The stimulus to profits and the stimulus to investment from government deficits bled away overseas, and the exceptional growth of the economy in 1984 proved to be a one-time affair.

But while profits and so total surplus recovered for a time, the growth of productive investment was undoubtedly much less. This resulted from the industrial structure fostered by the cost and income growth patterns of the Reagan expansion in the context of the U.S. role in international trade.

The United States is an LTP. Our export structure is weighted toward capital goods. Capital goods industries have cost structures that rely on American inputs: the silicon and steel they use are small components of cost in comparison with the engineering and research establishments they must support.

Capital goods industries do not usually survive on the domestic market alone. They must export to prosper in competition with rising producers of similar goods elsewhere in the world. This is an imperative partly of economies of scale but even more of technological development. In the capital goods sector, product advance occurs at the pace of production: each order is to some extent custom, and therefore more orders means a greater potential for development. The industry is like the great white shark: it must move forward, or it dies. If a country's capital goods sector cannot supply world markets, it may quickly lose its technological advantage. And at that point, only protection can save it from extinction.

The growth of productive investment will, however, be largest as a proportion of total profits in industrial sectors that are young; growing rapidly; suffused with technological and entrepreneurial optimism; still unburdened by legions of middle managers and lawyers; unconcerned with the need for distribution networks to reach mass markets; and requiring rapid turnover in capital equipment so as not to lose their competitive advantage. In an advanced economy these sectors are, of course, the capital goods producers of the most progressive kind.

But, such sectors were the ones least favored by the structure of the Reagan expansion. The cost/price environment of the high dollar, combined with America's high growth of demand relative to the rest of the world, was exceptionally favorable to inward-looking firms. Meanwhile the high dollar and world development depression from 1982 on meant just the reverse for outward-looking firms.

The industries that did grow the most, the big consumer goods manufacturers, generated less productive investment than capital goods producers for two reasons. First, they are technologically far less progressive. The great improvements of design that create the biggest technological advances are available to them only when they renew their equipment, which they generally do incrementally, replacing machines and factories only when their useful life is nearing an end. Only in moments of corporate crisis does an automaker, for example, abandon existing plants for a new start. Hence, consumer goods producers are competitive in an extensive sense: they operate on low and steady margins, and make their profits on a high volume of output. By contrast, for the capital goods producer, the next technology and the prospect of gigantic quasi-rents are no further away than the next order. By the same token, abandoning an obsolete process is virtually a way of life. Capital goods producers compete on the intensive margins of radical cost reduction—and since competitive success of this kind is cumulative, they often find that only one firm can survive and prosper in the cutthroat environment that such competition generates.

Second, consumer goods producers are older, established, mature bureaucracies, concerned with maintaining sales to a vast public. Distribution requires bureaucracy; capital goods producers who sell to but a few clients are free of this particular bureaucratic burden. Big consumer goods firms are also concerned with maintaining their position in a rarified, often oligopolistic, institutional world; they are subject to the competitive pathologies best explained by game theory in their relations with their corporate peers. Consumer goods producers therefore tend to absorb within their own operations a far larger fraction of the gross surplus they produce. *These are forms, analytically, of capitalists' consumption.* As such, they have a favorable effect, dollar for dollar, on gross profits by bidding consumer goods away from production workers. But they drive a wedge between measured profits, on the one hand, and the expansion of industrial capacity (investment), on the other.

For these reasons, it is fair to infer that a given rise in profits corresponded to less productive investment in the conditions of the 1980s than it did during the previous decade, when the expansion was weighted toward, if not concentrated in, firms whose success did not require disproportionate expenditures on managerial and promotional activities.

There is one further consideration, perhaps not so significant as a quantitative matter, which concerns how the productive assets of the capital goods sector came to be appropriated by government in the Reagan years. With the export markets dying or dead, the government did not abandon the advanced-technology, capital goods sector to its own (very considerable) devices. Rather, by expanding the military demand for advanced-technology products, the government converted some producers of investment made productive through export sales into absorbers of the reduced amount of economic surplus produced elsewhere. It thus compounded the productive investment problem. Whether the military breadline hones or dulls the capabilities of these people to generate productive investment in the future, when they are again released to private competition, is an open question, on whose outcome much evidently depends.

The palpable result of all this has been the decline in U.S. exports to the world, which began in 1982, and the rise in imports that took hold in 1984, leading to a current account deficit of over 3 percent of GNP in 1986 and 1987. This is truly a collapse of competitiveness in international markets. It is offset, for the present, by foreign direct investment and the sale of capital assets—from automobile plants in California and Tennessee to the Algonquin Hotel in New York City. The sale of assets is a process that can go on for a very long time: so long as the United States has capital assets to sell. But it is also a process that can end only when the United States no longer effectively controls the disposition of the profit income that its economy generates. And that is an end that no one with an eye to the future can wish.

A further result lies in the increasing hazard of a debt deflation within the U.S. economy. Since 1982, Americans have been accumulating the debts. No one else—not the Latins, not the Europeans and not the

Profits and Productive Investment

Japanese—has been doing so. If growth stops, it is now American households and businesses that are most subject to the risk of bankruptcy. This can already be seen in the shakeouts of financial institutions in Texas and elsewhere—a matter to which we shall return.

The Goal

These considerations lead to the central goal on which macroeconomic policy must focus. This is to raise the American economy's productive investment, and so permit an expansion of economic activity that lays a sounder foundation for the long-range improvement of living standards.

Advocates of industrial policy have glimpsed this goal, and have in various arguments set forth programs to achieve it. Their focus is, however, on the consumer goods manufacturing process. This is the thrust of Robert Reich's attacks on paper entrepreneurialism,[13] for example, or of Michael Piore and Charles Sabel's advocacy of flexible production.[14] It is the aim of Barry Bluestone and Bennett Harrison when they speak of business–labor–government productivity pacts or of temporary trade protection to help industries reorganize.[15] By a thorough institutional reform of current corporate structures, these authors and advocates seek to reduce the absorption of economic surplus in the corporate bureaucracy as it now exists.

What they do not see, or at least do not acknowledge, is the vast scale and practical impossibility of this task. Corporate bureaucracies exist to manage the affairs of producing units in a very complex financial, legal and marketing world. Financial divisions exist because financial markets and debt structures are complex and volatile; small savings of time and interest yield large savings of money. Legal divisions exist because the United States is a country with complex laws and litigious citizens. Marketing divisions exist because to maintain market share requires constant cultivation of a public image.

The growth of corporate bureaucracies may well be pathological. These bureaucracies may indeed have pathological effects on the efficiency of the larger economic system. But that does not make them unnecessary to the

129

survival and prosperity of the firm. If they were, then one could expect to find counterexamples: an auto producer without a legal division or a soap manufacturer with no advertising budget. None such exists. The defect of excessive capitalist consumption is not that it is always inessential or wasteful from the standpoint of the firm; the defect is rather that such consumption raises profits and the demand for output without adding to the capacity to produce.

Capital goods producers are not as subject to the demands of legal, financial and marketing complexity. To the extent that new technologies give rise to new enterprises, these are relatively free at first of long-term contracts and legal commitments. Venture capital is comparatively simple in form, and the investor expects to lose his stake in a large fraction of cases. The penny stock startup firm does not sell bonds. And sales relationships in the capital goods business are relatively straightforward compared with direct sales to the consumer. Customers are few, and they tend to know exactly what they want.

To foster the growth of independent capital goods production is thus an effective alternative to strategies that seek to raise productive investment by reforming the corporate structure of consumer goods producers. Such a strategy entails substitution: a larger share of capital goods production in total manufacturing output and employment, and a correspondingly smaller share of consumer goods. Hence it entails trade: more consumer goods imports paid for by capital goods exports. The substitution of industries whose profits are devoted, in larger measure, to investment for industries that absorb profits in distribution and management means a rise in productive investment in the economy as a whole.

Ironically, because of the apparent labor intensivity of the capital goods sector, a rise in the relative size of the capital goods sector would appear in the national income accounts as a *rise* in the share of national income going to wages and a *fall* in the share of profits. Total profits would rise, as before, with the rise in orders for capital goods. But now workers' incomes and total income would be rising even more rapidly, for so much of the permanent capital on which the profits were being earned is human capital—brainpower and education—which is, as a legal and practical matter, inseparable from the workers who own it.

As an increasing share of profit is spent on productive investment, a corresponding decline in some aspects of social consumption must necessarily also occur. Moreover, if nature is allowed to take its course, this will occur. What will fall is the consumption out of profits made in (and in servicing) the consumer goods sector. These companies are, as a rule, wholly inferior as producing units to capital goods producers within the United States. Adaptation and recovery for many of these firms are will-o'-the-wisps, unachievable even if wanted. Top American engineers have not entered the automotive or television industries for twenty years, and nothing in the world can induce them to do so. On the other hand, this is precisely what top Korean engineers have been doing. For this reason, the Korean industries are better; the A-Team in Korea or Brazil is better than the B-Team in the United States.

Overall, though painful to those affected, such changes are as progressive as they are unavoidable in the long run. Consumer goods markets will assuredly be absorbed by foreign production to an increasing degree as the major consumer goods producers shrink by attrition or bankruptcy. But in the meantime, U.S. production of capital goods for export must expand. This we cannot regard as a bad thing, despite the disruption and transitional hardship it causes. It is only the counterpart of an expanding and interconnected global economy. In particular, public resources should not be deployed to keep older industries halfway out of the grave or to maintain their managements and distribution and sales forces. There is plenty of useful work in the world economy if each country only concentrates on what, at its present stage of development, it does best.

What then will become of the lawyers, accountants, financial experts and headquarters staff? It is clear that any transformation of the gross surplus to productive investment must displace the absorption of surplus by capitalist consumption. A crash in commercial and residential real estate values in Greater New York, in vacation properties in Maine and Long Island, in trendy boutiques and perhaps even in the cocaine market, will be sidelights of an increase in productive investment. Engineers and scientists will again be in strong demand; MBAs will have to seek alternative employment. Can anyone doubt the social benefits of this change? A further shift to capital goods production will accomplish automatically much of what industrial policy advocates seek. This argument is not kind to the case for top-down restructuring that industrial policy advocates have proposed. And for a reason: their worthy goals are much more likely to be achieved by sweeping, indirect, macroeconomic means than by purposeful micro-intervention. Yet this does not mean that government has no direct role to play in helping the transition along. To the contrary, there is a large, neglected and vital micro-agenda for government, to which, along with further discussion of industrial policy proper, the next chapter is devoted.

CHAPTER 7

Industrial Intervention

THE INDUSTRIAL POLICY DEBATE, more than any other of our time, was fostered, shaped and finally doomed by congressional politics. The brief ascendancy of the idea did not occur because of the productivity crisis. Although the perception of such a crisis played a role, mainstream economists most concerned with that issue were often most resistant to the industrial policy solution. And those most in favor of industrial policy were often concerned with other things, particularly with preserving industries, communities and union organizations most threatened by the industrial transition of the 1970s.[1]

Rather, industrial policy arose to meet an explicitly political need, to fill a vacuum in the political agenda, specifically, of congressional Democrats. The vacuum itself stemmed from the political exhaustion of alternative ideas. A decade of policy experimentation, from Nixon's four phases of price control to Carter's moral equivalent of war over energy policy, had worn down the advocates of intervention in traditional forms. Conservative Republicans, backed by business interests, held a strong initiative on economic policy matters of all sorts. Industrial policy emerged into its brief limelight as a fresh response to this challenge.[2]

And then it faded again. Robert Reich's epitaph has been quoted: "industrial policy is one of those rare ideas that has moved swiftly from obscurity to meaninglessness without any intervening period of coherence."[3] Tax reform, an appealing alternative, shouldered it aside in Congress after 1984. For the present, schemes for trade regimentation are having their day. Nevertheless, some elements of the industrial policy debate appear newly attractive in light of what has succeeded them, and on their own merits are worth salvaging for incorporation in a fresh approach.

False Starts

As national attention in the late 1970s turned to policies for structural change in industry, there were difficulties that one might expect in any new endeavor. The United States has no cadre of industrial planners, and thus no academic reserve specifically trained in the art of industrial policy. Yet several sources of recent academic work to which a platform builder might look for inspiration did exist. They could be found in a subculture of specialists in industrial performance, in comparative management practices and in the comparative politics of industry. None of them had extensive contact with the mainstream of American political debate.

Several distinct perspectives existed among these groups. One, originating in the business schools, focused on the management habits of American corporations and sought to define areas where those of the Japanese or (in a few cases) Europeans were superior: attention to quality control, labor relations, a longer time frame for corporate planning.[4] But this view offered solutions to business, not to government. It suggested little that a politician could do that could be framed in legislation or as a plank in an electoral platform. Accordingly, it was and has remained marginal to the political debate.

A second set of ideas about what to do stemmed from studies of what other governments have done. Many mechanisms for intervention in industry do exist abroad. Sometimes these were established under Social Democratic governments in Europe; were clearly identified, for the purposes of U.S. political debate, as left-wing strategies (the postwar British and more recent French nationalizations, for example); and were therefore taboo. In other cases, interventions were the handiwork of conservative or nationalistic governments. These were attractive models for American advocates of industrial intervention, partly because of their political camouflage and perhaps also because they contradicted the idea that social conservatism is uniquely identified with free markets. Industry policy measures in France and Japan that work through control of capital flows, seemed particularly applicable to the United States, since they avoid the ideological trap of advocating direct or visible state control of industry.[5] But this nicety, while appealing to advocates and academicians, had little effect on the attitudes of responsible public officials.

For the Democratic politician, there was an unpleasant choice. One could draw on the industry policy expertise of the business consultants and end up on safe political ground, but without much to say. Or one could follow the advocates of foreign models and risk unwanted identification with the Left. In the end, Democrats shied away from both of these choices. Their alternative option was retreat to the relative safety of precedent in U.S. political history, a precedent that was embodied, for symbolic purposes, in the memory of the Reconstruction Finance Corporation (RFC).

Reinventing the RFC

Ever since the abolition of the RFC in the early 1950s there have been calls to restore it. Such calls were a fixture in the belief structure of old New Deal Democrats in Congress in the 1960s and 1970s, for whom the RFC represented the best efforts of government to help businesses out of hard times. Further, the RFC had a certain credibility and respectability in business circles that other New Deal agencies did not have. It was a relief agency for *business.* It had been created not under Roosevelt but under Hoover. And in its heyday, it provided an institutional link between strong governments of the Democratic party and the American business class. As such, the RFC maintained a following on Capitol Hill, at least among the aging congressional veterans of the Depression years.[6]

The post–World War II generation of congressional leaders did not share this view. They remembered the RFC mainly for the irregularities of its operations, for the problems that led to its dissolution in 1954. Nor was that generation of liberals, who set the agenda of the 1960s and early 1970s, particularly concerned with the political agenda of business. They presided over a time of general prosperity, and their work focused on human, social and, later, environmental issues in a way that presumed that economic growth could be taken for granted. And as the older, Depression-era generation passed away, so, for a time, did the active political constituency of the old RFC.

By 1978 the postwar generation of congressional leaders was nearing retirement. Once again, a younger set of politicians was near the levers of power within the Democratic party in Congress. This group, which had roots in the Vietnam War policy debate of the late 1960s and which had been greatly reinforced in the post-Watergate election of 1974, did not have strong ties to traditional Democratic constituencies such as labor. It was especially threatened by the rise of the Republicans, and it saw a need to deemphasize the traditional Democratic social agenda in favor of fostering economic growth and, not incidentally, to reestablish the Democratic party's deteriorated ties to business.

At the same time, because of the political crisis of the economic transition and inflation of the 1970s, the policy agenda of business was crowding its way back onto the agenda of Congress. Neoliberals wanted to be open-minded to the business agenda. If a strategy of growth required a slowdown in the pursuit of the final social objectives of growth—good health care, assured nutrition, quality public education, environmental control, full employment—then the neoliberals were prepared to see that price paid.

It is thus not surprising that the idea of industrial policy appealed to the rising moderate political leadership of the Democratic party. It was a "new idea," the identification with which distinguished the new generation. It addressed the issue of economic growth, newly important again after forty years and clearly secondary in the value structure of the older leadership. It was oriented to business while remaining attractive at least to the industrial unions, which have always sought a strong, acknowledged voice in the councils of national industrial decision making.

Industrial policy thus emerged for a time as the answer offered by the new centrist leadership of the congressional Democratic party to two challenges: the demands being made on Democratic officeholders by traditional Democratic constituencies, and the appeal to Democratic business constituencies of the Republicans' tax-based version of supply-side economics. Industrial policy preached at both sides of the party from the center. To the liberals, it carried a message of limits to resources and a counsel of patience while policy concentrated on the revitalization of the private sector. To conservatives, it offered a pro-business alternative to the Republican fiscal program.

As a practical matter, to favor industrial policy was to favor a development bank for business—a "Bank for Industrial Competitiveness," as the Subcommittee on Economic Stabilization proposed. There was then the question of what such a bank should do.

The Failed Case for a Development Bank

Two objectives, in particular, were commonly cited as goals for a reconstituted RFC. First, at a time when the false view of a falling share of investment in GNP was widely believed, there was the goal of directly raising the rate of gross capital formation and thus the share of such capital formation in GNP. Second was the aim of improving the international competitiveness of the economy as a whole. Unfortunately, neither result could logically have been expected, and in the end, arguments for a federal bank to achieve them could not be sustained.

There is no reputable argument that policies of loan channeling or subsidy, and so of direct intervention in the individual investment decisions of companies, can, by themselves, alter the share of investment in an unchanged volume of aggregate economic activity. Such an argument requires one to believe that microeconomic policies can alter the position of the aggregate supply curve of capital while having no effect on aggregate demand. In practice, aggregate demand is likely to move but aggregate supply is not.

If the government guarantees one company's investments, and so lowers the cost of borrowing for that company, it is promoting one particular activity at the expense of some other activity that would otherwise be chosen. Surely, then, the cost of borrowing for some other company must rise. (If government guarantees could lower the cost of borrowing for all investment simultaneously, why not have government guarantees for all borrowing?) That being so, the direction in which the overall supply curve for capital will actually shift in response to measures pushing part of it outward—if it shifts at all—is uncertain. Critics of industrial policy argued that any selective intervention was more likely to move away from the efficient choice than toward it, that losses from pushing the wrong things would more than offset any possible gains from outsmarting the market and choosing well.

Actual policy actions are, of course, unlikely to have effects restricted exclusively to the supply side. Unless the economy is already functioning at full utilization of resources, any effort to mobilize resources for industrial investment will likely increase aggregate demand as well as supply. However, since to raise demand is to raise consumption as well as investment, there is no reason why the share of capital formation in activity would rise. And to stimulate output and investment by raising profit expectations, lowering interest rates and increasing spending is not a novel trick or one that requires industrial policy. It is just the Keynesian exercise, perfectly valid but not what congressional politicians were looking for in 1981 and 1982.

There were many other arguments against selective intervention. At an early stage the public argument came to turn on a rhetorical Hobson's choice, constructed by the opponents of protection, subsidy and intervention so as to trap the advocates into an indefensible position. According to the syllogism, industries were of two kinds: *winners,* destined to succeed in the competitive environment of the future, and *losers,* destined to fail. One *should not* assist losers, the argument went, since to shore up failing industries merely subsidizes inefficiency, retards adjustment to new, more productive activities, and condemns the population to a lower than necessary standard of life. And one *cannot* pick winners, since mere mortals are incapable of figuring out in advance which the winners will be.[7]

Proponents of industrial policy soon developed their rhetorical counterstroke. To replace the concept of *losers,* the classification of *basic* industries was offered. And the term *sunrise industries* came to substitute for *winners.* Basic industries are surely, well, basic, and sunrises are predictable. Yet, though these semantic innovations helped to reverse the burden of proof, they, too, fell short of proving definitively persuasive.

There is the problem of defining a basic industry. Is automobile production a basic industry? If so, why? If the reasons are size and importance to the health of the economy, then what about housing? Or domestic oil production? Or agriculture? If domestic oil production is basic, what

Industrial Intervention

about solar power? If agriculture as a whole is a basic industry, what about strawberries and kiwi fruit? We are in uncharted territory: there are no criteria for separating an industry from its close and distant substitutes or for distinguishing within a generically basic industry between the essential and the frivolous.

Most people would agree that national security provides a minimal case for basic-ness. On this criterion, cases have been made for shipbuilding, for certain exotic metallurgies, for aerospace and atomic energy, of course, and for steel. Yet the argument is not a good one. There are a few clear cases: nuclear bombs, high-performance aircraft, ballistic missiles and atomic submarines and some of the associated electronics. But within this sphere, there is still room to debate what is essential and what is not. And outside it, the national security cover does not fit neatly over industries that are primarily civilian.

Consider steel. Leave aside, for the purposes of argument, doubts about the relevance of aircraft carriers and tanks to national security in the nuclear age and forget that steel, compared to aluminum and other metals, has become a less and less important component of military hardware since World War II. What about advanced-technology steel mills that roll out thin steel sheet for steel cans? If this is a basic activity, then what about the competition—glass, aluminum and plastic? If those are basic industries, what isn't? Problems of definition are endless, and criteria for basic-ness are never proposed. Instead, the term is defined around the industries that most need assistance.

Yet programs to assist an industry, however basic, don't operate through the industry as such. They operate through the companies in the industry. A trigger price mechanism may be intended, in principle, to help steel. What it does in practice is raise the revenues of United States Steel (now USX) and the other steel companies. Reinvestment in steel may or may not be the result. U.S. Steel's acquisition of Marathon Oil (for $6.2 billion in March 1982) was a widely noted counterexample at the time of the industrial policy debate. The problem of companies changing industries is endemic to a system in which companies are neither restricted to a particular segment of the industrial marketplace nor required to follow public guidelines in making investment decisions as the price of government market intervention in their favor.

Last, to preserve capacity for national security reasons may not be compatible with the use of the same capacity for civilian purposes in the peaceful interim. Domestic petroleum production is the most clear case: one cannot both encourage the domestic production of oil (to reduce imports) and plan to have that same oil in reserve for an emergency. The surge capacity that some argue we should maintain in steel and shipbuilding is a financial drain on private corporations and a resource cost to the civilian economy. With some exotic forges and specialized machine tools, and the entire industry of munitions and ordnance production, there is simply no link between the basic (national security) industry question and the question of civilian industrial policy.

The case for sunrise industries—meaning help to the currently successful—was and is no more compelling. Sunrise industries are easily defined in principle. What we don't have is any idea of what the appropriate eventual size of these industries should be. The semiconductor industry, untended, grew like Topsy for a while, despite calls from some outsiders for government help to make it grow still faster. And then certain parts of it collapsed. Had growth been aided, the collapse would have been more pervasive. Sooner or later, indiscriminate subsidies may return to haunt an industry in the form of low rates of profit. Indeed, given the herd instinct of the venture capital market, this may happen even without the benefit of subsidy.

The final argument for industrial intervention was that of comparison: didn't industrial policy work for the Europeans and the Japanese? Why, then, not for us? Industrial policies do exist overseas, and considerable adjustment of export and consumption patterns has occurred. But the link between the two is not clear.

The 1973–74 oil price shock created a rapid shift in the worldwide locus of purchasing power, first to the Organization of Petroleum Exporting Countries (OPEC) itself and then, in the latter half of the decade, to the Third World. This was because the industrial economies responded to the inflation induced by OPEC with restrictive policies; they slowed their domestic growth and permitted unemployment to rise. The principal economies of Latin America and Asia did not do this. The loans—recycled petrodollars—went where the activity was.

What was perceived as an adverse *supply shock* by the United States was therefore also a favorable *demand shock* for many industrialized economies. There were changes in the pattern of demand facing the industrialized economies. Internally, the shift was away from energy-intensive consumption activities first, along with some decline in goods with higher income elasticities of demand as real incomes fell. Externally, the shift was toward industries for export. It was apparent to some governments in Europe that faster adjustment and greater exports meant faster recovery with less political and economic stress.

And so, the Germans and the French scrambled for export contracts in Saudi Arabia, Iran, Korea and Brazil, mainly selling the products of industries that had already been developed for the European markets: capital equipment, heavy engineering, nuclear power plants, and armaments. No doubt, some aspects of national policy were helpful in securing large contracts from government buyers. (For the Japanese, the major adjustment was to a changed U.S. automobile and consumer goods market, which required far less structural adjustment than was demanded of the United States and Europe.) The important point is that in no case did government policy invent markets or industries that did not already exist. And as we have seen, many components of U.S. manufacturing did extremely well in the new export markets without the benefit of systematic government support.

Advocates of industrial policy looked at the gains achieved by the French, the Germans and the Japanese in the face of large induced changes in demand and in the pattern of worldwide growth in the mid-1970s, and inferred that similar results could be achieved by industrial policy alone in the 1980s in the United States. It was a serious error, a complete misconstruction of the true industrial position of the United States then and since.

Before 1981, industrial policy was unnecessary; afterward, it became impossible. For the situation was totally different after 1981 for OPEC and the Third World. We could have strengthened our Exim Bank, rebuilt our steel industry, perhaps subsidized aerospace and farm equipment and nuclear power industries, only to discover that these products could not be sold on the world market at any reasonable price. Without a policy to re-create the markets, policies to re-create the goods are useless.

If it had been clearly understood in the United States that European and Japanese industrial policies of the late 1970s were adjustment phenomena—in part the result of policy but often a simple response to changing markets—a good result in U.S. policy design would have more likely occured, though not necessarily. For the crucial difference remains that in the wake of OPEC's actions, the Europeans and the Japanese knew what they were adjusting to. In 1981 we did not.

Nor do we now. Who can say where the next shock is coming from? Will it be oil again? Or food, perhaps? Or a breakdown of manufacturing trade due to financial calamity in Latin America and elsewhere? Or a Depression-style freezing over of the private economy in the United States itself? We don't know. And an advance strategy conceived in ignorance of the future is likely to be quite different from one conceived as a response to an established threat.

A Course of Action

The case against industrial policy has been used as the case against all forms of industrial intervention. But while this argument is often effective, it too is not persuasive. The United States, we have seen, faces the task of industrial transformation. Advanced industries must be fostered, and older consumer goods sectors whose functions should pass to developing countries must be allowed to shrink. These tasks can be accomplished with grace and compassion or with a jagged brutality to workers, their communities and the social fabric of the nation. Government has a strong role to play in realizing the first option.

The valid goals of industrial policy in the United States can thus be organized around the idea of preparing for an uncertain future. Such an orientation leads to policies designed to foster success in a macroeconomic climate geared to outward-looking expansion in sectors that produce technologically progressive investment goods. The key is not to try to pick winners or sunrise firms; the aim is to foster the attributes that produce a climate of rapid technological change. These attributes are diversification and adaptability.

Diversification is the pertinent objective, for example, when considering policy toward education, research and development and support for basic science. The economic literature on the relationship between industrial structure, the rate of investment in research and development and the rate of diffusion of new technologies stresses how little we know. Theory does not tell us how government policies affecting industry will affect the rate of creation of new knowledge. But this is an area where, unlike the question of corporate culture central to other hypotheses, what little we do know is enough to allow us to take action.

Industrial Intervention

Policy that affects the creation and diffusion of new technical knowledge should not be concerned with speeding the process up. Instead, it can work to create a large range of opportunities for individuals and groups to foster new knowledge in the confident hope that something will turn up.

There are three arenas of policy that directly affect the diversity of technological opportunity. These are:

Support for science and *basic* research
Support for education, training and equal educational opportunity
Access to venture capital

There is nothing novel about any of these three policies. A strong science base, abetted by national research and development projects, is an established feature of our national scene. Government–university cooperation has a proven record of accomplishment, through laboratories from which vast numbers of fundamental innovations emerge. Not least, a strong commitment to science and technology research attracts the best scientific talent from overseas—a persistent glory of American intellectual life.

There are many examples. The space program was, in its prime, a hothouse of technological innovation. The National Institutes of Health and the Center for Disease Control today are at the forefront of cancer and AIDS research. The Naval Nuclear Propulsion Program gave us the electric power–generating reactor. Government-supported agricultural research gave the world the Green Revolution. Bell Labs, an institution whose extraordinary reach in mid-century was due to the government-protected position of AT&T, gave us the transistor. Even the Strategic Defense Initiative, the present employment project of government-sponsored physics, may one day yield some scientific results with commercial applications.

Likewise education. One cannot specify in advance which workers and technicians will best be suited to certain tasks. But it is certain that a broadly and well-educated population will be more productive on the whole than a poorly educated one, will be more receptive to constructive technological change and will be a better electorate. And there is no real mystery about how to improve public education. Good education requires money, and this is particularly true as the breakdown of professional barriers to women in other occupations continues and it becomes harder to attract highly educated and well-motivated personnel into a poorly paid field.

The main thing about science, education and training is that they compete with other disciplines for a limited pool of public funds. The danger is that in the enthusiasm for new and different means of implementing industrial policy, particularly for schemes involving the corporate sector, we will divert resources from established strategies that are known to work.

Capital access is a more subtle problem, since the United States continues to have the most open capital markets in the world. This is partly because of our immensely diverse and unconcentrated financial structure, but it is also a side effect of the distribution of household wealth: it is possible for many new enterprises to get started on the strength of an uncle's second mortgage or a little partnership capital scraped up among friends. There may be no way to augment this network of personal relations directly. But it is certain that the relative openness of our capital markets will diminish with a continuing decline in the wealth and security of American households. This source of innovation and diversity may be an incidental casualty of tight money, high interest rates and the loss of Schumpeterian quasi-rents as American technological advantage declines.

The pursuit of adaptability is in some ways more difficult than the pursuit of diversification, since in general it requires actual changes in the way governments and corporations operate. But here, too, there are measures—traditional government functions—that simply need to be addressed. In a mature society such as the United States, efficient use of social resources means conserving and reusing existing physical and human capital when the transition from some economic activities to others is made.

Our social capital is built up in our manufacturing cities. Streets, housing, water and sewer systems, schools, cultural facilities, urban transportation networks and other public activities that constitute a city's attractiveness are as vital to investors as to those who live there. Ports, airports, industrial land, roads and waste treatment are essential if a community is to attract manufacturing or science-based investment. It is a pattern in land-rich America for industry to choose its location and for the public to adapt—a pattern now showing its ugliest side along the Mexican frontier, in vast *colonias* with unpaved streets, no sewer connections, and water supplies from recycled fifty-five-gallon chemical drums. How much

Industrial Intervention

better it would be to make possible industrial transformations in fixed sites, bringing jobs where housing, water and sewers, roads and transport already exist! An industrial system that requires workers in trailer parks to pay taxes for welfare residents in tenements makes no sense.

In 1984, the Joint Economic Committee published an extensive survey of national infrastructure investment needs, covering highways and bridges, other transportation, water and sewer projects.[8] The survey, reflecting engineering estimates by twenty-two participating states, stated that about $400 billion worth of additional public capital investment, above what is scheduled to be financed at current rates of expenditure, could usefully be put in place over fifteen years. In a start toward this goal, the report proposed the creation of a National Infrastructure Fund, which would be a federally financed revolving fund and guarantee facility for the use of state and local governments to raise the rate of investment in basic public infrastructure. The fund would be large enough to meet about one-quarter of the estimated need and would work mainly by reducing interest costs and pooling risks for participating governments. Legislation, authored by Representatives Lee Hamilton (D–Ind.) and the late James Howard (D–N.J.), was introduced in 1985.

Infrastructure, too, is uniquely vulnerable to economic dislocation under a federal system of government. It does not take much erosion of the tax base to force service curtailment and rate increases. These, in turn, depress the climate for new investment, starting a downward cycle leading to emigration and, ultimately, to a need to recapture what was lost with vast new public investments elsewhere. A high priority of industrial policy should be to avoid this waste of resources through the conservation of industrial sites, irrespective of the manufacturing activities that go on there.

Beyond the National Infrastructure Fund, there is a need for an Infrastructure Support Facility to make long-term loans at low interest to communities hit by major industrial transitions: the closing of a large mill, furnace or manufacturing assembly plant. Communities could be declared eligible on the basis of the percentage diminution of their tax roles caused by economic dislocation. Criteria for eligibility would include the presentation of a plan for the application of the funds to the maintenance of public facilities. This would enable communities to preserve the quality of their public services and so make them more attractive as locations for new industrial development. It would also free resources and talent from

145

short-term crisis management for planning industrial transitions. Milwaukee and Lowell are the right models, while future Youngstowns and future Hamtramcks should by all efforts be avoided.

The recycling of workers is another and in some ways more daunting task, for human beings have life cycles and aging processes that are more definite and irreversible than those of capital stock. Hard economics indicate that no matter how capable a displaced miner or brake fitter in his forties may be, he is a less attractive candidate for a skilled job in a new industry than a younger person. This is partly because as educational standards have improved, younger people have gained an advantage over their elders. Partly it is because training costs are inevitably amortized (and future retirement costs discounted) for younger workers over longer periods. Partly it is because younger people expect and are accustomed to lower rates of pay. Subsidized retraining is therefore only part of the answer, and its role is often greatly overstated in public debate. For even if effective retraining for older workers were available and entirely free of cost to the firm, it is unlikely that many older workers would prevail in the competitive struggle for jobs as good as the ones they have lost.

Another part of the problem is that work life in the United States is not well organized to facilitate mid-life transitions to new careers. It doesn't have to be this way. A great merit of the Japanese labor market is that workers are constantly being retrained on the job so that they can move with relative ease between jobs requiring diverse skills.[9] But these moves almost always tend to be moves within the firm; the movement between tasks requires the preservation of an overarching corporate environment. Even in Japan, workers lose their position on the wage ladder when they leave their firms. In the United States, whose competitive corporate environment is faced with inevitable industrial transitions, even the reorganization of manufacturing methods has only a limited ability to prepare workers for interindustry moves.

A focus on industrial transformation necessarily implies a relaxed attitude toward job transformation. Policies fostering direct preservation of communities can help make such transformations easier by bringing new jobs to areas with good homes near good schools. Retraining and relocation assistance can help older workers with transferable skills take advantage of new opportunities that may exist. In the end, however, overpowering market forces will dictate the outcome. Many, if not most, manufacturing workers displaced in industrial transformation will have to find new work at lower wages in the service sector, just as they do when faced with (often involuntary) early retirement in Japan.

The market can be brutal. And so, perhaps the most important and useful challenge for government in an era of transition and modernization lies in helping to buffer the worst effects of job displacement on the income, social surroundings and life itself of older manufacturing workers. Social insurance, such as the Trade Adjustment Assistance program of the 1970s, can be revived for this purpose. Public employment can favor older and displaced workers in certain capacities, because the public sector is not subject to the same competitive pressures as private firms; perhaps with employment preferences it can save money that would otherwise be spent fruitlessly on welfare or retraining. Perhaps most important would be to expand the access to capital at low rates of interest for small business development, so as to foster a proliferation of useful private sector service job opportunities for older workers.

This is a painful area in which more study is clearly required, for it has been a substantially neglected part of the progressive agenda. It is politically more acceptable to discuss retraining of older workers for comparable jobs and easiest of all to talk about preventing plant closings in the first place. No one likes to hear that their jobs are doomed. But the fact is that many existing manufacturing jobs *are* doomed. The question of transition for workers is therefore an urgent one that must be faced, and not denied, in progressive discussions of labor market policy.

Displaced, unemployed and welfare-dependent workers are extremely diverse and so have a range of needs requiring a very large range of specialized programs. Nevertheless, the government does have effective experience in dealing with some of their problems, having established programs in the past to support students, for postsecondary vocational education, to assist displaced workers in middle age and to help senior citizens. Funding for labor market programs reached a peak at $9 billion in 1980 but fell sharply to about $4 billion in 1986. Nevertheless, as the Joint Economic Committee observes, "these budget cuts do not necessarily reflect informed judgment on the actual success or failure of past programs."[10] In fact, the cuts reflect nothing more than the administration's own differing priorities, now ripe for reversal.

A final weakness of the U.S. political structure appears periodically when a large corporate entity—Lockheed, Chrysler, the Penn Central Railroad, New York City—shows up on the federal doorstep on the brink of financial collapse. There is considerable admiration in the United States, perhaps among those who have not looked too closely, at the quiet and allegedly efficient way the French handled their steel crisis in 1978–79 or the German banks the agony of AEG-Telefunken. Some wish for a quasi-public institution, flush with funds, that could handle comparable crises in the United States far from the klieg lights of Congress.

The enthusiasm in some quarters for depoliticizing large bailouts— again the RFC model—is misplaced. With any public financing vehicle, adverse selection is a major hazard. But there are few companies indeed that would voluntarily endure the public humiliations visited on Chrysler, Lockheed and New York City before the banking committees of the House and Senate. Moreover, where bankruptcy and reorganization are the preferable route, Congress occasionally finds the courage to say so, as it did in 1970 when Congressman Wright Patman derailed the bailout of the Penn Central.

What Congress does need is a better ability to impose technical performance criteria on the corporations it helps to restructure with public money, and to monitor those criteria over the lifetime of a financial-aid program. For example, when Chrysler came before the House Banking Committee, there was no disinterested technical expert on whom Congress could rely to evaluate Chrysler's plans for future investment and return to profitability. Without this expertise, provisions written into law designed to ensure that public money would not be wasted were unenforceable.[11] In the total absence of effective supervision Chrysler did in fact survive, but this had everything to do with the change in economic circumstances after 1981 and nothing whatever with the quality of the guidance the company received from the government.[12]

Adaptability is served by selected bits of public entrepreneurship, particularly where large-scale organizational tasks are required. In 1982 in its annual *Report,* the Joint Economic Committee identified two such areas in the United States: passenger rail transport and the mining and transport of coal.[13] No doubt more such projects can be developed with thought and careful planning.

Major improvements in public or semipublic transportation networks, including freight raillines, slurry pipelines and ports, would be rewarded by large increases in U.S. coal production and export. Greater coal production would, of course, reduce the market power of any future OPEC.[14]

148

Industrial Intervention

A program of high-speed passenger railroads, similar to the Shinkansen in Japan and the marvelous TGV in France, could be constructed in up to thirty intercity corridors in the United States where population densities are similar to those in Europe. Such a system, or set of systems, with its great contribution to the efficiency of point-to-point transit, would help determine industrial location patterns for decades to come. Specifically, it would focus such investments on the endpoints of the rail corridors. As such, a high-speed passenger rail system would powerfully complement a community preservation strategy implemented in the major manufacturing cities.[15]

How much can we afford to spend on such endeavors? The answer to that question is given, I think, by the implicit framework of public consent to the size of the government sector. At present, no grand projects occupy the policy planning horizon; there have been no claims staked on the normal and accepted growth of federal government spending. This normal growth is an estimated 1 percent of all spending per year,[16] which would allow for about $10 billion in immediate new annual spending on public investment, education, training and research. This would not be a bad beginning. Additional funds can be found as the reversal of Reagan-era priorities takes effect. A reduction of 8 percent in the military budget would free another $20 billion. Finally, if lower interest rates drive down the net interest payments due on the national debt, at least $10 billion more could be found within a year. A total of at least $40 billion in new annual federal spending could thus be accommodated easily by these means, with no change in the normal size of government or in the prescribed course of fiscal policy. This stream of investments could then rise to 1 percent of GNP per year (about $50 billion) and be sustained at that level for a decade or longer.

There is a valid role for industrial intervention in the United States. It consists in generalized preparation for a future about which we know little. To meet it, we should be strong in science and research, broadly and well educated, open in our access to employment and to capital. We need attractive cities with modern water and sewer systems and plenty of good transport. Governments and large corporations must develop flexible procedures to restructure capital, retrain workers and make transitions easier. In all of these matters there is the need for a strong public role to reverse the public capital starvation of the past decade. Yet, industrial policy will not create full employment. It will not cure inflation. It will not raise the rate of investment in the economy or the rate of productivity growth, nor will it lead to a stable trade balance. To do these things, a coherent macroeconomic program is necessary, accompanied by income policies designed to prevent periodic inflation crises from derailing economic expansion. Industrial policy is no substitute for such measures.

CHAPTER 8

The Case for a Limited Tax Shock

NOW: what should (and can) be done about the budget?

The budget remains the most visible feature of the political landscape, and step 1 in any macroeconomic strategy must address it. Yet the economic measure and meaning of the budget differ importantly from the popular perception, and so it is a topic that must be approached with care. We must first establish accurately the dimensions of the budget problem from the perspective of the needs of the economy; only then can we sensibly estimate the direction, size and path of appropriate budget action.

The numbers that follow are approximate and doubtless differ in particulars from what they were when these words were written. Nevertheless the message they convey is straightforward, and will remain valid so long as neither high inflation nor renewed recession supervenes. As of late 1988, this had not happened, despite uncertainties created by the worldwide crash of stock prices in October, 1987.

Some Budget Background

In 1988, federal government spending (as measured in the national income accounts) was expected to total about $1.06 trillion and receipts to come to $899 billion, leaving a deficit of $161 billion. The expected deficit for fiscal year 1989, as reported by the Congressional Budget Office (CBO) in March 1988, was $165 billion.[1]

CBO also foresaw a decline in the budget deficit to the neighborhood of $100 billion by fiscal year 1993 under certain special assumptions known as the *baseline.* Generally, the baseline is a forecast conditioned on a standard set of economic projections (for growth, unemployment, inflation and interest rates) and on the assumption that there will be no change in current spending policies or in the current (post-reform) tax law.

As a rule, the current spending policy assumption is generally interpreted to mean the spending level implied in present law.[2] This means that spending innovations—new programs or projects—are reflected in the baseline only if they are built into laws already enacted. And since new expenditure programs are not typically enacted years before they are actually to go into effect, growth in the baseline dollar level of spending converges toward the expected rate of inflation (zero real growth in spending) as the forecast looks further into the future.

CBO's baseline projections are appropriate for their purpose, which is to assist Congress in planning for the fiscal consequences of departures from current law. They should not be considered to be (as commonly they are) a forecast of what is likely to happen. There are two reasons for preserving a distinction between the concept of baseline and that of forecast.

First, the baseline economic assumptions are, as a rule, too optimistic. In particular, CBO normally projects sustained economic growth, steady or somewhat rising inflation and steady or falling nominal interest rates. For example, the baseline budget forecast published in early 1988, covering fiscal years through 1993, was conditioned on steady real expansion at a rate of 2.6 to 2.7 percent, constant inflation at 4.1 percent and a short-term interest rate falling from 6.7 to 5.9 percent over five years. None of these are unreasonable individually. But the combination, which will tend to maximize growth in revenues, minimize growth in expenditure, and hold down growth in net interest obligations, is always unlikely to occur on a sustained basis in practice.

The Case for a Limited Tax Shock

For example, the rise in inflation past 4 percent, already a fact, could well provoke a tighter monetary policy and higher interest rates. This would then be likely to be followed by a new round of slower real economic growth. The net result would be a sharper reduction than expected in the deficit at first, as nominal GNP and revenues rise relative to spending, followed by a rapid increase in the deficit in the ensuing slowdown. CBO's economic assumptions are no worse than those of its competitors in the private sector and elsewhere in the government, but they share a long-range optimism and an inability to pick up turning points with all modern econometric models.[3]

The second reason why the CBO baseline generally proves optimistic in comparison with experience is that the baseline assumption of no future innovations in discretionary expenditure, while again not inappropriate for a baseline exercise, conflicts with observed patterns of expenditure behavior. The president and Congress have for many years followed a pattern of increasing real expenditures, often by adding new functions, as resources and the condition of the economy permit. These are changes in policy, but they are (at least in the abstract) predictable changes, and therefore appropriate for inclusion in a forecast. This tendency to change policy by augmenting real government activity was not interrupted by the Reagan administration, which added substantially to procurement and to research and development in the military sector. It is a pattern that seems unlikely to be interrupted as (and if) a more overtly interventionist generation of politicians comes to power.

The CBO assumption of no change in tax policy, on the other hand, *is* realistic both as a baseline and as a forecast. Tax policy generates tax revenues in a given proportion to GNP. The assumption of no change in policy therefore provides for tax revenues to rise as private income rises, which is a realistic approximation of the degree to which tax revenues actually will be permitted to rise.

A Behavioral Budget Baseline

We may therefore imagine the construction of an alternative baseline forecast, based not on current law but on behavioral trends in expenditure and revenue. For the sake of convenience and in order to isolate the consequences of this one change, we will continue to use the CBO's economic assumptions, merely noting that their optimism establishes these estimates as a lower bound for what is actually likely to happen to the deficit over a reasonable future time frame.

The principal difference between a behavioral-baseline forecast and that constructed under the CBO rules is on the spending side. A behavioral forecast respects the past pattern of annual real growth of spending, which is in the range of 3 percent per year, while the CBO forecast calls for a reduction in real spending growth to below 1 percent five years ahead. By 1993, a behavioral track for spending implies a level of outlays about $100 billion higher than under the CBO baseline.

The net result is to show larger deficits than those projected by the CBO continuing over the forecast horizon. Without attempting to place too rigid an interpretation on the estimate, one can allow for a normal deficit in the range of $180 to $200 billion through the early 1990s— anything much lower would imply policy changes for which actual spending and tax data as yet provide no evidence. This is a stark contrast to the cautious optimism of the CBO baseline, let alone the zero-deficit 1993 targets embodied in law in the Gramm–Rudman–Hollings legislation of 1986, as amended. Note, moreover, that this is a so-called structural deficit: it is based on assumptions that account fully for the recent decline of unemployment to the vicinity of 6 percent and which expect unemployment to remain at that comparatively modest level.

Necessary Budget Economics

In economic terms, however, the deficit just predicted is not so terrible as it appears. To appreciate the economic consequences of sustaining a deficit on the order of $200 billion in the federal budget, even a structural deficit of this size, we must examine two mitigating factors that prove to be substantial.

The first is the size of the surplus, if any, in the budgets of state and local governments. Federal grants-in-aid to states and localities total nearly $100 billion. This expenditure item for the federal government (and revenue item for the states) does not affect spending in the economy

The Case for a Limited Tax Shock

until it is respent by the state or local government that receives it. In any given year, therefore, unspent grants-in-aid or equivalent monies in state and local accounts should be deducted from federal expenditure to arrive at a number that has economic meaning. The "unspent" portion may be measured, for practical purposes, by the surplus of the state and local government sector.

Before 1977, the surplus of the state and local government sector was very small and could safely be neglected. But in recent years this surplus has risen sharply, doubling to about $30 billion from 1977 to 1982 and then doubling again in 1983–84. It seems to have stabilized at around $60 billion in 1985 and 1986, or about 1.5 percent of GNP before declining to $45 billion in 1987. Probably the size of the surplus in relation to GNP will decline in the years ahead, as states particularly favored either reduce their tax rates or raise their expenditures. Still, an allowance for a continuing state and local surplus of $50 billion annually for the immediate future would be prudent.

The rate of inflation is the second, more volatile, and even more important factor. Inflation affects the deficit because, as Robert Eisner in particular has recently shown, inflation reduces the real value of the outstanding federal debt.[4] Government bonds, a form of financial wealth in the hands of the public, lose purchasing power in inflation. Their holders commensurately lose wealth. In effect, inflation imposes a tax on holders of public debt equal to the rate of inflation times the amount of debt they hold. The proper measure of the debt to deflate for this purpose is probably the value of government debt in the hands of the public, a measure which excludes that part of the whole national debt held by the government's own agencies, such as at the Federal Reserve.[5] Publicly held government debt came to around $1.9 trillion in fiscal year 1987, and it is expected to rise, under the baseline, to $2.5 trillion by 1991 (at book value—we ignore another adjustment to market value here for the purpose of keeping things comparatively simple). Under the behavioral forecast given here, the increase in the debt would be to about $2.8 trillion. At the present 3 percent inflation rate, the uncounted tax is now $63 billion and its expected value in 1991 is on the order of $85 billion—no minor sum.[6]

Taken together, these two adjustments reduce the size of the deficit by a very large amount, as figure 8–1 shows.[7] For the future, allowing again that the behavioral baseline is highly approximate, the reduction is from around $180 to around $70 billion in fiscal year 1989 and from $200

FIGURE 8–1
Deficits: Official and Adjusted

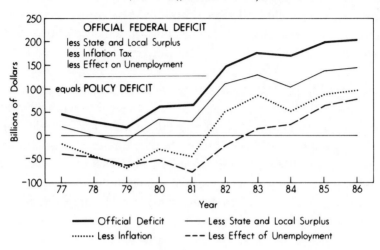

SOURCES: *Economic Report of the President* and author's calculations.

billion to around $65 billion in 1991. In relation to present GNP, the reduction is from around 4.0 to around 1.4 percent, and for 1991 the adjustment in relation to the then expected GNP is from 3.4 to 1.1 percent. At an inflation rate in the vicinity of 6 percent the budget in real terms in 1991 would be in balance!

Goals for the Deficit

Unfortunately, neither nominal dollar amounts for the deficit nor its share in GNP tell us what we want to know. We are not, or ought not to be, interested in hitting some arbitrarily specified accounting target. We are, or ought to be, interested in choosing a target for the deficit that will be appropriate to a strategy for sustained, outward-looking economic expansion—for the economic objectives that we have in mind.

What, then, does the budget deficit do, and how does it fit into the patterns of international performance of the U.S. economy? Most important, in conjunction with monetary policy, the deficit forces the United States as a nation to borrow money abroad, incurring rising foreign debts

The Case for a Limited Tax Shock

and interest obligations. In conjunction with monetary policy, the deficit forces up the interest rate, raising the exchange value of the dollar. And this, we have seen, erodes our current trade competitiveness and compromises future living standards for the sake of high levels of current import consumption.

To cut the budget deficit and government borrowing, holding everything else equal—whether achieved by lower spending or higher taxes—would mean a decline in demand, in imports, and in the trade deficit. Conversely, to raise exports, everything else being equal, would mean a lower trade deficit, higher national income, higher tax revenues and a lower budget deficit. There is thus a strong link between the two deficits, and policies to reduce one will strongly affect the other.

As we have already seen, in terms of their effect on gross profits the two deficits are offsetting. A budget deficit increases U.S. business profits; a trade deficit reduces them. If our goal is to end the foreign debt pileup without jeopardizing U.S. prospects for profitability, and therefore for confidence and investment, then we may wish to design policies that reduce the two deficits in tandem. The desired change in the price-adjusted, all-government deficit may thus be set with a view toward the desired change in the current account.

The current account deficit, over 3 percent of GNP in 1986, 1987 and 1988, is, like the budget deficit, partly structural and partly cyclical. The structural element is due to the imbalance of U.S. fiscal and monetary policies, and the cyclical element is caused by the weaker growth performance of the world economy compared to the U.S. economy since 1982. Since world recovery, our reserve currency status, and the competitiveness of our export industries all require that the United States return to a situation of net capital outflow, the whole current account deficit ultimately should be eliminated. But not at once, and not wholly by fiscal tightening and reduction of imports: that would induce recession. Instead, the goal should be to achieve a balance between export improvement and import slowdown, partly through budget deficit reduction and easier money, and partly through more rapid growth in the external markets of the United States.

A return of real (gross) exports to their average 1979–80 share in U.S. GNP alone would in 1986 have constituted a rise of 1.6 percent relative to U.S. GNP. We may take this as a crude estimate of the cyclical component in our current account deficit: this is the amount by which

U.S. exports might rise if world income were in some sense fully recovered from recession levels. The estimate is conservative: in 1973 and 1979, following worldwide catch-ups to U.S. recoveries, exports rose by 2.4 and 2.6 percent of GNP, respectively, in a single year. Thus a strong world recovery could accomplish substantially more than allowed for here.

Subtracting the cyclical element would leave a structural current account deficit of about 1.7 percent of GNP in 1986—about $70 billion. A useful rule of thumb, then, might be to seek from domestic measures, from budget tightening together with falling interest rates and dollar depreciation, a trade improvement in both imports and exports equivalent to the structural component of the current account deficit. And then we should press our trading partners to accomplish the rest, through their own economic expansions, enlarged foreign aid and lending, and consequent increase in demand for our exports. To the extent that they can be pressured to comply, the U.S. current account deficit would fall more rapidly than the budget deficit, raising profits in the United States. This would tend to stimulate a profits-led investment boom, raising tax revenues still more.

The value of the present structural budget deficit, when corrected for inflation and the state/local surplus, is nearly equal to the above-presumed value of the present structural current account deficit. To assure a neutral effect on profits, policy could thus be set so that the interim current account target is achieved together with a target reduction of the price-adjusted, all-government deficit to zero. We then have a short-term policy problem that is about $70 billion at present and likely to stick near that figure for the next several years, since both the structural current account deficit and the structural budget deficit are falling as shares of GNP under the pressure of policy changes already made. This is a far cry from the panicky perceptions that led to the enactment of the Gramm–Rudman–Hollings law in 1985.

Our internal fiscal goal therefore should be to stabilize the nominal (measured, official) deficit at around 2.2 percent of GNP, which is the sum of the uncounted inflation tax and the expected state and local government surplus. For fiscal year 1989 this total comes to around $110 billion, assuming that current inflation rates continue and that the other CBO assumptions hold good. To get this would require a large short-term fiscal change on about the same scale as was called for under Gramm–Rudman–Hollings for 1988 in the original deficit target set for that year of $108

The Case for a Limited Tax Shock

billion. But the same nominal reduction is also roughly right for future years. In 1991, for example, an appropriate *ex ante* deficit target is about $125 billion—below the officially reported baseline by only $20-odd billion and below the more reasonable behavioral baseline, once again, by about $70 billion.

At about that point, budget deficit reduction by fiscal tightening should stop. We should on no account set policy on a path toward official budget balance by 1993, 1994, or any other year. To do so only invites—indeed, guarantees—an epoch of slow growth and probable recession.[8]

There are many good ways to solve a $70 billion problem. Expenditures may be foregone or taxes raised. However, there is the objection of extreme political difficulty to expenditure cuts. Expenditure plans just do not respond in our political system to budget-related efforts to alter their rate of growth. Defense and interest cuts, which are certainly feasible and perhaps inevitable, will be reabsorbed by the high unmet needs of the domestic sector. Even President Reagan at his moment of greatest strength could not bring about a shift in the growth of total expenditure. It is unlikely that his successor will make any more headway than could the most powerful and popular conservative president of the twentieth century.

Taxation presents a different and more promising picture. Tax revenues remain, since 1983, well below levels that would have been consistent with the long-standing prior patterns of tax policy behavior. As it happens, the shortfall of tax revenues below past norms corresponds closely in quantity to the excess of the deficit above its desired level. True, current tax policy baselines are reasonable forecasts of what tax revenues will be. But tax policy, unlike expenditure policy, was redirected in 1981. Why not change it again?

Total corporate and personal income tax receipts for fiscal year 1991 are expected to be about $670 billion. Thus nearly the whole $70 billion deficit reduction that needs to be achieved could be accomplished by a 10 percent increase in income taxes on individuals and corporations, applied in that year to the new low rates that are presently effective under the tax reform law of 1986. That is, a rise in the marginal rate on income now taxed at 15 percent to 16.5 percent would nearly do the trick; the corresponding rise in the rate on income now taxed at 28 percent would be to 30.8 percent.

Such action would be roughly equivalent in size to the repeal, delayed now for half a decade, of the third year of the Kemp–Roth Economic Recovery Tax Act (ERTA) tax cuts, the part that took effect in July 1983. Since the first two stages of that cut corresponded to necessary postinflation adjustments and antirecession stimulus, while many of the corporate provisions of ERTA were rewritten in 1986, this measure would constitute a final act in undoing the Reagan administration's tax legacy and restoring the fiscal base for effective government in the United States.

In principle, the tax increase described above should be implemented at once. However, this calculation depends critically on two assumptions: that the 1987 stock crash will not by itself set off a downward spiral toward recession and that, on the other hand, inflation will not rise.

Original estimates were that up to $1 trillion in paper gains were destroyed between October 12 and October 20, 1987. Normally, economists would estimate a first-year effect on spending of such a wealth loss at between 3 and 6 percent, and thus a reduction in demand on the order of 0.75 to 1.5 percent of GNP. This by itself would not be enough to cause a recession in an economy whose base rate of growth is on the order of 4 percent per year—the growth rate in the third quarter of 1987. Moreover the effect would be smaller to the extent that the stock losses were from unanticipated gains which had been made only since the beginning of 1987, and to the extent that the aggressive easing of monetary policy after the crash succeeded in restoring asset prices. By the middle of 1988, fears of a large or lasting effect from the stock crash had generally abated.

If inflation does rise, the uncounted inflation tax revenues will rise with it, creating a degree of fiscal tightness that would be unnecessary and unintended. Therefore, should the inflation rate rise temporarily above its present values (on the order of 4 to 5 percent), the projected path of nominal deficit reduction should be adjusted so as to keep the real budget accounts from shifting sharply and catastrophically into surplus. Since further dollar depreciation and other measures described in the next chapters would entail a one-time rise in the inflation rate, an integrated tax and monetary strategy would require delaying the effective date of nominal tax increases until the uncounted taxes imposed by a year or so of high inflation have been, so to speak, collected.

It might be added that income tax rate changes are the instrument of choice for fiscal policy changes not only in general and on the political and administrative grounds emphasized above, but also in the specific economic circumstances the United States faces at the present writing.

The Case for a Limited Tax Shock

Our compelling need, we have seen, is to raise the sustainable rate of productive investment and, at the same time, to slow the growth rate of imports of consumer goods so as to achieve trade and budget deficit reductions in tandem. It seems clear that meeting the investment objective requires the expansion of certain types of public investment expenditures that complement those of the private sector. Moreover, it is certain that the propensity to import consumer goods is a rising function of income. Therefore a rise in progressive income tax rates, affecting consumers' marginal demand for compact-disk players, imported cars and cocaine, would be a more efficient import reducer than cuts in public investment or in transfers to the elderly and poor for health care, housing and food.

The income tax is also demonstrably superior to a proposed national value-added or sales tax (VAT), despite the substantial support that such proposals have received from respected figures in the financial community and from some economists. The drawbacks of the VAT are well known: it is regressive in effect, it is inflationary when first implemented, and it competes with the established tax bases of state and local governments. On the other side, the VAT's allegedly superior incentives to saving are doubtful. A tax that raises the absolute and relative tax burden on lower-income people who have no net savings to begin with can be expected to induce hardship, not saving. Economists widely accept, moreover, that the main effect of higher taxes on national saving lies not in any induced change in personal savings behavior but in the reduction of dissaving (the deficit) by the government; for this purpose, the income tax is as good as any other instrument.

The income tax has another, less noted, administrative advantage. It exists. It can be changed, in principle, by the simple device of altering the marginal tax rate. If income tax rates are raised with a future effective date, and in the meantime economic conditions deteriorate, the income tax rate can be cut. The VAT would have to be created. The process of its creation would be stormy, and once in place, it would be irreversible.

The superior flexibility of the income tax has been greatly enhanced, since 1986, by the enactment of tax reform. Under the earlier tax code, horizontal inequities presented a powerful bar to simple legislation adjusting average income tax rates, since any such legislation entailed major changes in the value to taxpayers of the many possible exemptions and deductions. The substantial reduction of exemptions and deductions under the new law means that uniform adjustments in tax rates will have much more uniform effects than heretofore. They have therefore become a much more desirable instrument for changing the gross level of purchasing power in the private economy, particularly in comparison with proposals for a national sales tax or VAT, which would require the imposition of an entirely new federal tax structure alongside the existing one.

As it happens, then, a total-government, price-adjusted, balanced budget is equivalent in 1993 to a measured deficit on the order of $145 billion, and that is, by coincidence, not much above the CBO baseline projection of $139 billion for that year, contingent on the same economic assumptions. The difference between the two is political. CBO's baseline could be achieved in practice only by unprecedented political change, bringing about near-zero real growth in spending, while at the same time leaving tax laws unchanged. This alternative would save the futile political struggle by taking instead the path of restoring tax norms to past accustomed values, while leaving gross expenditure growth norms as they have been.

There is, in short, no reason whatever to continue the fiscal deadlock and sense of crisis that hangs perpetually over the budget deficit. A new administration need not, and should not, accept the prevailing cant that has kept expenditure cuts at the top of the budget agenda for a decade. Normal growth of expenditures can continue in the 1990s, and rising total expenditures in key areas can be accommodated out of normal growth and resource reallocation.

To achieve budget stabilization at continuing high levels of nominal deficit, and to be content with that deficit while the forces of world growth help put the trade picture back to rights, will require not only a new strategy but also a new political dialogue about the nature of budget formation. For this a few words are devoted here to the budget-making process.

Budget Process and Feasible Fiscal Policy

The congressional budget process came into being with the Budget Reform and Impoundment Control Act of 1974. The process has always been subject to ambiguous interpretation. Its primary original intent was to impose discipline on the consideration of expenditure programs, to establish a framework for disciplining the aggregate growth of expenditure and a workable calendar for the consideration of appropriations bills. Over this, over the years, has been superimposed a concern with fiscal policy as such—with the relation of tax revenues to spending and therefore with the deficit.

However, the design of the process does not foster effective congressional decision making on the broader fiscal issues. Rather, the process provides a telling illustration of the pernicious effects that procedures can have on the substance of a debate. The budget process obscures and obstructs a clear-minded debate over desired economic outcomes by substituting budget criteria for economic criteria in making judgments about programs.

The core of the existing budget process is its system of spending and revenue targets. These five-year (and longer) projections for each functional area have a useful microeconomic program-evaluation function, in particular guarding against the "camel's nose" syndrome in the introduction of new expenditure programs. The budget process is indeed a useful, perhaps indispensable, device for considering the long-range implications of adopting new expenditure programs.

But in the consideration of fiscal policy at the aggregate level, three- and five-year projections for expenditure, revenue and especially deficits take on a different role. They become, effectively, in and of themselves, the final *goals* for fiscal policy. This is a function which they should not be made to serve in a rational system.

The mutation of projections into goals seems to happen for technical reasons, almost incidentally, without great forethought or deliberate intention, as a by-product of CBO operating procedures and of the formal independence of monetary policy from the budget process.

Budget process participants, members of Congress who must evaluate alternative revenue and expenditure streams, find it necessary to place each alternative on as nearly comparable a basis as possible. To establish ground rules for comparability, Congress uses CBO, which is a nonpartisan organization that commands general respect. In addition to its own baselines, CBO generates cost estimates for various alternative expenditure proposals and revenue estimates for tax proposals, beginning with those in the president's budget and including all proposals that might be presented as alternative plans by members of the Budget Committees in the House or Senate.

CBO has developed standard, professional techniques for costing out such proposals. But herein lies the difficulty. There is no standard, professional, nonpartisan methodology for evaluating the most important aspect of the effect that any tax/expenditure program might have—namely, its consequences for macroeconomic performance. In Congress, competing economic theories are inherently political. There are no Democratic supply-siders, no Republican post-Keynesians. CBO is obliged to skirt this difficulty, and it does so by assuming that all budget programs have the *same* long-run economic impact. Hence, at any given time, the same (baseline) economic assumptions underlie every budget alternative brought before Congress.

Consequently, it is impossible to use the budget process to design policies for their macroeconomic effect and then to incorporate such effects into estimates of the budget consequences of the policy. All efforts to do so are suspect, tainted by politics, and thwarted by the procedure. Submit the program to CBO for costing out, and it comes back with any presumed economic improvements removed. Refrain from submitting your program, and your revenue and expenditure estimates will carry little weight with your colleagues and cannot hope to be adopted as part of the official framework of the budget.

This is particularly true of proposals that would change monetary policy in conjunction with fiscal policy (as the scenario set out above would certainly require). The Federal Reserve is, in the parlance, a "creature of Congress," which acknowledges as a formal matter its obligation to respect any instructions it may receive from Congress.[9] But Congress is extremely reluctant to issue instructions and unable, because of divisions of jurisdiction between the Banking and Budget Committees, to do so through the budget process. In the early 1980s, budget programs worked out in conjunction with the Joint Economic Committee staff sought to incorporate in an explicit and professional way their own macroeconomic implications and directions for the course of monetary policy. These plans (Moynihan–Riegle–Sasser in 1982, Hart–Moynihan in 1983) were minority efforts within the Senate Budget Committee, and thus short-lived. In 1982, Congress set precedent by including a general instruction to the Federal Reserve in the budget resolution. But this accomplishment was possible only under the crisis conditions of an election-year recession; later efforts to extend the new precedent were easily defeated.

Since achieving economic performance different from the assumptions of the baseline cannot be a target, the budget deficit itself becomes the target. Each year, the president's budget, and every congressional alterna-

The Case for a Limited Tax Shock

tive at every level, is geared to hitting, under specified economic assumptions, an "out-year" target for the budget deficit. The target may have a general logic (economists agree that the deficit should decline rather than rise), but its quantitative value is a matter, at best, of habit. The Gramm–Rudman–Hollings plan of a five-year path to budget balance illustrates the worst features of the system: budget balance is the ultimate target because the budget process focuses political attention on the nominal budget deficit; five years was the time frame because five years is the planning period for which the budget process provides. Both elements of this plan were process-determined; neither bore any perceptible sign of having been thought through as matters of fiscal policy.

Gramm–Rudman–Hollings, though a law rather than a mere budget proposal, was no exception to the general rule of process determination in congressional budgeting. All budget alternatives are judged by their ability to meet or better a given deficit target, and not according to whether they promise better or worse economic performance. Indeed, alternatives survive despite the fact that they guarantee a worse economic performance. Indeed, many members of Congress who voted for the Gramm–Rudman–Hollings bill surely recognized that actually to achieve nominal budget balance by 1991 through the cuts that it specified would generate a deep (and, from the budget standpoint, self-defeating) recession.

Complicating matters further is the rolling aspect of a multiyear target system. Each year is year one of a new five-year plan. Deviations from the previous year's targets, for whatever reason, are forgotten and superseded with each new budget message. Hence the endpoint of the process never falls within the time horizon of the sitting legislature, and political accountability is remote, if not impossible. In the year before each election, the administration and Congress are just as far from ultimate realization of their current goals as they were the day they took office. By then, the goals issued earlier have long since been rendered obsolete by the failure of the economy to track its previous projections, and have been forgotten. This creates every incentive to pass budget resolutions each year that appear to meet the objectives under specified economic and interest rate assumptions, but which then routinely fail to do so. And indeed, unspecified cuts, "magic asterisks," hyperthyroid economic performances and mysterious drops in the interest rate litter the budget documents, executive and congressional, of recent years.

The rolling target is a safety valve (one that Gramm–Rudman–Hollings tried to close); it renders the pursuit of arbitrary budget objectives less immediately pernicious than it would otherwise be. It is true that under a rolling multiyear target system a mindless target need never be achieved: draconian measures enacted in one year and scheduled to take effect in three years can be offset, one way or another, within the next two years— and after all the commotion, nothing, in the end, will have happened. All the same, this is no defense of a procedure that obstructs clear thinking about the objectives of economic policy, wastes legislative time and fosters inaction or pointless action when purposeful action is what the country needs.

The difficulties of the budget process arise from extending its purposes past the point for which the process is best designed. The remedy lies essentially in retracing steps. The budget process is effective and necessary when used to evaluate the long-range implications of alternative spending decisions. It fails when it is used to change the long-run growth path of government spending and when it is made the centerpiece of fiscal policy decision making. These roles should be removed from the budget process.

It may be too much to ask for the development of an explicit policy consensus on the appropriate size and growth of government spending in the aggregate—even one that actually conforms to well-established practice. But it would be preferable if administrations implicitly adjusted their gross expenditure requests so as to acknowledge, at least indirectly, the stability of the underlying political bargain. We need to end the pointless stalemates that arise when the executive branch persists in calling settled questions back up for reconsideration. This would reduce the workload required each year to arrive at a revalidation of the basic, long-standing budget bargain. It would greatly ease the burden of planning and sensible administration of government programs. There is no serious point in maintaining the pretense that what defeated Reagan can practicably be done by someone else. An end to the phony war over the size of government is thus an essential element in making the process of fiscal policy decision making easier, more responsive to economic conditions, and more effective.

The remaining instrument of short-term fiscal policy would then be tax policy. And there is no need for tax policy to be a concern of the budget committees. Let the administration send its tax program, with its deficit implications, first to the Joint Economic Committee and then directly to the tax committees themselves. Let executive and legislature argue the

The Case for a Limited Tax Shock

basic fiscal issues in those forums, taking for this purpose the growth of expenditure as a given, or exogenous, force. Such a change would acknowledge the superior practical flexibility of the tax instrument for countercyclical purposes, and it would remove the temptation to advertise fraudulent, unachievable expenditure reduction as a substitute for necessary tax increases. With a focus strictly on taxes and deficits, it would be a much simpler political matter to make the accounting corrections, for inflation and for the surplus position of other levels of government, as predicates to a fiscal policy debate.

In sum, a restructured congressional process should aim to separate medium- and long-term resource allocation decisions from short- and medium-term fiscal policy decisions. The former is the task for which the budget committees and the CBO are best suited, and the budget process works well in assuring that resource allocation decisions are taken with full regard to their out-year spending consequences. But the budget committees, with their presumption of given economic conditions and their focus on accounting targets and five-year planning horizons, are of no use in making short-run fiscal policy decisions affecting the deficit. This, under the newly redesigned tax code, is the comparative advantage of the joint economic and tax-writing committees. To focus fiscal decision making on the tax instrument alone would help restore the possibility of effective, flexible, short-run fiscal decision making.

CHAPTER 9

Real Money and
Real Interest Rates

I HAVE ALREADY described the macroeconomic policy history of the present decade in terms that leave no doubt of the importance to it of Federal Reserve action. It was a sharp monetary contraction, above all, that drove the economy into recession in 1981. It was only with a sharp reversal of monetary gears that the tax cuts of mid-1982 were able to induce a recovery. It was monetary action in mid-1983 and the consequent tight-money, loose-fiscal-policy mix that produced the continuing high real interest rates and high dollar of the mid-decade. And in the aftermath of Black Monday, October 19, 1987, it was easy money that, for a time, staved off disaster.

A longer review of the history of monetary policy would reveal that this pattern of activism is not extraordinary. Monetary tightenings have been systematic elements of anti-inflation strategy at least since the credit crunch of 1967. They contributed the early and vital blows that led to recession in 1970, 1974 and 1980. Monetary reversals in each case, accompanied by changes in tax policy, helped lead the recoveries. Sustained monetary expansion and negative real interest rates, both at home and for

Real Money and Real Interest Rates

the credit that the United States was extending to the developing world, were the hallmark of the expansionary period under President Carter until October 6, 1979.

Still, there remains a very widely held public perception that monetary policy is a junior partner in macroeconomic policy as a whole. This is due in part to the more public nature of the setting of fiscal policy; public attention focuses where public access is permitted. In part there is a protective attitude of the economic and financial community toward the freedom of action of the Federal Reserve, so that outsiders rarely take their recommendations and complaints to Congress or to the press. In part there is confusion, rooted in academic controversy, over what the instruments of monetary policy are and how they work. And in part the fault rests with the formal structure of decision-making relations, which allows for a large measure of deliberate ambiguity as to who in the U.S. government is actually responsible for monetary actions.

In the United States, the central bank is formally independent of the president, governed by a board appointed for long terms precisely to assure such independence. To what extent, then, should one expect conformity of monetary policy to an administration's objectives? The record since 1913 is filled with arguments between the White House and the Federal Reserve, accompanied now and then by public criticism.[1] Nevertheless, virtually without exception these incidents have the overtone of strain and not of breach. The Federal Reserve is formally independent, but from the political standpoint that independence is fragile; in any open battle before Congress with a president, the Federal Reserve would lose. The central bank therefore cannot afford to stand alone.

There has not been, in the period with which we are concerned, sustained Federal Reserve defiance of an administration's clearly stated monetary wishes. In the Volcker period, where a breach is most commonly alleged, a strong Federal Reserve chairman confronted weak, divided and indecisive counterparts in two administrations. Yet here the problem lay not in a conflict of wills, but in the presence of will at the Federal Reserve and its absence at the White House. On critical occasions when the White House demanded action (March–April 1981, June–August 1982, October 1987), action was forthcoming. Equally important, the administration stood by the Federal Reserve on political matters when the chips were down.

There is a fascinating interplay of politics and press relations between the Federal Reserve and the White House, especially when the economy is performing poorly. On such occasions, Treasury secretaries love to call top reporters and vent their apparent displeasure. In late 1981 and early 1982, as the recession gathered momentum, the hand of Secretary Donald Regan could be seen in a stream of reported complaints that money supply growth was too "volatile" for the Treasury Department's taste. This was reported with straight faces all around, although in fact the money supply's growth was being held nearly constant at 0 percent and the extreme volatility was in interest rates, including a 20 percent prime rate. Regan's charge was insubstantial, and when called before Congress, no administration official would press it. Instead, in that official forum, subject to cross-examination and verbatim public transcripts, the administration consistently averred its basic support for Federal Reserve policy. The Joint Economic Committee made a point of raising the question with every official witness it questioned in this period, and documented a consistent pattern of administration support for Federal Reserve policy in its annual report in March 1982.[2]

As the Federal Reserve and Congress moved toward a confrontation over interest rates in the summer of 1982, the game became more serious. Legislation was introduced by Democratic leaders in both houses (House Majority Leader Jim Wright, Senate Minority Leader Robert Byrd) that would have required direct targeting of interest rates by the Federal Reserve. There was substantial support for these bills on Capitol Hill, though the intent was simply to step up pressure for an easier policy. Now the administration withdrew from the stage. The Federal Reserve abandoned the supertight course in June 1982, and the volatility issue has not been heard of since.

For these reasons, we will treat the conduct of monetary policy as a matter of the strategic preferences of the administration in power, while including the chairman of the Federal Reserve as a major player in determining what those preferences are.

We then turn to the question of how monetary policy works, and try to show in a more precise way why changes in monetary policy occur and how they have affected economic performance.

Real Money and Real Interest Rates

Real Money

Theory teaches that monetary policy works first and foremost on the state of demand. Money in circulation is effectively a debt owed to the holder by the government. Private actors, individuals and businesses, therefore view money, like other receivables, as part of their private financial wealth. If the central bank can increase the real size of the money stock, it is increasing wealth holdings. Economic actors will feel themselves enriched and will step up their real purchases. This demand stimulus is exactly the same in principle as a direct increase in government spending.[3]

From this perspective, the variable to be controlled is not the raw money stock as such—the quantity whose ups and downs from week to week make regular reading in the *Wall Street Journal.* It is the size of this quantity in relation to the price level. If prices go up by the same percentage as the nominal stock of money, the purchasing power of money has not changed, and spending habits will not be much affected. Only when the *real,* after-inflation size of the money stock changes can important effects on real demand, production and employment be expected.

To what extent, then, does the government exercise discretionary control over changes in the real money stock? In particular, has the Reagan administration exercised such control? And to what extent has the Reagan administration pursued a monetary strategy different from that of its predecessors?

Economic conditions that normally affect the growth of real money are readily identified. We expect, first and most obviously, that a high rate of inflation would be associated with slow growth in the real money stock. The central bank leans against an inflationary wind; it usually does not create new money rapidly enough to offset the fall in money's purchasing power. There are elements of demand as well as of supply in this relation: as inflation rises, individuals reduce their desired money holdings (which are losing value) relative to transactions, even as the central bank seeks to fight inflation by making money tight. Statistical estimates show that the leaning effect is quite strong: a 1 percent rise in the annual inflation rate from one calendar quarter to the next produces a more than proportionate drop in the real value of circulating money.[4] Correspondingly, a fall in inflation produces a rise in the real value of money, partly to accommodate a rising demand for money holdings and partly to compensate for the prior fall in real demand that is usually the cause of the fall in inflation.

Second, rising real production should be expected to generate an expansion of real money. In a time of economic growth, individuals and businesses require more of the economy's transacting medium, which is money, to finance the higher volume of purchases and sales that they must make. The central bank is moved to accommodate this demand, though not completely: the bank resists too strong a real growth rate, and also allows for a rising velocity of circulation of real money to absorb some of the real increase in the demand for money. Estimates show that an accommodating effect is present but is quite stingy: a 1 percent rise in real GNP tends to be accommodated by a rise in the real money stock that is only about one-sixth as large. For this reason, interest rates tend to rise with economic growth as the demand for new money outstrips the supply, and those companies and individuals without ready access to credit feel the pinch.

Third, we might expect that monetary policy responds to economic distress, as may be measured by the unemployment rate. In our estimates, this effect is present and very strong: a rise in unemployment of 1 percentage point will generate an increase of 2 percentage points in the growth rate of the real money stock. Thus the Federal Reserve is sensitive to the human and political consequences of the unemployment that its own policies partly cause.

Taking these three factors into consideration, a simple linear regression can explain over half of the quarterly change in the growth rate of the real stock of money for the period from 1970 to the advent of the Reagan administration. Extending this sample period to include the following five years has no effect on the estimates of the effects of inflation, real growth, and unemployment on money creation. Thus we may say that the arrival of Reagan did not change, at least along these dimensions, the pattern of response of the Federal Reserve to changing economic conditions.

But there is an enormous difference of a blunter kind. Beginning in late 1979 with the appointment of Paul Volcker, and continuing through the first five years of the Reagan era, there is a dramatic downshift in the *average rate* of real money growth.[5] This was a major policy change that occurred even though the pattern of responsiveness of the Federal Reserve to changing economic conditions remained about what it had been before. For every state of the economy, in other words, real money growth fell sharply. Statistical estimates value this downshift at nearly a full 5 percentage points off the growth rate for real M2 for each year from 1980 on. In other words, the real money supply every year under Reagan grew at perhaps half the average rate of the 1970s, even after accounting for the effects of all economic variables on the rate, including the fall in inflation.

Figure 9-1 compares the actual growth rate of real money in the Reagan era with a forecast based on the behavioral conditions of the 1970s, adjusted for the economic conditions of the present decade. The chart leaves no doubt of the size or importance of the money slowdown.

The Great Money Slowdown confirms, that like tax policy, monetary policy is capable of undergoing a true "change of regime," independent of the normal influences of economic conditions on policymakers' behavior. Monetary policy changed regime in 1979; the Reagan administration continued a new regime already inaugurated, under conservative pressure, by Carter. And given the change in regime in 1979, the 1981 supertightening now appears as a predictable (though nonetheless extreme) reaction to the extraordinary inflation run-up of late 1980. (Evidently, contrary to the famous dictum of rational expectations theory, even predictable events can have powerful effects.)

Two conclusions follow. First, we must give the Great Money Slowdown

FIGURE 9–1
*Real Money Growth vs. Projection (fitted 1970–80,
forecast 1981–85)*

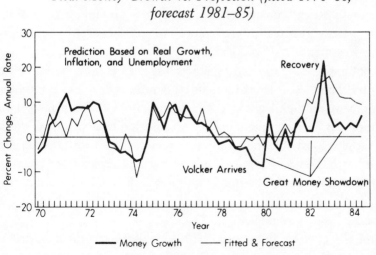

Sources: Citibase and author's calculations.

due weight in accounting for the financial and economic events of the 1980s. These include the recession with which the decade began in 1980, the panic and collapse of financial values in the summer of 1981—so widely ascribed at the time to legislative action on taxes and spending—and the subsequent recovery. Most of all, it must include the high level of real short-term interest rates that characterized the entire first half of the decade and the consequent enormous rise in the foreign exchange value of the dollar. The fact that supply-siders have for their own reasons adopted and to some extent discredited this viewpoint does not make it false.

Second, consideration of the future must allow that a large discretionary reversal in monetary policy is both a possibility and a policy option. The real interest rate and the dollar may fall without the assistance of action on the budget. It can happen. It may or may not be desirable under given circumstances. It may indeed have been happening for a time under the pressure of circumstance, and was certainly desirable, in the aftermath of the stock market crash of October 1987.

Real Interest Rates

We have so far restricted our focus to the effects of monetary policy on the growth of the real value of the money stock. Theory teaches, however, that there is a second important channel of monetary influence, which is through the effect of real interest rates on credit-financed consumption and on investment.

It is not appropriate to regard real interest rates as the sole preserve of the central bank. Real short-term interest rates reflect the return that lenders receive on their loans after the depreciation of their principal due to inflation has been subtracted. They are affected by demand, as well as by the supply of loanable funds, and may therefore vary with the business cycle and with the size of public sector borrowing (deficits). Nevertheless, real interest rates may be treated as an intermediate financial variable of interest to the administration as a whole, and on this ground an analysis may proceed much as above.

On the evidence for the period 1970–85, real interest rates depend on both the size of the federal deficit (measured as the change in the value of the federal debt after adjusting for inflation) and the rate of change of the real money stock. Both effects are as one would expect. A rise in the real deficit of 1 percent of GNP raises the short-term real interest rate by over 0.5 percent. A decline in the growth rate of the real money stock of 1 percentage point tends to raise the real interest rate by about one-third of a point. In principle, either or both actions can make the real interest rate rise.

In practice, the Federal Reserve's assault on real interest rates came first. Real money growth turned extremely tight with the accession of Paul Volcker in late 1979, even though the real budget was still strongly in surplus. Real interest rates nevertheless rose sharply as money tightened, as one might have expected. But real deficits did not soar until mid-1982, which was also when the real money stock, responding to recession, started once again to grow. At that time, the burden of sustaining a 5 percent real short-term interest rate (and the high dollar it produced) shifted, in effect, from the Federal Reserve to the budget. Thus, over the decade as a whole, the sharp drop in real money growth under Volcker and the sharp rise in real deficits under Reagan are *together* responsible for the increase in real short-term interest rates from an average in the 1970s of −1 percent to an average since late 1979 of over 5 percent.

The rate of inflation is the only other readily identified factor that strongly affects real interest rates. A rise in inflation depresses real interest rates, and a decline increases them. In the short run, this reflects the slow adjustment of expectations, of policy and of financial market conditions to changes in the actual inflation rate. Thus the steadily declining inflation of the Reagan–Volcker years constitutes a third factor that, at least in the statistical sense, accounts for the dramatic increase in real interest rates over the same period.

In sum, the good news is that policy does work. The bad news, is that policy often works in depressingly predictable and unproductive ways. The question is: What role should monetary policy now play?

Monetary Strategy Ahead

A sharp though limited deficit cut—whether arrived at by the tax shock advocated in the previous chapter or otherwise—will reduce the growth of aggregate demand, and so tend to reduce the economy's real rate of growth. Moreover, the economic growth rate is already below a 4 percent target and shows no signs of climbing back up there on its own. To get growth back on a high but sustainable long-run track despite a contractionary fiscal shift is the next task that policy design must address.

Real growth is a matter of real spending, and real spending is a matter of two partially independent factors: real incomes on the one hand and perceived profit opportunities on the other. Little can be done for domestic real disposable incomes in the short run, since fiscal policy must move to reduce such incomes either through higher taxes or reductions in spending. That leaves two main arenas for growth: *foreign* real incomes and *domestic* expected profits.

There is room for progress on both of these fronts, and monetary policy must be the instrument for action on both. And, as with tax policy, the way to act is through a once-and-for-all change of regime. In essence, a permanent reversal of the Volcker–Carter–Reagan regime of worldwide high real interest rates and slow real money growth is now called for.

Such a reversal would affect domestic profit opportunities through two channels. First, there are housing, automobiles, and the major consumer durables sectors of the domestic economy. Sales in these sectors are financed, and so are sensitive to the supply and price of credit. When interest rates fall, sales will increase and so will profits. But here there are two problems.

The first is one of capacity. The expansion of 1983–87 was largely led by housing and other interest-sensitive consumer industries in the wake of the previous bout of monetary easing in 1982; by the end of 1986, production in these sectors was well past its previous peaks. And so, it is doubtful that there can be rapid growth in these sectors now. Should the demand grow strongly, bottlenecks in supply will emerge, attenuating the opportunity for potential profits to be realized.

The second issue stems from the fact that purchases in these sectors are debt financed. Consumer debt loads, having been brought down sharply in the recessions of 1980–82, have risen once again in the expansion, as illustrated in figure 9–2. They have been an engine for the growth of business profits under Reagan. By 1987 they stood well above past peaks in relation to income. It is certain that private debt loads cannot continue to rise indefinitely, and it is doubtful that they can continue even for very long. Sustained industrial expansion cannot be carried mainly on the backs of the American consumer.

Real Money and Real Interest Rates

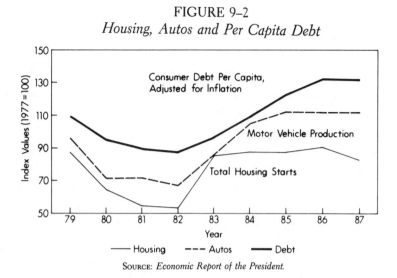

FIGURE 9-2
Housing, Autos and Per Capita Debt

SOURCE: *Economic Report of the President.*

The more promising source of growth lies in net exports. In this sector, there was effectively no growth from 1981 to 1986. In 1987 exports did recover, growing about 15 percent in real terms. But the largest share of this growth (about two-thirds of the total) was in exports to Japan and East Asia; the expansion of exports to Europe and to Latin America was far less. Hence, despite some recovery in 1987 and 1988, the potential for export growth remains very large if ways can be found to exploit it.

This is partly a second channel of monetary effect. An immediate, credible and sustained cut in U.S. real interest rates relative to those abroad, and a consequent sharp depreciation of the dollar, would produce a decline in the real burden of U.S.–denominated debt. Since a decline in debt is a rise in net worth, and a rise in net worth amounts to income, such an event would be tantamount to a rise in foreign real income. At the same time, it would induce substitution toward U.S.–produced export commodities.

The dollar has been falling since September 1985. It has fallen especially far with respect to the yen and to the deutsche mark, and this is already having an effect on Japanese and German exports relative to our own. But this is not enough. A dollar fall with respect to the yen and the deutsche mark does indeed affect relative prices between U.S., Japanese and German goods. But all of Europe and Japan together now account for only 40 percent of U.S. trade. It is equally (and perhaps more) important to affect the real incomes of those nations that account for the other

177

60 percent of U.S. trade and an even larger portion of U.S. exports. Yet this will not occur until the dollar falls with respect to the currencies of those countries—something which, as of mid 1988, had not occurred.

Ideally, how much more should the dollar fall? One can provide an *average* or trade-weighted answer for this question. It is not a matter for the faint of heart. The fact is that in 1980, when the dollar stood roughly 22 percent below trade-weighted values in 1986 (18 percent in real terms), our current account was balanced and our export and capital goods performance was satisfactory. They have not been so since. While accelerating inflation may have artificially depressed the dollar a little in this period, especially in 1980, this effect cannot have been very large (and in real terms, the dollar appreciated in 1980 over 1979). We should therefore probably take a value not too far above the 1980 value as the correct one from the standpoint of U.S. competitiveness *at that time.* But we have been losing competitive ground in the key capital goods exporting sectors in the interim. To regain lost ground will require an overshoot. Therefore the correct trade-weighted dollar value, from a trade and competitiveness perspective, is probably 30 percent or more below its already fallen value in the summer of 1987 (before the stock crash).[6]

Accordingly, regaining lost export and capital goods ground will require a substantial additional depreciation of the dollar. This must go far beyond the tentative, halting, and drawn-out process set in motion by the Plaza Accords. We are back at the brink of the post–Vietnam War adjustments, and we need the grit to deliver a comparable shock, in our own interest, to the world system.

The problem of achieving depreciation breaks down into two components. The first of these concerns financial relations among developed countries with convertible currencies and efficient financial markets. The second concerns depreciation of the dollar with respect to the more fragile and, in some cases, deeply indebted economies of the developing world, whose renewed growth is essential to the success of U.S. trade.

In the world of efficient financial markets, it may be that a relatively *small* decline in U.S. nominal interest rates—say, 2 percent—could, if presented by the authorities to the markets and to foreign central banks with vigor, be sufficient to bring the necessary depreciation about. The reason concerns the way in which foreign exchange markets bring themselves into equilibrium, and this deserves a short discussion.

Foreign exchange has become, since the breakdown of the Bretton

Real Money and Real Interest Rates

Woods arrangements for exchange-rate stabilization in 1971, the quintessential market for speculative assets. The ephemera of short-term profit expectations rule the roost; so-called fundamental forces are on the sidelines. Trade and current account imbalances, which for a time were thought central to foreign exchange equilibration, have become, for the major currencies, essentially irrelevant in comparison with the smallest movements of overnight market sentiment.

In particular, investors at the international level must concern themselves with two issues. First is the nominal rate of return to an instrument, such as a bond. Second is the prospective change in the relative value of the currency in which the bond is denominated. At the margin, an investor will equalize the sum of these returns over the holding period. That is, he will take a yen bond (for example) at a lower interest rate than a comparable dollar bond if he believes that appreciation of the yen is likely to cover the interest rate differential. So long as the bet that the yen will rise seems to be a good one, the investor will hold the bond, even though each month or quarter the coupon payment is lower than he could have gotten on a dollar bond.

In practice, investors have widely disparate perceptions at any one time—some are bulls, some are bears—and so portfolios of all kinds—some are long, some are short—are always being held. This is especially true in the treacherous market for foreign exchange. Nevertheless, *changes* in crowd sentiment are likely to develop in response to given *changes* in the environment, and this movement is often predictable. Thus a change in U.S. policy (expanding the real money supply and cutting interest rates, for example) will likely make bulls more bullish and bears less bearish. And so, such changes will influence market movements in a fairly predictable way.

The Baker–Volcker duet of 1985–87, beginning with the Plaza Accords of September 1985 and ending with Volcker's resignation in July 1987, consisted of a long series of conflicting signals about the future course of monetary policy in the United States. On the one hand, Baker and Volcker (Baker more than Volcker) signaled that U.S. monetary authorities feared a recession and were prepared to lower the dollar sporadically to avert one. On the other hand, they made it clear (Volcker more than Baker) that they feared inflation and were afraid to do anything sudden. The monetary authorities were thus resisting action until forced to it by adverse news, and then were taking only the minimum action required to keep the news from getting worse.

Obviously, this decision rule could not work to make the news better. Because it was predictable, it fostered speculation against the authorities' position. Investors looking at the U.S. situation under these circumstances foresaw a continuing but slow decline in the dollar, interrupted episodically by U.S. efforts to defend it. From this expectation one can make money, and, clearly, many did.

An investor foreseeing a *future* decline in a currency must insist on a higher nominal interest return at present, or else he will transfer his assets elsewhere. And higher interest must be paid, lest the currency value fall further yet. Thus the Baker–Volcker duet, so long as it lasted, had the effect of keeping U.S. interest rates higher, and the dollar much higher, than they would otherwise have been. This helps to explain the continuing high differential between U.S. nominal interest rates and U.S. inflation, and consequently the high real interest rate and the sluggish performance of the U.S. investment sector in 1986 and 1987.

Yet, the Baker–Volcker duet contained an internal tension: high interest rates impede growth, and so the high dollar was incompatible with sustained economic expansion, to which the administration was evidently committed. Speculation against the Baker–Volcker duet began in earnest in early 1987 as high interest rates began to cut into housing, automotive and consumer durables sales. Anticipating a policy response and an unavoidable decline in the dollar, private foreign investors ceased purchasing U.S. assets altogether. From February 1987 on, virtually the entire U.S. current account was financed by increased dollar holdings at foreign central banks.[7] This helped keep the dollar from collapsing in immediate response to speculation, at the price of making additional speculation even more profitable than it was before.

The growing dependence of the dollar on foreign official intervention could not help, temporarily at least, but weaken the negotiating position of the United States in seeking coordinated international expansion. With Volcker's resignation, the picture clouded; U.S. intentions and leadership became momentarily uncertain. For a few crucial months, U.S. authorities actually fell under the sway of German monetary leadership, and a pattern of American followership developed: U.S. interest rates rose in response to German initiatives, so as to defend the dollar. The inconsistency between defense of the dollar and economic expansion grew acute.

The stock crash in October was precipitated in part by fear of German monetary hegemony, which came to a head in mid-October when Secre-

Real Money and Real Interest Rates

tary Baker failed to secure Bundesbank cooperation on a coordinated interest rate reduction. And mercifully for the administration, the stock crash forced the American hand. With brokerage houses, banks and possibly the economy at risk, the Federal Reserve reacted by breaking free of German influence and filling its role as the lender of last resort. From that point, with the election on the line, U.S. interest rates had to fall, little by little, so as to keep a collapse of values and a threatened recession at bay. So the dollar's fall resumed—again against the major-country currencies of Europe and Japan.

The fall of the dollar in late 1987 demonstrated that when the monetary authorities act quickly, decisively and publicly to cut interest rates, with all the means that they use to convey conviction, the markets respond by adjusting currency values in a very substantial way.

The reason for this can be most easily seen in an example. Consider the situation the morning after a drop in U.S. nominal interest rates, say from 6 to 4 percent. At this moment, nominal returns in the United States are down by a full 33 percent. Investors will now wish to adjust their portfolios to reduce their exposure in dollars. They will register orders to sell. But if the price of the dollar is allowed to fall freely, *it will have already fallen* by the time this process goes very far. Stock and currency crashes can occur in a day.

After the fall, the prospective situation looks very different. The marginal investor is confronted with a dollar portfolio on which he has already sustained (to the benefit of U.S. debtors, including the government) a capital loss. But if the loss is big enough, then looking to the future, he will conclude that the prospect is now for dollar appreciation. The period of decline has concluded. With sorrow for the past, the investor will look to a future of capital gains on his diminished fortune. What is the point now of selling any more? And that being so, the investor will hold his depleted dollars at a *lower nominal interest rate than existed earlier,* when he expected the overvalued dollar to decline. Such is the psychology of markets.

With respect to the major currencies, then, the problem is simply that, as of the present writing, monetary policy has not yet moved forcefully enough. Alan Greenspan and James Baker (and more recently, Nicholas Brady) have continued on a gradualist path, hoping to find an alternative path out of the world's low-growth dilemma. They are hoping to persuade the Germans, in particular, to move with us, lowering their interest rates, and so bring about a coordinated worldwide monetary expansion. Should our allies move with us, and lower their interest rates alongside ours, exchange rates would not change so much. But the worldwide monetary expansion would be greater, U.S. exports would recover due to foreign real income expansion, and the inflation shock would occur nevertheless, though later rather than sooner.

And so, a word needs to be said about international coordination. It might be best, in an ideal world, to work out offsetting fiscal–monetary shifts in Japan, Germany and Great Britain (at least), as the administration and the Federal Reserve have been attempting, in a limited way, to do. But the ideological composition and competitive interests of the governments of those nations make such coordination in advance on the scale required unrealistic. And so international coordination has become, under these circumstances, an obstacle to effective policy change. What could be a coordinated expansion can become a prisoner's dilemma, a coordination trap, a drag on the world system that requires every country to conform to the financial conservatism of its most recalcitrant government.

The second best method is to act first and consult later. Faced with lower U.S. interest rates, our advanced industrial allies could either abandon their own overly contractionary policies or see their currencies rise and lose the trading advantages they presently enjoy. The United States could live with either outcome, and the world would be much better off with either. Nothing, indeed, would be lost except face for Gerhard Stoltenberg and Otto Pohl. But their problems of personal prestige need not detain us.

If the dollar falls, the authorities could then move to create a climate of expected stability in exchange rates at the restored competitive levels. This will slow down any expected appreciation and prolong the low interest rate equilibrium. An international agreement to stabilize exchange rates could move right to the top of the monetary agenda once the fundamental parities and interest rate structure had been put right.

Far more difficult problems arise in connection with the developing countries. As figure 9-3 shows, falling interest rates have not produced dollar depreciation with respect to Latin America, the Pacific Rim or Canada. Indeed, in comparison with these regions, the dollar has continued to appreciate despite falling U.S. interest rates since the time of the Plaza Accords.

FIGURE 9–3

The Undeclining Dollar

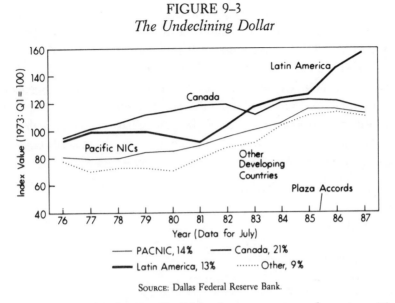

SOURCE: Dallas Federal Reserve Bank.

With respect to the Pacific Rim, the matter is perhaps transitional. Korea, for example, runs a trade surplus with the United States but a large deficit with Japan, from which it buys industrial equipment (Hyundai, for example, imports Mitsubishi equipment to produce cars for the American market). Thus a rise in the yen relative to the won (which has remained at a constant parity with the dollar) must mean a hard squeeze on Korean profits. This can be mitigated if and only if Japanese suppliers cut their yen prices in Korea, and so cut their profit margins, which to some extent has occurred. But this also gets to the heart of a competitive correction sooner or later, and so a temporary continuation of a high dollar with countries in Korea's situation need not be regarded as an indefinite structural problem.

It is the debt problem that is difficult and crucial. Latin American countries now account for less than 15 percent of U.S. trade, but the potential for a vast expansion exists. Yet Latin American nations are battling for survival. To survive, they must export, since export surpluses are required if interest payments on past debts are to be paid. The available market is, as it always has been, in the United States. Export surpluses therefore require that Latin currencies be kept cheap relative to the dollar, and this impedes Latin purchasing power over American goods.

Thus there is a structural reason why the dollar remains high against

183

a group of currencies which, though not substantial in the world economy, are linked intimately and inextricably to the trading fate of the United States. Lower interest rates alone will not correct the failure of U.S. exports in Mexico and Brazil. Something more is needed. The solution is to eliminate the need for Latin export surpluses. Debt relief, therefore, has a structural role in reestablishing the world position of U.S. trade. And the revival of development worldwide has, as we have seen and shall now again consider, a structural role in sustaining U.S. investment, employment *and* competitive advantage in the advanced sectors.

CHAPTER 10

World Growth and the Debt

To RAISE PRODUCTIVE INVESTMENT and speed the pace of industrial transformation in the United States has turned out to be the heart of the matter. Rising living standards over the long period are what we seek. These depend on investment in machines and in the skills to design, create and run them. That investment must occur on a sufficient scale. And it also must be investment of the right kind, given the opportunities and challenges of the position the United States occupies in the structure of world trade.

Total gross investment, the scale of investment *grosso modo*, depends on confidence in an expected run of profitability sufficient to make the investment worthwhile. It is within the power of government to create an environment in which such confidence exists. Kennedy and Johnson did it, Nixon did it, Ford and Carter did it and Reagan did it in the middle of his term. The basic technique is to exploit the conditions that normally follow a recession, which include low indebtedness and quiescent labor and commodity markets. When government in such circumstances commits itself to policies of sustained expansion, speculators respond by running up the stock market, and businesses respond to that event by taking out loans to expand capital and to bring the construction and capital goods sectors back to high employment.

This technique effectively raises total surplus and creates the warm glow of an incipient boom. But it is not a durable way to raise productive investment. Businesses that sell into the internal market are well aware of the business cycle and of its limits. They know that there can be too much productive investment as well as too little. If a business overinvests in the expansion, it will find itself caught between its debt obligations and its unused capacity in the subsequent downturn. Especially as the expansion ages, it is better for business to use existing capital equipment more intensively, and to divert profit income toward the struggle for market share and toward consumption. This is one reason that measured productivity growth falls in late expansions: consumer goods producers are hedging their positions for the upcoming slump.

To raise productive investment durably thus requires structural change of two kinds. The first task is to change the climate of expectations for long-term demand growth and to reestablish faith in the lasting expansion. The second task is to change the market incentives facing those who make business investment decisions, so that they devote their resources to expanded capacity rather than to expanded surplus absorption and sales effort.

Yet, to achieve either type of structural change in a business-dominated economy is difficult, and perhaps impossible to do directly. Businesses that sell to the U.S. market act rationally in deciding to absorb the surplus available to them and will not change their view on the probability of a future downturn simply because they are asked to do so. The best that government can hope for from direct measures is to capture some of the absorbed surplus for productive public purposes, including investment in public infrastructure, in community amenities and in environmental protection. No strategy has yet been devised to raise productive investment by changing the internal structure of the managerial firm.

By working through product markets, however, the desired result *can* be achieved. The capital goods producer is less concerned with distribution and more concerned with development, production and reaching the technological frontier. Comfortable careers are made in consumer goods, on high volume, low margins and the free spending of corporate slack. The great fortunes are made in capital goods, in the lean pursuit of the big killing. To raise the sustainable share of capital goods in all of production is therefore *pro tanto* to raise the sustained rate of renewal of the capital stock.

World Growth and the Debt

To expand the capital goods share means to expand trade. The elementary reason is that each capital goods worker supports many more workers in the consumer goods sector; the ratio may be as high as four to one.[1] Without trade, significant expansion of the domestic capital goods sector must entail massive expansion of domestic consumer goods employment at the expense of services. Within the United States alone, there would soon be a scarcity of available workers. More subtly, the conditions that would bring about a rise in consumer goods production within the United States—as the demand and price conditions of the 1980s have done—also foster (and have fostered) a rising share of imports in all production of capital goods (as well as of consumer goods). And this defeats the final purpose of the exercise.

To raise the share of capital goods in industrial production is therefore tantamount to raising the share of exports in GNP.[2] And so, the strategy to do so must be a strategy for global economic growth, for global reconstruction and for development. There are many actual and potential manufacturing workers throughout the world; they would be far better off if supplied with the capital equipment that the United States is capable of producing. They would, in turn, agree happily to share with us, in payment, a substantial fraction of the new consumer goods that would then be produced.

A global growth strategy must have two elements: a demand element and a price element. The demand element must stem from an increase in worldwide investment spending, in the ability and willingness of all countries to purchase capital goods. The price element must be there to assure that the United States remains or is restored as a competitive supplier of those goods.

To raise investment spending worldwide is a daunting objective, but one which remains well within the scope of the power of Western governments. It requires a concentration of financial resources in the hands of governments and enterprises around the world, including those in Latin America, East Asia, the Soviet Union, China and India, that are prepared to gamble on development. For this, an end to the present debt crisis is essential, as will be discussed later. A new set of worldwide financial arrangements, to expand liquidity in conjunction with expanded investment spending, would be helpful. These seem prohibitive conditions, but they are not. The problems here lie not in the technical difficulties but in a lack of political will, which in turn is greatly exacerbated by the dominating position of commercial bankers in reputable political discussions of finance. Breaking that monopoly with an alternative vision can go far toward establishing the political conditions for action.

Worldwide growth of investment spending generates a pattern of trend-and-cycle expectations very different from that created by spending growth within a single country. At the global level, there is no balance of payments constraint. Cycles in relative commodity product prices, which affect individual producer countries, tend to even out over the whole world. Cycles in the domestic politics of different countries offset one another. Therefore, there is no reason to expect a uniform world business cycle other than what might stem from coordinated actions in the developed world. Once the conditions are ripe, capital goods production for export can expand, and go on expanding, for a much longer period without encountering the expectation that world development will peter out. Saturation need not occur for decades, and the final limit comes only when the last laggard achieves a comfortable living standard and eliminates the backlog of technologies from which it has suffered with respect to the United States, Europe and Japan. This is safely far in the future.

Price competitiveness for U.S. capital goods on world markets can be achieved, in principle, in many ways. The alternatives include subsidization of capital goods industry, provision of credit on favorable terms to the purchaser through the Export-Import Bank and other intermediaries and exchange rate depreciation.

I have argued that the practical problems of efficient direct subsidy to advanced industry are insurmountable if the essential character of successful capital goods production is to be preserved. This rules out industrial policy administered under the tripartite business–labor–government model, as favored by certain elements of big business and labor. Destructive for similar reasons would be wage controls in the capital goods sectors to keep prices down. Capital goods firms must have independence in their investment decisions and the flexibility to share quasi-rents with their employees.

The direct role of the state must therefore be primarily that of providing the social overhead that is necessary for capital goods firms to take root and prosper. This includes public infrastructure to support the creation of new plants. It includes education of high quality accessible to those youngsters still attracted to science and engineering in preference to accounting, management and law. It includes fostering financial markets with many decision makers prepared to scatter resources over many uncertain investment options. It includes providing a good measure of social security so that workers entering volatile industries will not be dissuaded by a forbidding level of personal risk. Making public goods available to the capital goods sector is the most effective form of subsidization to which government can aspire.

A low dollar exchange rate is indispensable at least for a transition period, while capital goods producers seek to prevent the Japanese and Germans from capturing too large a share of the new markets that a rise in worldwide investment spending would create. Much of what is necessary with respect to the yen and deutsche mark may, as of the end of 1987, have been achieved. However, the dollar must fall still further to provide purchasing power over U.S. goods to the countries most prone to buy them. Against Canada, the Pacific rim and the rest of the world, there had been negligible dollar depreciation by the end of the year. Against the crucial Latin American market, the dollar continued to appreciate throughout 1987 and into 1988.

Why was this so? The answer has everything to do with the debt crisis. The Latin debtors, Brazil and Mexico above all, must maintain large trade surpluses if they are to continue any significant debt service. For this, their goods must remain price competitive in American markets.[3] American markets are their historical markets and are the only relatively unprotected, growing markets available in the world. So it is imperative that when the dollar falls, the peso, the crusado and the others must fall too.

Better credit conditions for indebted buyers of U.S. exports would be helpful. But it is certainly unrealistic to expect that the Export-Import Bank will assume this task, particularly when no comparable program of loan subsidy can be plausibly extended to indebted American farmers and small businessmen. Congress would never appropriate the money. Nor can sufficient funds be channeled through the World Bank, for the same reason. Liquidation of the present debt crisis is the only way out, the only way to relieve the finance constraint that is destroying development in South and Central America.

As a world strategy for growth and investment succeeds, the jobs created in the U.S. capital goods sectors will be good jobs—the best available on a mass basis in the world. They will, of course, be risky. Capital goods producers must therefore be allowed to bid employees— scientists, engineers, skilled employees—away from alternative employment by offering them a scarcity wage and by compensating them for taking risks. A rise in the size of a high-income sector will mean rising average wages in the economy overall and in the share of wages in national income (even though profits will also be rising). This will remove some of the debilitating pressure on secondary workers to seek employment and so ease the competition of workers for jobs in services. Hence, service wages as well as capital goods wages will rise relative to wages in the traditional consumer goods manufacturing sector. The net result will be a strengthening of workers in these sectors, even though the erosion of traditional (unionized) consumer goods industry in the United States will be destined to continue. One of the challenges facing U.S. unions will be to move from this traditional arena toward a new power base in the advanced sectors.

The reward for export of capital goods is the ability to import for the purpose of consumption. A low exchange rate would make consumer goods imports more expensive at first than they have been recently. This is an unavoidable consequence of eliminating the structural current account deficit and debt-based consumption we have been running. But it is purely a transitional event.

As worldwide consumer goods production grows, real prices for the First World consumer must fall, and fall sharply. The terms on which capital goods are traded for consumer goods are very favorable in the first place, and they become even more so when total production is rising. There is no competition in capital goods like that between alternative producers of the identical consumer product. It is imperative for full development that consumer goods become cheap, cheap enough so that even the lowest strata of society can afford them. To extend this principle to the Third World is to make consumer goods cheap beyond all present imagining and so to extend the consumption possibilities of the wealthy all the more. The transition to higher capital goods production entails a lower consumption standard at first, but it will yield a much higher and more sustainable consumption standard as time goes on.

We may take conditions at the end of the 1980s as given. The U.S. economy is, at present, debt ridden and expansion bloated. Consumption standards, financed by debt, have been unsustainably high. The falling dollar portends rising inflation. An adjustment must be made in order to reduce American imports to levels that can be sustained by the future growth of American exports. How is it all to be done? There are two alternatives.

World Growth and the Debt

The first is easy, vulgar and painful. The United States could simply break the back, once again, of its consumer goods sector with a recession, and follow that with a massive stimulus to world production through a high-deficit, low real interest rate, low-dollar expansion. The essential tools for this, monetary and fiscal policy, are readily at hand. After six years of expansion, the debt structures of U.S. businesses and of households are such as to make both highly vulnerable. Moreover, the strategy might work. Imports would fall immediately, so there would be gratifying progress on the current account. A recession would eliminate the marginal tier of domestic consumer goods manufacturers and would again stimulate demand for imports in the recovery. The capital goods sector would be hurt in the recession, but it would bounce back quickly, though the consumer goods sector would not. With a powerful enough stimulus at that point, a new trade distorting cycle could probably get underway.

Yet there are certain drawbacks to this course of action. The initial tight money policy would drive U.S. real interest rates up, and the subsequent recession would increase the deficit. This policy combination would work initially to raise the value of the dollar. Getting the dollar back down again might prove difficult, for the interest rate reaches a floor at zero. If the dollar stayed high, imports would rise in the ensuing expansion, but U.S. exports would be no more competitive. Import demand might therefore flow, as it has in the 1980s, to countries that buy their capital goods not from us but from our competitors, Japan and Germany. The final result could be merely another enlargement of the trade deficit—so long as U.S. credit held good.

The initial revaluation of the dollar would also mean a revaluation of dollar-denominated sovereign debts, foreclosing early recovery in the debt-crisis countries. Perhaps the political systems of Mexico, Brazil, Argentina and the Philippines would withstand the strain, perhaps not. Those that, like Mexico, have accumulated foreign exchange reserves at great sacrifice in recent years would find those reserves gone in a flash. It would be a bitter blow for countries clinging to hope against hope after six years of depression. A crisis of default and debt repudiation cannot be ruled out.

One might also mention in passing the bankruptcies and mass unemployment that would engulf the American political and social scene. The American unemployment rate reached 11 percent at the trough of the recession in 1982; in the next recession, it might go higher. No administration presiding over such a fiasco at election time would survive.

Therefore, a managed transition without recession seems obligatory as well as reasonable. A smooth transition would limit the pace of slowdown in the U.S. consumer goods sector until export demand and the growth of investment-sector jobs actually took hold. It could help avoid the next domestic bankruptcy crisis. It would help keep the costs of the transition within the resource limits available as a practical matter to the American state. It would help stave off a Latin collapse. Most of all, it would enable world growth to resume from a higher base of American real wealth, production and consumption. There is simply no good sense in throwing away what we already have simply to speed up the transition to something better.

To achieve the growth of world demand is primarily a matter of monetary expansion and foreign debt relief initiated by the United States and of fiscal expansion in the other advanced countries with good credit. The goal for the United States should be a growth of exports sufficient to eliminate the cyclical component of the U.S. current account deficit without, however, curtailing much or any of the absolute level of U.S. demand for imports. Immediate monetary expansion is the U.S. instrument of choice because it is the instrument in which we enjoy a degree of maneuverability. Fiscal expansion should be urged, and if that fails, pushed on the rest of the industrial West, because that is the instrument on which they likewise enjoy a margin of maneuverability.

The best prospects for worldwide demand growth are in the debt-ridden developing countries, in the East, and on the periphery of Europe. The developing world alone supplied 25 percent of the U.S. export demand in 1980, but by 1987 this share had declined to only 20 percent. By one estimate, growth and a reversal of financial flows could restore U.S. exports to the Third World by as much as $30 billion by 1991.[4]

Second in quantity terms is the absorptive capacity of Europe (about 23 percent of U.S. exports in 1987). Within the European community there has been minimal industrial expansion for a decade, just over 0.5 percent per year on average. Evidently, a prisoners' dilemma holds: all countries would benefit from higher growth, but such policies are sustainable only if all participate. In practice, all have been hostage to the hyperconservative *rentier* policies of the Germans. Economic incentives for a possible solution can emerge from the strong pressure of improved American competitiveness on the profitability of German exports within Europe. Still, strong political pressure will no doubt continue to be necessary.

World Growth and the Debt

U.S. trade with the East is very small: exports to the Soviet Union and China combined were about $5 billion in 1987. But the potential is very large. Both Eastern giants are good credit risks and very short on capital goods. *Perestroika* and arms control may provide an opportunity for the capture of expanding capital goods markets. It is unfortunate that so much damage was done to trade relations, particularly with the Soviets, by dubious U.S. policies affecting technology transfer. Perhaps, though, in an improved political climate, much of the damage can be undone.

As world demand growth takes hold, the United States must move to restrain the growth of (but not to cut) its own imports so as to permit the current account deficit to end. The best means of accomplishing this is with a general increase in the average rate of U.S. income taxation, levied on the newly reformed and simplified tax structure. Transfers of purchasing power within the United States to lower-income groups, through expanded welfare programs financed by higher taxation, would also reduce the propensity to import. Thus, U.S. policy toward the budget deficit should be directed at closing the trade gap in the context of continued U.S. growth. The particulars of the strategy are discussed in chapter 8.

Other things being equal, a tighter fiscal policy and a more expansionary monetary strategy together imply a further fall in the dollar. This will work to correct any price disadvantages still afflicting U.S. capital goods exporters in foreign markets in competition with Japanese, German and other suppliers. As noted, relative U.S. capital goods prices may already be low enough, and it would be better still if the threat of a sharply lower dollar drove the governments of those countries to coordinate their own real interest rates with ours. This would permit global monetary expansion to occur on a multicurrency basis. It would effect the necessary further trade-weighted depreciation of the dollar by raising the purchasing power of Third World currencies at current rates of exchange between the dollar, deutsche mark and yen. However, this result cannot be relied on.

Dollar depreciation and global monetary expansion would ease the debt crisis. Countries requiring dollars for their imports would find their costs reduced. Those exporting directly in large volumes to the United States would be affected by declining U.S. demand for consumer imports, but their absolute earnings would remain strong. The burden of the debt in real terms would decline. Falling U.S. interest rates would ease the servicing burden. Commodity prices would probably rise as interest rates (the opportunity cost of inventory holdings) fell. Most fundamentally, once the United States again became a capital surplus nation, the capital so generated would seek an outlet, and unless Europe and Japan changed their own policies even more radically than ourselves (and in the opposite direction), that capital would eventually make its way to the developing world.

Still, even if all this happened, the debt overhang would continue to thwart the efforts, particularly of Latin American debtors, to expand their own industrial bases. Such expansion is essential for a recovery of U.S. capital goods exports, since beating out the Japanese in the rapidly growing Asian markets (including Japan's own) is by now probably impossible. The United States must place its bets, for better or worse, on Brazil, Mexico and Argentina.

Comprehensive debt relief initiated by the creditors has been proposed. Senator Bill Bradley, a leader in the American debate, has suggested what amounts to a worldwide bankruptcy proceeding that would bring debtors and creditors together to seek a settlement under the auspices of the president of the United States.[5] Others have proposed the creation of a a writedown or discount facility, administered either by the United States or by the World Bank, that would lighten the burden of losses from bad debt writedowns otherwise facing commercial banks.[6] Still others (not in Congress) have ventured brave talk about a debtors' cartel.

There is a persuasive argument that *any* means of lifting the debt burden would serve the national interest of the United States. The Federal Reserve could, for example, buy the notes of the debtor countries from the banks at an appropriate discount and cancel them outright.[7] Alternatively, it could trade them back to the debtors in exchange for bonds with long maturities and low interest rates. A multinational facility could be set up for the same purpose,[8] along the lines of an International Monetary Fund (IMF) adjustment facility but much larger, and financed with bonds guaranteed by participating governments. Japan and the United States, acting alone, as the most deeply affected parties among the advanced countries, could jointly bring about the same result.

The difficulties are, once again, not technical but political. Intractable disagreements over the means of debt relief stem from the unwillingness of lending banks to acknowledge the loan losses that have already occurred, and from a corresponding unwillingness by regulating authorities to commit the resources necessary to restore confidence in the banks.

In fact, the banking system as a whole is not seriously at risk. The eight largest U.S. banks, representing less than 20 percent of U.S. bank equity, all hold shaky foreign debts whose face value exceeds 100 percent of their primary (liquid) capital. But these debts are of uneven quality and would not all, even in the worst case, lose all of their value, particularly since, with an adequate writedown of part of the debt, the rest would gain in market value. Perhaps in a crisis only one large money center bank would fail, or perhaps two or more would fail, provoking the authorities to repeat the acrobatics of the Continental Illinois reorganization of 1984. Beyond the large banks, U.S. exposure to the risk of foreign default is quite small and has fallen sharply since 1982. There is little doubt that, with aggressive management of a writedown, the damage to the U.S. banking system would be entirely manageable.[9]

The disagreement is therefore rooted in the dynamics of a credit crisis as it affects the self-interest of the largest American commercial banks. Only a few such banks are at risk from the Latin debt crisis. But for them, Latin debts are life-threatening assets and are becoming riskier as time passes and as prices for such debts on the secondary markets fall. In this situation, any bank with all of its equity exposed faces perverse incentives. From an economic standpoint, it should quickly realize and so limit its losses by selling as many of the devalued debts as possible. But it cannot do so, since it would then be forced to admit their loss of value, write them off against equity and acknowledge the bankruptcy that as a matter of valuation has already occurred. The alternative is to hold on, making new loans to cover interest and counting the inflow as earnings, in the Micawberish hope that something will turn up. But as the banks hold on, they further erode their own positions by maintaining high rates of divided payment on their common stock.

If, by a miracle, the debts recover their value (as defaulted Brazilian bonds did in the 1940s), the bankers are saved. Otherwise, they are in no worse condition by delaying, since in any event the federal government must eventually pick up the pieces. And common stockholders are better off, since with continuing dividends they are effectively receiving a distribution of the bank's capital that they would not get in a bankruptcy proceeding. The losers from delay are bondholders, other noninsured creditors, and the public, which is denied a banking sector interested in ordinary business loans at ordinary levels of risk.

The heart of the question is this: At what price should the nonperforming foreign assets held by the banks be valued? High enough to preserve shareholders' equity? Or low enough to force a reorganization of the weakest institutions while strengthening the remainder? Also, to what new authority over banking practices is the public sector entitled in exchange for its participation in a rescue?

The largest commercial banks in danger from the Latin debts do not want any settlement of the debt crisis. They want delay instead. They have had loyal allies and supporters in the Reagan Treasury Department and at the IMF, as was shown in September 1987, when a Brazilian plan to settle the debt at secondary market prices was torpedoed by Secretary James Baker.[10] It is fair to state that U.S. strategy on the debt has worked both sides of the street to prolong the crisis, encouraging U.S. banks to fund interest payments due with new loans, on the one hand, and discouraging comprehensive solutions that would set a precedent for settlement of the crisis, on the other. Thus, U.S. policy has so far dovetailed with the interests of the large American commercial banks.

The adjustment plans of the IMF have served essentially the same purpose: they do not produce adjustment, but they do produce delay. Adjustment would require expanded investment in the export sectors of developing countries, and, as Lance Taylor has argued,[11] private investment in developing countries is complementary to investment in the public sector. Thus, when an indebted country cuts public spending under an IMF program, private investment falls and adjustment does not occur. Instead, falling demand for imports creates an export surplus, which permits debt service to continue. It is easily shown that the export surpluses of the Latin debtors stem almost entirely from falling imports and not at all from rising exports.[12] Needless to say, the interests of U.S. exporters are wholly neglected in this process.

Delay worsens the crisis as a whole by piling new debts on old, but it correspondingly strengthens the political position of the affected banks. In this way, the weaker institutions drag down the stronger, until pressures for a bailout of the whole mass of large American commercial banks become irresistible and the option of cutting losses no longer exists.

Happily, a new administration need not be bound by the same political commitments, and there remains time to cut losses and end the crisis. There are ways to achieve a debt settlement, moreover, that are not demanding from an administrative or technical standpoint but that can be based almost wholly on orthodox principles of private contract, free competition and self-interest. For the fact is that virtually all of the legal cards and bargaining chips in the modern world lie on the side of the

World Growth and the Debt

debtors. There are no effective provisions under international or American law for *legal* recourse in the event of sovereign default. For this reason, actions by Brazil, Peru, Bolivia and others to limit interest outflows have so far gone unopposed. The creditors, with large investments in banking facilities in the Latin debtor nations, have far more to lose than do the debtors. In the past, foreign debt commitments were enforced by backing the creditors with the political and military weight of their governments, but in the postcolonial (and post-Vietnam) world this is far harder to do than formerly. Repayment of foreign sovereign debts is, as a practical matter, essentially optional for the debtor.

Thus, the solution: U.S. public policy should be strengthened, as necessary, to protect depositors in the vulnerable banks, to assure continuity of banking services, and to preserve confidence in the system of payments. And then the U.S. government should sharply distance the national interests of the United States from the private financial transactions between large multinational banking institutions and foreign governments. In particular, the government should make it clear that there is no compelling public case for preserving shareholders' equity in those banks. The public attitude should let the losses fall where they may.

Under these circumstances, the bargaining position of the debtors would strengthen. There would be further defaults, negotiated and conciliatory or otherwise. Writedowns at individual banks would consequently occur. Can we survive this? Of course we can.

Default is the coming impeachment crisis of the 1990s—something greatly feared until it happens. Individual banks are at risk, but the U.S. banking system as a whole is not. Given responsible (that is, aggressive) monetary management, nothing untoward need happen to the system except for the managements and market shares of particular institutions. The management of those transitions will require resources, but far less than will ultimately be required if the crisis drags on.

And indeed, the system would benefit strongly from a new generation of prudent bankers with a heightened awareness of the importance of a stable government supervisory role in banking and of the limits to the extent that government can insure shareholders against financial risk. Such a new conservative generation would quickly emerge, once the debris from the Ponzi game of the past decade and a half has been cleared away.

It may be that at present the monetary authorities are aware of the final inevitability of default and writedowns of the international debt. The actions of Citicorp, Chase Manhattan and others in setting aside reserves in 1987 constituted an acknowledgment of this fact; Chairman-Designate Alan Greenspan of the Federal Reserve alluded to it at his confirmation hearings before the Senate in July 1987. The obstacle may lie not in a disagreement about the underlying situation but in a concern that the politically available resources of government may not be sufficient to handle the task of reorganizing those commercial banks most deeply damaged by their overextension in sovereign lending. If this is the case, the remedy lies in the delegation to the Federal Reserve of further financial powers, together with stronger powers of regulatory control suitable to dealing with the reorganization of large banks.

If worldwide, multicurrency monetary expansion takes hold alongside effective debt relief, there may be a long period of real growth before inflation impinges from the external sector. If, instead, a dollar devaluation comes quickly because the U.S. must go it alone, inflationary pressures will be with us almost at once. Either way, an inflation problem is in store; an incomes policy is not available on the world scale. Given that the United States will probably have to go it alone, avoiding an inflation crisis before the transition period is complete will be a major problem.

I have argued that the key to a solution lies in changing the perception of the inflation problem. Shock inflation, here today and gone tomorrow, need not cause lasting concern or generate a political crisis, provided always that its effects on the real bearing of fiscal policy on the economy, through debt depreciation, are understood and allowed for. The key is to create conditions for postshock stabilization that do not foster a desperate spiral of run-forward and slide-back.

Achieving a compressed external shock, more likely sooner than later, is, as history reveals, readily within the scope of macro- and exchange-rate management. Getting the shock through and out of the system in a hurry is more difficult. Shocks are transformed into crisis when they become entangled in the complex, overlapping calendars of the labor market. What is needed is to reform the structure of relationships within that market.

The grand objective, in short, is to re-create the industrial transformations of the 1970s and, on a more sustainable basis, the world development surge that went with them. Yet it is obvious that these conditions cannot

World Growth and the Debt

be re-created by the same methods that were used at that time. Equally, the gross instability and transition costs that accompanied the unanticipated transformations of the 1970s must, if possible, be avoided. For this inflation must not again be allowed to degenerate into political crisis. And so we turn to the means of coping with the rising inflation rate that sustained growth and trade correction will bring to the United States. This will prove to be the most daunting, yet indispensable, of balancing acts.

CHAPTER 11

Incomes Policies

———

ALL SOCIETIES POSSESS incomes arrangements, or patterns of normal behavior affecting wage and price determination, including, in particular, patterns of collective bargaining. An incomes policy may be defined as government actions that alter these patterns so as to influence inflation, or inflation expectations, or both. Usually such policies work to change the institutions of the factor markets. For example, the German policy of concerted action in the 1970s brought the trade union leadership into extensive direct contact with top policymakers—indeed, with the chancellor himself—and in this way sought to coordinate the inflation expectations of workers with those of the government. Wage guidelines place the government at the collective bargaining table as an advisory participant in the proceedings. Direct price and wage controls interfere with bargaining in a more drastic way.

Incomes arrangements structure the formation of inflation expectations. For example, if the normal life of a labor contract is three years (and there is no automatic cost-of-living indexing), it is necessary for workers to formulate inflation expectations over a three-year horizon so as to offset, as nearly as possible, the expected effects of inflation on the purchasing power of their expected wage. If, however, wage rates can be recontracted once a year, it is not necessary for economic agents to form inflation expectations for more than a year in advance. If annual cost-of-living adjustments are provided, it may not be necessary to form any opinion whatever about the future course of inflation.

The objectives of anti-inflation policy in general, as we have seen, are twofold: (1) to help assure price stabilization in its own right and (2) to help maintain reasonable inflation expectations and to restore such expectations when they are threatened. Incomes policies can contribute to both goals. Yet, most forms of incomes policy are not designed with both objectives in mind. In principle, there are three possible combinations of effect. We may have policies that stabilize prices and price expectations, or policies that stabilize prices but affect expectations perversely, or policies that stabilize price expectations but allow the price level to adjust from time to time as external conditions require. The first combination is optimal, but when it is unattainable, the third combination is clearly second best. In recent practice, sadly and avoidably, incomes policies have often delivered the second combination: temporary price stability at the expense of destabilized expectations, a formula for deferred crisis.

Types of Incomes Policy: Once and Future

CONTROLS AND GUIDELINES

Direct controls over wages and prices are the most familiar form of incomes policy in the United States; their history dates back to colonial times.[1] With controls, the dual effect on prices and price expectations is or ought to be clear. All controls programs, whether comprehensive or selective, affect wages, prices and inflation directly. Controls slow the pace of price increases relative to the trend predicted by the so-called fundamentals—deficits, money growth and inflation expectations or inertia.[2] *Effective* controls programs, however, also help to create a public *expectation* of future price stability. This is achieved partly through the efficiency of administration and enforcement but, above all, through direct communication to the public of the government's determination to keep inflation at bay. Because they are such drastic measures, effective controls are a powerful signal and concentrator of private expectations.

World War II's controls worked, while those of the Nixon period are commonly thought to have failed.[3] A major difference between them was the perceived impermanence and lack of effectively conveyed determination of the latter. The Office of Price Administration's accomplishment, in the face of massive expansion of demand, real output and money incomes in 1942, was to persuade the public that inflation would not be permitted, so that from the outset rising money incomes were willingly saved in low-interest bonds and bank accounts for the duration of the war.[4] This persuasion had to have immediate effect; it could not rely, except in exemplary cases, on the process of enforcement. At the beginning, effectiveness was therefore almost wholly a matter of prestige and clear determination: the public cooperated because they felt it was right, necessary and patriotic to do so. The Nixon controls were likewise greeted at first by wide approval and compliance. But they were undermined, in a short time, by the administration's own assertions that controls would be temporary, and then by its failure to put in place either complementary changes in economic fundamentals or a full complement of enforcers. Thus, under the Nixon controls, inflation expectations increased as time went on.[5]

Nevertheless, it is the Nixon controls, and not those of Roosevelt, that define the practical role of controls in the late twentieth century. Controls may well return one day. They were advocated, in the late 1970s, as a means of breaking inflationary expectations. On this basis they became, for a brief time, a plank in the platform of Edward Kennedy's 1980 insurgency against President Carter. This discussion, which became moot with Carter's renomination, probably defined the outside limit of the future usefulness of peacetime controls. That is, if controls are ever again used, it will be, Nixon-like, as a temporary device to break existing contracts so as (in the best case) to halt inflation while the government puts the fundamentals right and designs a new form of incomes policy. No permanent institutional framework based on administrative control of prices can be considered seriously as a political option in the United States.

GUIDELINES

Wage guidelines, formally abolished only in 1981, are certain to reemerge in the near future. Guidelines are simply controls without enforcement.

Incomes Policies

They incorporate no direct incentives for individual cooperation other than the initial goodwill that all initiatives tend to enjoy. The purpose of guidelines is therefore *only* to influence the climate of inflation expectations; the hope is to slow the incorporation of worst-case inflation fears into prospective wage bargains. Guidelines are subject, of course, to free rider problems: those who defy the guidelines are better off, in all respects, than those who abide by them. The effectiveness of guidelines is therefore a rapidly wasting asset: guidelines burn the political capital of the president. And presidential political capital continues to burn as the effort to keep a structure of guidelines in place is carried on from year to year.

TIPS

Tax-based incomes policies (TIPs) do not actually exist, nor have they ever been tried. They would operate, as their name suggests, through the tax code. In some versions, workers receive a tax credit for accepting wage increases less than or equal to a guideline. In other, more plausible versions, the credit is transformed into a tax penalty for exceeding the guideline.[6]

TIPs are designed to structure wage bargaining incentives so as to achieve noninflationary behavior patterns. They do so, interestingly, in ways that have a minimal auxiliary effect on inflation expectations.

TIP proposals are designed to work, as it were, on the subconscious level of the bargaining process. They bring about wage growth deceleration as a by-product of utility maximization, by creating the conditions under which worker self-interest lies in wage restraint. This is done through the operation of impersonal rules in the tax system and without the intervention of politics. In a correctly functioning TIP system, workers find themselves repeatedly surprised that the inflation rate proved to be lower, and real incomes therefore higher, than their expectations.

TIP advocates count this aspect of their proposals as a strength: TIPs foster satisfaction *ex post* with the way the system *had* worked. But if one accepts the structure of the price stabilization objective offered in chapter 4, this is not good enough. Workers as political beings are forward-looking; what matters is not their satisfaction with past performance but their confidence in the future. The TIP system can affect inflation expectations only insofar as actual success against inflation is achieved. But as disinflation may occur slowly, TIPs contain the seeds of a prolonged political crisis of inflation expectations. Inattention to the means of bringing about a speedy realignment of inflation expectations in the design of TIPs is, from this perspective, not strength but a great weakness.

MONETARY TARGETS

At another extreme lies the only formal incomes policy mechanism directly available to the Federal Reserve, a weak but not uninteresting device. This is the process by which the Federal Reserve sets annual targets for the growth of the money supply and reports on them, under the provisions of the Humphrey–Hawkins Act, to Congress.

The conventional tight-money policy works against inflation by exploiting the short-run Phillips curve trade-off. That is, it creates unemployment, excess capacity, undesired inventories and commodity gluts, and so places a general downward supply-and-demand pressure on prices. Such policies undeniably work: recessions cut the rate of inflation. They are feasible: tight policies readily bring on recession, as they did in 1970, 1974, 1980 and 1981. However, the conventional policy is restricted in a crucial political respect: it can be called upon in practice only *after* inflation has emerged as an important problem. The preemptive or preventive value of this policy is nil.

The new idea in monetary control of inflation, since 1979 in both the United Kingdom and the United States, has been an effort to alter private perceptions of the maximum rate of inflation that the monetary authorities will tolerate, and so to create a preemptive barrier to inflation. If it is known, the argument goes, that rising inflation will provoke an overpowering tight-money response, then individual actors will be deterred from seeking price and wage settlements incommensurate with official objectives. In this way a subjective cost, the fear of unemployment, is introduced in the hope of reducing the actual unemployment cost of achieving a given anti-inflation objective.

In principle there is something obviously desirable about this effort. If effective, it substitutes an internalized deterrence for part of the direct material impoverishment on which monetary anti-inflation policies otherwise depend.

However, it is doubtful that net economic cost savings can be achieved, even in principle. The basic problem is that the extra persuasion which monetary targets provide does not come free. There is a cost of credibility: distinct output and employment costs of reducing inflation expectations.[7] This will be true whenever a contractionary policy must be amplified or prolonged, so as to wring inflation expectations, as well as inflation itself, out of the system.

Expectations-altering monetary regimes actually work to deter inflationary price and wage behavior by making a large, early impression on private parties of the ultimate costs of such behavior. That is, they impose real preemptive costs, over and above what would be required to reduce inflation to acceptable levels in a conventional monetary regime, and then seek to persuade all concerned that a return to inflationary wage-price setting will bring a return of the same repressive policies and associated costs. To this extent, expectations-altering regimes are immediately *more costly* than conventional regimes. The credibility of a tight monetary policy is bought dearly, by demonstrating just how deep and long a recession the authorities are prepared to tolerate in order to maintain it. Such a policy can be justified only if the deterrence works—if workers "learn their lesson"—and so, the success in keeping inflation down is more durable under such regimes as production and employment recover than would otherwise be the case.

Once the consequences of inflationary behavior have been spelled out through example, expectations-altering monetary regimes seek to continue effective deterrence by establishing norms for social behavior in the aggregate. This is the function of the annual money supply targets, which imply a composite annual target for acceptable inflation and real output growth. Ideally, workers and employers interpret the official monetary targets in the appropriate way and learn from them the appropriate expected rate of inflation. This supposedly allows wage bargaining to take place in real terms, within the real resource constraints of a high-employment economy and without inertial inflationary pressure.

Yet, it is most unlikely that this aspect of the new monetary policy has any actual effect on public behavior. For the monetary targets provide no explicit, readily interpreted guidance to individuals, unions or companies on appropriate wage-price settlement behavior. The targets are obscure to begin with, and agents do not know what to make of them even if they know what they are. The issue is further confused by the authorities' ideologically motivated denial that monetary targeting/signaling policies could, in principle, be construed as a disguised incomes policy and translated into wage guidelines. The targets may be credible and even fear-inspiring to the cognoscenti,[8] but yet provide no practical guidance for ordinary people.

Finally, even if monetary signals were translated into wage-price targets, it would not follow that particular individuals have incentives to abide by them. To the contrary, there is the free rider problem again. Anyone can gain, though all may later lose, by acting in a way that is incommensurate with the official stabilization objectives. And so long as one person succumbs to the temptation to cheat, all others must join in or else lose their comparative position.

Costs and Effectiveness

Against the tangible and intangible benefits of an incomes policy must be weighed its economic and political costs. These may include distortions in resource allocation due to misalignment of relative prices, restrictions on the economic discretion otherwise available to labor and business and the political effort and opportunities foregone in striving to keep the policy in place. Alternatively, depending on policy design, these problems may be small, even unimportant.

Two general points may be made about the costs and effectiveness of incomes policy. First, there is no policy yet discovered that will deliver guaranteed price stability without friction, effort or distress. It is therefore no criticism of policies to point out that they have risks, difficulties and a potential for failure; they all do.

Design matters in equal measure. Some policies are likely to work better than others. Some are misconceived and doomed to fail. Distinctions can and should be drawn.

The elements of a desirable design begin to emerge from the features of our typology. Incomes policy should work so as to influence directly the formation of inflation expectations. It should make explicit to individuals and firms which wage behavior is and which behavior is not consistent with price stabilization goals. It should provide incentives for behavior in conformity with those goals. And it should be credible but should not require a costly recession so as to become credible in the first place.

ELEMENTS OF EFFECTIVENESS

It is clear, to begin with, that *incentives* matter. Good incentives economize necessary enforcement. If a system structures the opportunities available to individuals so that they will be inclined to behave in ways conducive to the system's objectives, limited enforcement resources may suffice to cope with limited efforts at evasion. On this criterion, TIPs are a strong policy: they work to shape self-interest through a tax system that already exists. Controls are an intermediate case: whether individuals see their interest as lying in compliance or in defiance depends on the rigor of the occasion and the atmosphere of enforcement. Guidelines fall on the weak side of this spectrum. Monetary targeting is weakest of all. Workers may well understand that to avoid unemployment under such targeting requires general discipline on wages, and yet still feel an individual incentive to press their own wage demands.

As the example of controls makes clear, the *credibility* of a policy strongly affects its chances of being enforced effectively. Credibility therefore affects incentives. Will the policy stick once it is in place? Does it make sense to plan as though the policy is likely to prove permanent? Credibility is a matter of demonstrating commitment. It is achieved through actions whose success is of palpable importance to those who take them—thus the evident importance of *resolve* to the image of the price controller or that of the chairman of the Federal Reserve. If a similar level of credibility can be achieved at a lower real economic sacrifice, that must be chalked up as a desirable feature of policy design.

Here again, in principle, TIPs have an advantage: once on the books, they would be matters of law, and the implicit presumption of permanence would exist, although this is qualified by the possibility of amendment. Controls in peacetime operate under a severe credibility gap: no such controls have been sustained for long except during war. Monetary targeting operates under an equally severe credibility gap: the Federal Reserve's record in respecting its own previous annual monetary targets is weak to nonexistent,[9] with the result that the Federal Reserve's institutional credibility appears to rest almost entirely on the reputation of its chairmen. (Such reputation, moreover, must be reconstituted with each new chairman—a costly business.)

Underpinning credibility is a question of what may be called *time-frame matching.* Will the policy prove effective within the time it may be expected to survive? A price freeze might be an adequate device if it effectively breaks inflation expectations, but not if expectations are sticky past the 90 or 180 days that the freeze will last. "Disinflation by credible threat"[10] might also work if expectations respond quickly to threats. The longer the threat must be maintained, the less credible (and more costly to validate) it is likely to become. On this count, TIPs are constitutionally weak. They are designed to operate at a gradual pace—so slowly, indeed, that their incentives may well be eroded by legislative amendment before they can be counted a success. In general, any feature of design that shortens the lag between implementation and results must be counted in favor, since all such features reduce the cumulative political effort involved in achieving given results.

ELEMENTS OF COST

Finally, one must consider the real resource costs, administrative and political, that are required to make even a well-designed policy work. Administrative costs are related to complexity, political costs to the perception of fairness. An incomes policy must be as administratively simple and distributionally neutral as possible.

For controls, both types of cost are high, and rise with time and resistance. With TIPs, their extent is controversial. One recent collection of papers contained the argument that TIPs are not inherently easier to administer than guidelines or controls;[11] other authors disagree.[12] The political costs of TIPs must, however, necessarily rise with time, since continuing pressure for exceptions will be felt in the political process.[13] Monetary targets have low administrative and political costs, but the point is moot, since as an inflation preventive their effectiveness is also nil.

We may now further characterize desirable incomes policy designs. They should be as credible as possible; this turns on the relationship between the incentives for individual behavior within the system and the tools available to control that behavior. But a policy need *remain* credible only long enough to achieve its desired objective. Hence, unsustainable policies that are effective in the short run are better than policies that are sustainable but ineffective in the long run. And if a policy must operate in the long run to be effective, it should not contain the political seeds of its own premature destruction. Unfortunately, all of the alternatives considered so far—controls, TIPs, and disinflation by credible threat—fall short on one of these counts or another.

Incomes Policies

Share Economy and Bonus Schemes

In recent work, Martin Weitzman,[14] Lester Thurow[15] and others have introduced yet another proposed anti-inflationary regime. This is the concept of a *share economy,* in which fixed hourly wages are subordinated to a discretionary bonus or to a formula based on gross revenue.

BONUS PLANS

Thurow's variant of the share proposal suggests adoption of the Japanese system of bonus payments, in which labor compensation is divided between a fixed and a discretionary component, with the expected value of the latter representing a very significant fraction (say one-third) of the whole. Under Weitzman's more radical pure-share economy, all of labor compensation would be determined as a fixed share of gross company revenue. For a practical beginning, Weitzman has urged a 25 percent bonus; this is substantially more than most existing American bonus arrangements, where the typical figure is closer to 10 percent.

The bonus system addresses the nominal wage inflexibility that many economists believe is the cause of disequilibrium phenomena in the labor market. Because of such inflexibility, the argument runs, profits rather than wages must fall to absorb the effects of an external shock. Producers then necessarily seek to stabilize their situation either by raising prices or by curtailing output. A bonus system would permit employers to transfer to their employees part of a cost shock, such as a rise in raw materials prices, and so make possible a more stable level of final goods prices, profits, investment and employment.

SHARE ECONOMY

The pure-share proposal is more ambitious still. Its extreme version would rewrite all labor compensation contracts in terms of *sharing ratios;* instead of hourly pay, workers would receive a specific proportion of gross company revenue. Weitzman argues that such a system would have the effect of assuring perpetual excess demand for labor, effectively eliminating unemployment.

Weitzman compares the large firm in a share economy to a vacuum cleaner in the labor market, scouring neglected corners and even under carpets for new workers to hire. In such an enterprise, each additional worker hired would slightly reduce the compensation of all existing workers, since the gross revenue would now be shared by one additional worker. In effect, some of the cost of new employees would be transferred directly to existing workers, making the last-hired or marginal worker less costly for the firm to hire. Firms thus would have continuing incentives to add workers and to increase production and sales, well past the point at which the marginal revenue gained by adding workers would ordinarily have fallen below their marginal cost and expansion would stop. (Existing workers would clearly resist overexpansion of the workforce at their expense; Weitzman's argument rests on the presumption that this resistance would be overcome.[16]) Yet the stimulus to demand from rising levels of employment would (it is argued) stop the system as a whole from sinking into an underconsumptionist trap. Under the share system, the economy as a whole would acquire a built-in tendency toward full employment, yet without the present built-in tendency of full employment to generate inflation.

RESPONSE TO SHOCKS

How, in practice, would these ideas work? How would they react to the disturbances, shocks and political insults that afflict real economies in everyday life? First, it should be noted that the bonus and share systems appear to work in quite different ways, so much so that they almost seem designed to deal with separate aspects of the stagflation issue.

The bonus system would provide a means of rapid adjustment of labor compensation to a cost shock originating on the supply side. By cutting the bonus, firms could stabilize gross profits at the expense of gross wages, rather than always having to make the reverse adjustment. So, the bonus system would reduce the employer's tendency to shore up profits by passing on the supply shock to his customers, an action which would show up in the price index and risk becoming embedded in contractual cost-of-living adjustments, inflation expectations and inflation. Instead, the bonus system would make it possible to pass such a shock backward to workers, but without disrupting production through layoffs. This system could therefore tend to shorten any transitory (shock-induced) inflationary episode, translating a decline in real earnings effected gradually through a rising price level into one effected suddenly through a one-time cut in the

Incomes Policies

bonus. This, as we have seen, would be a highly useful feature for the political management of an inflation shock.

Whether the bonus system would also effectively stabilize employment is more doubtful. It is unlikely that a variable bonus can be made compatible with a stable level of aggregate demand. If, as some suppose, the institution of the bonus came to govern workers' savings behavior, a variable bonus might merely mean a variable savings rate—and stable aggregate spending and employment, as well as more stable prices. But this is not very likely. Introduction of the bonus system would not raise workers' incomes per se, and so an increase in savings to the same scale, in relation to wages, as the proposed bonuses would require a voluntary *prior* decline in real consumption standards, and there is no strong reason to suppose that such a decline would occur. It is true that the bonus system is associated with high savings rates in Japan, but this is a historical development associated with rising real wages and consumption. It does not follow that the same pattern could be established in the United States, where to achieve it would require a sharp fall in real consumption standards for a given real wage.

If there are no changes in savings behavior, a cut in the bonus would mean a variability in real effective demand roughly equivalent to that achieved by layoffs and by higher final goods prices relative to wages. "Lumpy" purchases, such as appliances, would be deferred. The goods would appear on the shelves at unchanged prices, but they would not sell. To clear markets, prices would have to fall, and this would lower profits and reestablish the real wage. In that case, confidence and therefore investment would suffer. Alternatively, prices might be maintained; in that case, markets would not clear, and firms would cancel orders and (eventually, after there were no more bonuses to cut) lay off workers just as they would under the straight wage system.

Supporters of the bonus plan point to the much greater stability of measured unemployment in Japan (where bonus plans are widely used) compared to the United States. There is something to this comparison, but it is also somewhat misleading. *Hours worked* in Japan fluctuated nearly as much in the business cycles of the 1970s as in the United States. The difference in *unemployment rates* is accounted for partly by the greater variability of mandatory overtime in Japan, and by the fact that in Japan major changes in the manufacturing workforce through involuntary retirement and the furloughing of married female employees (who

211

then leave the labor force) are not officially counted as unemployment.[17] These artificially stabilizing factors have nothing to do with the bonus.

The pure-share system differs from the bonus system in that it assures a stable *share* for labor compensation, and so also for profits, in all revenues (while under the bonus system, the labor share normally fluctuates to permit greater stability of profits). In normal times, the bonus system does not reduce the *marginal* cost of labor; the share system, on the other hand, is designed precisely for this purpose. The share system, therefore, relieves a constraint on output that is thought to be endemic to a monopolistically competitive industrial structure. Its principal merit, if Weitzman is right, would be to eliminate chronic unemployment, which it would do by creating for large manufacturing firms (in the pure form) an essentially unlimited opportunity to add to profits by adding workers and production.

But would a pure-share system be effective against inflation? As Weitzman points out, the share system tends to dissociate unemployment from inflation, and so makes the pursuit of stable prices at the macroeconomic level less costly. But it is also possible to imagine policy regimes under the share system that would have perverse effects on the rate of inflation. This would be the case, for example, if the government responded to calls for help in stabilizing the nominal level of total company profits in the wake of a cost shock.

In the immediate aftermath of a cost shock, gross company revenues are unchanged. And so, under a share system, workers' compensation is unaffected. Profits take the whole hit (as they do not in the bonus system). Prices would then rise as companies attempted to restore part of the lost profits at the expense of their consumers. This would raise the demand for money to finance transactions, which (under the assumption that the government was concerned with company profits) would be supplied. But if raising the price increases the revenue, it must also increase labor compensation. The share system thus appears vulnerable to a labor-cost/resource-cost inflation cycle. In the case of a cost shock, the share system would not have inbuilt stabilizing properties unless the government held absolutely firm against the temptation to validate pass-through price increases.

Another disturbing possibility is that the share system could generate an internal inflation cycle based purely on relative rates of sharing. Sharing ratios would be negotiated by free collective bargaining, company by company or industry by industry, on a staggered calendar. Workers would evaluate the fairness of their own contract, as they do today, by comparison with contracts negotiated just prior to their own. There appears to be no good reason to suppose that such a system would generate a mutually consistent, stable set of share bargains. While it is certain that a firm with too high a sharing ratio that tried to stabilize net profits by raising its prices and revenues would fail in the long run, if other firms maintained their existing contracts, it is possible that the long run would never be reached. In the short run, one excessively high share contract could lead to another, with each firm validating the price increases of the one before it by raising its own prices, and thus its workers' pay and nominal disposable incomes. Adrian Wood has provided a theoretical discussion of the dynamics of unstable relative pay arrangements that would seem applicable to the share system.[18]

An interesting feature of bonus and share proposals is that neither costs anything once put into effect. If the proposals work as advertised, workers do not lose income or employment, employers do not lose profits, and there is no increase in the administrative or political overhead of the government.

Transition costs and transfers of wealth and political power between groups of workers are more worrisome. Share and bonus proposals directly attack the present arrangements by which some workers exact high wages at the expense of output and future competitiveness in their industries, and by which some union officials retain support and authority by delivering to workers high nominal wage increases (but wages that cannot be validated in real terms). While it may be true that the general material welfare would be enhanced by neglecting these considerations, economists cannot afford to overlook either the real costs imposed on these special interests or the political difficulties inherent in an attempt to get by them.

Bonus proposals leave the decision regarding the size of the bonus in the hands of management; thus they remove from labor a measure of control and power which labor currently possesses. Share proposals penalize the relative income of senior workers so as to foster new hiring. At the least, either system would require substantial changes in labor–management relations to establish a climate of trust and good faith which is now generally lacking. Without such changes, bonus and share schemes would have to be introduced either in a general climate of worker weakness (they are already spreading rapidly in parts of the manufacturing sector that face desperate alternatives in the struggle for competitive survival) or as part of a broader bargain transferring equivalent authority over some other aspect of work life from management to labor.

Bonus and share proposals have been discussed mainly in a domestic, closed-economy setting. A telling objection to them arises, however, when international competitive pressures are considered. For such proposals are, above all, defensive: they are ways and means for improving the cost competitiveness of existing manufacturing processes. Where competition arises not from new facilities in an advanced country paying high wages but from advanced facilities in a low-wage setting, the practical effect of both bonus and share plans will be to facilitate a rapid fall of real wages in the advanced country. The sequence here is straightforward under either scheme: falling sales yield falling revenues, which in turn trigger falling worker compensation.

But these schemes cannot turn an older, depreciated and obsolete facility into a modern one. They can, at most, delay job loss and scrapping, and so keep an otherwise doomed facility open for longer than would otherwise be the case. This benefit has a broader cost: it helps to preserve the excess capacity that depresses profits and new investment in industry as a whole. Thus bonus and share schemes work to help clear labor markets, but at the expense of dynamic transitions toward more advanced structures of production and higher real standards of living. They cope poorly with the most serious challenges put before an advanced country by the pressures of trade.

Where does this leave us? Radical shifts of regime all share the property—not necessarily a defect—that their steady-state equilibrium cannot easily be foreseen. In addition, the transition to a wholly new regime is traumatic, incurs resistance, and courts the risk of political defeat. Traditional incomes policies suffer further under the incubus of past failures; no one can look to them with more than desperate hope. Tax-based policies face insuperable obstacles of design, administration and politics. And bonus and share schemes, though a welcome breath of fresh thinking, seem to work against the strategy of transition to high growth in the world economy for which we ought to be working.

Is there something else? In the next chapter, we will explore a proposal with two new and unique features. First, it is designed explicitly with the subtle goal of *expected price stabilization* in mind—rather than the wholesale repression of all changes in the aggregate price level. It is thus a more limited proposal than those aimed at the broader goal. Second, where other proposals seek an automatic mechanism for curing inflation, the one to be presented rests on the premise that political problems must engage the political system. Therefore it consists largely in effecting a major shift in the existing structure of political responsibility for expected price stabilization, from the Federal Reserve to the presidency, and in securing for the latter adequate powers to make the new responsibilities effective.

CHAPTER 12

National Expectations:
A Proposal

———

T HE FOLLOWING PROPOSAL is divided into two parts. The first concerns a matter of politicoeconomic organization, namely, the means whereby individuals receiving income flows from the public sector are protected, or not protected, from inflation. The second concerns the organization of the private labor market, specifically, the timing of contract negotiations, the role of reference wages in determining the outcome of collective bargaining arrangements and the mechanisms whereby such reference wages are set.

Discretionary Prospective Indexation

Presently, some 60 to 70 million Americans receive income streams from the federal government, including current and retired civilian and military employees, Social Security recipients, and welfare clients.[1] Most (those

National Expectations: A Proposal

receiving Aid to Families with Dependent Children [AFDC] are a significant exception) receive, as part of their benefit package, some protection from inflation. However, the degree of coverage varies sharply. Current government employees, for example, rarely receive a cost-of-living adjustment equal to the full value of the previous year's consumer price inflation rate; when inflation is rising, it is all too convenient to delay or pare down such adjustments. Social Security recipients, on the other hand, generally receive full consumer price indexation as a matter of right.

This system of variable indexation, which was not designed with any thought for its feedback effects on inflation and inflation expectations, has two undesirable characteristics. First, indexation is retrospective when it exists: the high inflation rates of one year are carried forward and translated into high income increments in the next, and in this way inflationary pressure is maintained from year to year. Second, inflation arbitrarily changes the distribution of real income in a way wholly unintended by statute. Those who are partly indexed or unindexed (federal workers, welfare recipients) lose their comparative position, while those who are completely indexed (retirees, Social Security recipients) gain. This is particularly unfair when a supply shock has raised prices and lowered real incomes in the economy as a whole, for then the redistribution involves restoring real incomes almost exactly for the most favored groups while cutting real incomes for everyone else.

A reform of the present inflation compensation system is possible that preserves the essential public purpose—equitable adjustment for a changing price level—while incorporating favorable feedback effects on the formation of inflation expectations. The proposed system is called *discretionary prospective indexation (DPI)*, suppressing in the name a third essential feature, that is, its uniform application on all recipients of regular income from the federal government. Each characteristic deserves attention.

First, benefit indexation should be converted from its present retrospective to a *prospective* basis. That is, in each year, benefits should be raised by the amount of inflation expected in the year ahead, not by the amount previously incurred. The theoretical benefits of forward-looking wage indexation are well established among economists, in particular through the work of Stanley Fischer, Rudiger Dornbusch and others who have studied the recent stabilization experience in Argentina, Brazil and Israel.[2] The benefits are threefold. First, forward-looking indexation breaks the link

217

between past inflation and current pay, and so permits the government to assign to public income recipients the same real income losses that are experienced in an inflationary cost shock by everyone else. In addition, forward-looking indexation eliminates the lag between price increases and wage adjustments, which in high inertial inflations produces large real income losses even when full backward-looking indexation exists. Third, if timed properly, forward-looking indexation tends to influence inflation expectations directly, not only among benefit recipients but in the economy as a whole.

Second, prospective benefit indexation should be, within broad limits, *discretionary:* proposed and implemented by order of the president. The purpose of this is to establish maximum political responsibility for the level at which prospective benefit indexation is set. The president should have to pick a number and then defend it, perhaps against the test of an expedited vote of approval in Congress. Faced with such a responsibility, the president would be led to establish the broadest possible advance consensus on the expected inflation rate and to devote his political capital to assuring that the population understands the basis for his decision.

It follows inescapably that the discretionary benefit indexation proposed by the president must be *uniform.* There is only one general inflation rate. Any variation in the degree of inflation protection across groups would destroy the information value of the prospective indexation number, while permitting political actors to pit the distributive interests of some groups against others.

It may be objected that these features would politicize the expected inflation rate. That is precisely the objective—to bring national attention to focus sharply on it. A single national expected inflation rate would tend to narrow the range of private estimates of this rate. And if the officially expected and rationally expected rates of inflation tend to converge, it would therefore reduce the unanticipated, relative to the anticipated, component of inflation.

All forecasts are subject to error. A single advance adjustment for expected inflation will not eliminate all winners or losers from inflation. It will still be true that on any given occasion some individuals will be proved right and others wrong by events.

But to eliminate error is not the purpose. The goal should be, first, to free private forecasts as much as possible from *systematic error* and, second, to reduce the remaining *range of random error.* Systematic error arises when individuals find reasons to be persistently oversanguine or overfearful. The range of random error rises when individuals base their information on widely diverse sources of information. We say that expectations are *rational* when individuals are using a common base of information (economic model) and when their forecasts are free of systematic error.[3] The objective is then to foster rationality in popular expectations of the rate of inflation.

Economists of the rational expectations school usually proceed by *assuming* that expectations are formed rationally, that what ought to happen does in fact happen. But this is to assume that the information available to ordinary members of the public is good information, freely available and that individuals have the wherewithal and processing ability to build good economic models for use with that information. In the real world, such information and processing ability are extremely expensive. Most individuals, ordinary workers and businessmen, make do with inexpensive substitutes, derived perhaps from daily experience, the newspapers and television. Rationality from such sources is far from assured.

If the government itself has rational expectations, however, it can transmit those expectations to the public at a very low cost and solve the problem of the private costliness of information. Expectations formation would become to a certain extent a nationalized sector, subject to the vast decreasing costs of large-scale information dissemination. The rational expectation would become the *national expectation.* The DPI adjustment would serve as an ideal vehicle for dissemination.

With government providing the cues for private inflation forecasts, systematic errors need arise only if government introduces them. Here there is a distinct danger from the ideological crusade. That is, the main risk of systematic bias would stem from efforts to use the DPI to alter the distribution of income, as between governmental benefit recipients and everyone else. In a democratic system, there can be no ironclad guarantee against this danger. Still, the requirements that the DPI be comprehensive and uniform would make such action politically risky in the extreme: to tamper with the forecast would mean giving identical offense to very large numbers of people. On occasion a determined ideologue—like Reagan—might forge ahead, but not many would be tempted to follow; even the Reagan administration in 1981 found deep cuts in Social Security impossible, for political reasons.[4] We therefore note this problem and set it aside, passing on to the second and more interesting difficulty: how to make the inflation forecast implicit in the DPI credible to most people, so that individuals come to base their own inflation forecasts on it.

Pay Calendar Synchronization

Having created a mechanism to generate an annual debate and a process of consensus formation about the expected rate of inflation, how can we assure that the actual inflation rate falls into line (on average) with the manufactured expectation?[5]

If all private expectations were truly rational, there would, of course, be nothing to improve on. The optimal government forecast would merely mimic the uniform private forecast. However, as just noted, information in the real economy is very costly; people base their inflation expectations on whatever information is close at hand and have no assurance that such information is free of systematic bias. In particular, significant groups of workers base their inflation expectations on the wage settlements of selected elements among their peers. These may be a neighboring union local in a related industry or a nationally salient collective bargaining pact.[6] The late Arthur Okun described the general phenomenon of wage followership, outside explicit bargaining relations, as the "invisible handshake."

Reference wages thus are one argument, among others, in the function determining price expectations. They are a powerful argument, since they can be summarized in a single number, a percentage growth rate, and so convey local information with great efficiency, as local commodity and consumer goods prices do not.[7] Yet reference wages in multiyear contracts necessarily incorporate lagged and extraneous information (such as changes in patterns of industrial competitiveness and consumer demand) that is irrelevant to changes in the general price level. The issue is whether, in principle, a better indicator can be found and whether, in practice, workers' behavior can be modified so as to purge reference wages of their price expectations formation functions in its favor.

Clearly, the proposed DPI expected inflation signal, which would be entirely free of local influences, would be a better indicator. So, we turn to the practical question: how can we get the DPI signal, once it exists,

National Expectations: A Proposal

into general use as a tool for price expectations formation, and how can we get traditional reference wages out?

As problems in social engineering go, this one is easy. Reference wages are important to workers because they link the immediate past to the medium-term future: to base my three-year wage demand on your settlement of last month assures that over the next thirty-five months our relative positions will remain unaltered. On the other hand, in order to do this, I must know what your settlement was before I am too far along in negotiating mine. What I don't know can't help.

Breaking the reliance on reference wages can thus be accomplished substantially by the simple device of holding *simultaneous* annual wage negotiations. Such negotiations would prevent workers and employers from knowing what settlements were being reached in other sectors. They would then have to make their own decisions, based on the information available *in advance,* such as, conspicuously, from the DPI. *Pay calendar synchronization (PCS)* is the second part of the proposal. A simple statute setting a uniform expiration date for all wage agreements (as in Japan), thereby outlawing automatic cost-of-living adjustments (as in Germany), would accomplish what is required.

With current reference wages thus rendered more or less inaccessible to bargaining parties, the uniform, national DPI signal could readily substitute in most workers' price expectation formation functions. It would become a national reference inflation adjustment, all the more palpable because one-third of the population would actually be slated to receive it as a rising wage, pension, or welfare adjustment. With appropriate sequencing, the DPI signal could become virtually the sole piece of information available to workers and employers at the time they need to make a judgment about the expected inflation for the forthcoming year. For example, the DPI adjustment could be announced on February 1 each year (perhaps as part of the president's budget), with April 1 as the date on which it would take effect. Wage contract negotiations could then be set to begin March 1, with resulting bargains also effective on April 1.

How the System Would Work

Suppose the president decided that an inflation rate of 4 percent was reasonable to expect in the coming year. On February 1, he would simply declare a prospective April-to-April DPI adjustment of 4 percent. By early February, workers and employers would be aware that this was coming. In February, these parties would decide on their own offers and demands. These might be higher or lower than expected inflation, depending on whether each industry faced a market that was tighter or easier than the average. Workers in the booming computer sector might ask for 6 percent, while those in the slumping coal industry might decide to settle for 2 percent. At the end of the process, an average wage settlement can be calculated from the results of all the disparate bargains.

The main contribution of the DPI is simply to center the calculation of offers and demands around a common perception of the *average* expected increase in prices. This would work particularly to avoid situations in which workers in weak situations demand high wage increases simply because they have distorted inflation fears. It would also relieve a compulsion on the part of unionists to seek gains simply to stay level with workers in other sectors: each bargaining unit would now bargain on the basis of its own economic situation. This might be expected to reduce conflict, since it would remove a major source of functionless conflict which lies in differing macroeconomic perceptions. Since, however, there are no direct controls over outcomes, a majority of workers might still demand, and get, wage settlements higher than the expected average. But this is tolerable because of productivity increases (as will be seen).

The operation of the joint DPI–PCS system may be assessed in light of the criteria for a cost-effective incomes policy discussed in the preceding chapter: credibility, speed of action, administrative and resource costs and political fairness.

Credibility for this system would not be automatic. Given a presidential edict setting the DPI at 4 percent, it would not instantly follow that inflation expectations would zero in on 4 percent. But the president would have the strongest possible incentives to try to bring this about—to choose a reasonable DPI target in the first place, to secure national agreement around it, and to set other national policies so as to be consistent with the DPI inflation expectation. If he failed, he would have either one-third or two-thirds of the population to answer to: the one-third receiving benefits if the DPI adjustment proved too low, the other two-thirds if it proved too high. Only a conscientious effort to pick the right number, and widespread agreement around it at the time, could serve *ex post* as a defense for error. Hence the system would place the onus for achieving credibility on the one federal officer who, with hard work, might be able to do just that.

The system would operate with great speed. Indeed, its chief built-in strength is its careful timing of policy actions and their effects, which would tend to minimize the rigidities, lags and extraneous influences that usually impinge on the formation of inflation expectations. The DPI–PCS system would introduce an unbiased estimator of the inflation rate directly into inflation expectations formation, and so reduce or eliminate the present reliance on individual judgment, implicit economic models and expectations functions of varying quality and rationality. It would also reduce or eliminate errors that stem from incorporating short-term inflation expectations into long-term contracts, as currently happens for example when a high one-year inflation rate is built into a three-year wage contract simply because there is no good information on how long today's inflation will last.

After the transition to the new system, continuing administrative costs would be low in comparison with those of every potentially effective alternative. Aside from the resources required to conduct technical discussions with economists, business and labor before settling on the DPI signal, and the minor costs of disseminating that signal through the mass media, there would be no need for an administrative bureaucracy. A prohibition or tax penalty on out-of-sequence wage settlements could make that aspect essentially self-enforcing. Since the government would not be involved in collective bargaining or concerned with the outcome of individual wage bargains, there would be no need for an agency like the Council on Wage and Price Stability to explain complex regulations to the public. The most that would be required would be a small staff, to monitor labor market developments with a view to providing continuing expertise in developing the DPI signal.[8]

Direct resource costs to the private economy would be small: the DPI–PCS system would merely reschedule and reshape activities that in any event already take place. The one significant risk stems from changing the power structure of labor relations. Because of the coordination of the timing of wage negotiations, PCS poses a risk of coordinated, and therefore mutually reinforcing, strike activity. A simultaneous strike in multiple industries would be a costly possibility. But by the same token, the political pressure on both labor and management to reach a settlement without a strike would also be stronger. It is not clear that the balance of these effects is toward more strikes. Certainly the record shows that the United States and the United Kingdom, with decentralized and uncoordinated labor markets, experience more strikes than does Germany, where a coordinated system has been in force.[9]

Finally, as to fairness: would this system amount, as might seem at first glance, to a form of wage control, affecting only the public sector and the old? Clearly not. It would merely systematize the inflation adjustment mechanisms already in place in the public sector, with a view to compensating for expected inflation and so preserving expected real wages. This would remove a gross inequity in the present system, wherein some subgroups in the public sector routinely lose real income in inflation while others do not. The vast size of the population receiving the prospective indexation, and the need for a substantial consensus to make it stick, would serve to guard against deliberate attempts by the president to set the number too high or too low—the latter being the common fate of federal employees in the present system.

Social Security recipients, in particular, might be expected to resist the change to the DPI–PCS system on the ground that it would be worse for them than the full cost-of-living adjustments they presently enjoy. But careful analysis suggests that this is not necessarily correct. The present cost-of-living adjustments are *retrospective:* they only compensate retirees for the losses from inflation in the previous year. Thus, during inflation, Social Security recipients suffer declining real incomes from the month in which they receive a cost-of-living adjustment until the month before they receive the next one, and their annual real incomes do not, in fact, fully compensate them for continuing inflation. A prospective system would put them one step ahead, rather than one step behind, the inflationary game.

Suppose (for purposes of simpler comparison) that cost-of-living adjustments (like the DPI) are paid in April. With 12 percent annual inflation, a retirement benefit paid the following March is worth just 89 percent of what the same dollar amount was worth a year previously, and average real income over the year is 5.5 percent lower than it would have been without inflation. A 12 percent increase in monthly benefits in April *of the follow-*

ing year (the present system) restores real income to what it was twelve months before. But even if inflation then stops, this does not replace the one-time real income loss already suffered in the previous year. And so long as inflation continues, these real, intrayear, uncompensated income losses recur every year.

Under DPI–PCS, the Social Security recipient receives in April a commitment to full compensation for inflation expected over the whole of the coming year. He is thus buffered in advance against running losses if inflation continues. For example, suppose the DPI adjustment is 6 percent and inflation over the year turns out to match the forecast. Now real income is 6 percent higher in April. By October, prices are up 3 percent and half the real gain is gone. By March, real income is back to April's levels. There has now been, however, a 3 percent average real income gain over the year, which will not be taken away even if inflation and the DPI fall to zero the next year. In fact, actual inflation (proceedingly smoothly from month to month) would have to run past 12 percent before a 6 percent DPI increase granted in April turns into a real income loss for that year. This permits some room for understating the DPI that is actually granted in the first place, and so placing downward pressure on nominal wages and on the inflation rate generally.[10]

If inflation stops unexpectedly after the DPI has been granted, Social Security recipients receive an additional real windfall (so that, despite the above, it is not necessarily in their interest to see inflation continue). The main risk to their real incomes comes from the converse situation, when an adverse shock (such as a rise in the price of oil) forces prices up unexpectedly after the DPI adjustment has taken place. For this there is no compensation, in contrast to the present system. Why, indeed, should there be? The nation as a whole, in such a case, is poorer. Should a single segment of the population be compensated when all others are not?[11]

It is particularly worthwhile to compare the DPI–PCS proposal not with the present system of full retrospective cost-of-living adjustments for Social Security recipients but with the leading candidate for replacing that system, which is Martin Feldstein's proposal to index benefits at 2 percent *less* than the prevailing rate of inflation. Under this system, known as the *CPI-minus-two* proposal, Social Security recipients would suffer automatic real income losses of about 2 percent every time the inflation rate exceeded that value. And these losses would be in addition to the effect of the running loss stemming from the retrospective character of the index, as discussed earlier. Over a decade of this system (with inflation at slightly more than 2 percent), real benefits would fall by 18 percent! Under the DPI–PCS system (without adverse shocks), real incomes would be maintained more or less exactly.

What, then, would be the incentives facing workers, whose behavior would ultimately determine the success of the system? Paul Davidson has provided a skeptical, but vivid analogy: that DPI–PCS would amount to placing a selective speed limit on a highway—say, only on those cars that happened to be blue:

> . . . it is as if the President announced speed limits of 55 mph on federally funded roads and the enforcement of such a speed limit led to the conviction of a significant part of the speeding population—but only those who drove in "blue" cars. Thus blue car drivers would know that speeding would cost them something and hence would attempt to stay within the speed limits—but what pressure could blue car drivers put on the rest of us to obey the speed limit?[12]

Davidson's analogy is suggestive, but it can be improved upon. It is *more* as if the federal government by remote signal were suddenly to acquire control over the cruise control on all cars that are blue. Suppose the government then set that control at fifty miles per hour for all such vehicles, not changing the average speed driven at all, but simply slowing the hard chargers and speeding up the slowpokes. Would this sudden *synchronization* of the speeds of blue cars—say one-third of all those on the highway—have an effect on the behavior of the rest of us? It would indeed—a modest effect, perhaps, but inexpensive to achieve, hence very high in added social value.[13] Suppose, too, that the government simultaneously jammed the citizens' band airwaves, preventing the formation of double-bottomed truck convoys traveling uniformly at seventy miles per hour. Would this also tend to reduce the average speed of trucks formerly in the convoy? Again, of course, it would.

There is some flexibility in the system. The working population in the private sector generates annual (measured) productivity increases, which the dependent population and public sector employees do not. Yet average price increases for the whole economy tend to equal the average rate of wage increase *minus* the average rate of measured productivity increase. If everyone is receiving a wage supplement equal only to the *expected* rate of price increase, and there is then positive average productivity growth, the *actual* rate of price increase must fall below the expected rate.

Hence, individual workers and firms can freely exceed the DPI expected-inflation speed limit to the extent that they expect productivity increases; this will not raise the realized (after-the-fact) inflation rate above the DPI forecast. So can workers in expanding export trades, whose increased incomes are being earned by high profit (quasi-rent) income in the advanced export sectors. Only if average wage settlements exceed the DPI by more than average productivity gains will average price increases exceed the DPI, inflicting losses of real income on the DPI-indexed population.

A numerical example may help make this clear. Suppose that a DPI of 4 percent is announced. Now, all workers individually may seek to do better than this average expected rate of inflation. And so, suppose the average nominal demand for wage increases is 8 percent, reflecting a desire for 4 percent real increases. But not all workers are in industries that can afford such real increases. So, suppose that when the dust settles, the average rate of wage increases that has been granted is 6 percent. No problem. If productivity growth is maintained at 2 percent (about the average for recent periods of economic expansion), price inflation over the year will come to 4 percent.

The DPI, in that case, has succeeded in keeping actual inflation on par with the forecast, and real incomes of government support recipients have been held constant! Real incomes of workers have risen by 2 percent, and real profits have been held constant. Everyone should be happy. Next year, the president can try to lower the DPI by a point. If economic conditions are unchanged, 7 percent demands will produce 5 percent settlements and 3 percent inflation. Soon the system will settle at a near-stable price level.

It is possible, in principle, that the entire private sector might set out to demand real wage increases above expected productivity gains (and so nominal wage increases above expected productivity plus the DPI), and that they will succeed. In that case, an inflationary redistribution of income would occur at the expense of government employees and transfer recipients. But for this to happen, cartel-like action across the whole private sector would have to occur, which is highly unlikely. In addition, the fact of the synchronized decentralization of the DPI–PCS system would make coordination and cartel behavior very difficult. Administered wages and prices produce inflationary spirals under the present system only through their interaction with rising general inflation expectations; it is hard to see how they could do so in a system with no mechanism for escalating such expectations.

The DPI–PCS system, by itself, is not a complete policy for absolute price stabilization. Individuals may rationally include diverse forecasts of the oil price, the wheat harvest, and Japanese monetary policy in their expectations functions. Shocks from such sources may unbalance the system, imposing costs on those whose expectations are proved wrong, and result in arbitrary transfers of wealth, depending on the source of the shock and the composition of individuals' portfolios. A political revolt by labor against presidential wage leadership could also inflict damage. In any of these cases, the performance of the system could be marked by individual episodes when prices move radically out of synchronization with *ex ante* expectations. But the system would permit quick passage over these episodes, so that they need not become built into an inflationary syndrome. Thus DPI–PCS would work to prevent the psychology of inflation from generating a political crisis.

To some extent, the DPI–PCS system and a political stake in its success might foster the implementation of additional supply management or selective intervention policies to minimize price variance from external sources. For example, control over commodity buffer stocks and more aggressive use of the strategic petroleum reserve would give the president additional levers over the average price level. But the main virtue of the system in the face of inflationary shocks from either external events or internal political breakdown is its ability to recover.

Each year would be a new start, without leftover wage contracts propping up wage expectations. Hence it should be much easier under DPI–PCS than under the present system to break a cycle of inflation expectations quickly or to prevent one from developing in the first place. Even if this meant an occasional higher one-shot price change in the very short term—because a larger fraction of wage settlements would respond to a shock or a political crisis—it would involve lower and more stable inflation expectations over both the short and the long run. Inflationary episodes, properly managed, would end quickly, restoring the general climate of price stability that people widely and wisely desire.

As observed earlier, inflationary pressures have been endemic to postwar American capitalism for two basic reasons. First, as time passes in an economic expansion, workers and employers are emboldened to seek larger shares of total income. This occurs through higher rates of growth of nominal wages, demanded by workers, and through the expansion of consumption out of profit incomes. Worker militancy is an interdependent phenomenon: once set off by one group of workers, it tends to spread throughout the system. The resulting pressure of demand and high utilization rates on existing capital equipment causes productivity growth to decline, while the anticipation of recession (and perhaps capacity limits in the investment goods sector) prevents an expansion of the means of production necessary to meet the current effective demand. Given rising wages and falling productivity growth, prices must rise unless forestalled for a time by a rapid growth of imports.

The second source of inflationary pressure has stemmed from slow, long catch-up periods followed by sudden external price shocks, such as result when import prices go up in a dollar devaluation or when the dollar prices of commodities rise. This is a matter that involves the structure of long-term wage bargains. Workers first try to catch up with the price of oil. Then they try to catch up with each other. The cycle continues until it is broken by a strong negative shock, such as a recession.

DPI–PCS would provide the president with a powerful counter to the purely internal, inertia-building competition for higher nominal wages. This would be a substitute for the costly club of periodic recessions. The standard would focus attention on the prospects for future inflation rather than on the experience of the past. The influence of the guideline would not be completely persuasive. But to the extent that it does work, it would produce longer, less inflationary expansions than we have enjoyed in the past two decades. Moreover, if and when disinflationary demand policies became necessary, their purposes could be accomplished in a shorter time and at less economic cost. Once growth stopped, militancy would quickly decline, saving the system much of the functionless conflict that has characterized it since 1965.

Against inflation caused by external shocks the system would be especially useful. In the immediate aftermath of a shock, real wages would fall. Any adjustments—catch-ups—would be strongly conditioned by national policy and would take place all at once in the next bargaining season. There would be no reason for the initial shocks to persist into a second season.

Isolating price instability on the external front, even if that were all that were achieved, would imply substantial gains in the perception of internal price stability. Beyond this are the real economic gains that the DPI–PCS system would achieve. The recession and unemployment incurred to establish policy credibility over the long term would no longer be necessary, since policy would have a chance to become credible and effective in the short run. Perhaps additional stabilizing weapons would have to be brought to bear from time to time. DPI–PCS is not a panacea, for there are no panaceas. But DPI–PCS would offer the hope of preventing the political crises that emerge in the United States when high inflation becomes chronic.

A Concluding Thought

A hundred years ago, at the urging of the great railroad companies, America undertook a remarkable experiment in social coordination. This was the reform of the system of time: the creation of the four standard time zones and the synchronization of watches, clocks, and—most important—timetables. Prior to this reform, each city maintained its own standard, often differing by no more than a few minutes from that of others, and travelers, telegraphists and train switchmen faced nightmares of translation and coordination.

Time reform was perhaps not necessary to the progress of economic life. The advent of the computer (in another seventy years) could theoretically have kept everything sorted out. But time reform greatly reduced various inefficiencies involved in running a large national system of railroads. It was a practical measure, virtually without economic cost, and it was put into effect largely by voluntary action.

Today, fighting inflation can be seen as approximately the same sort of problem. We ask our price system to convey very large amounts of information. Each actor in the wage and price determination process views the whole from his or her own subjective standpoint, weighting the available information in idiosyncratic ways. Differential benefit indexation atomizes popular opinion. Differential contract timing distorts worker perspectives. The result is a pattern of action with a large economic and social cost: misused and misinterpreted economic information, wasted effort based on misguided forecasts and the erosion of national self-assurance and confidence in political institutions, all of which follow from inflation.

National Expectations: A Proposal

To avoid these threats, we apply macroeconomic instruments that vastly amplify economic cost, and which, moreover, engender real human suffering and hardship. It is as though a century ago we had cured the national neurosis over timetables by slowing the trains or even shutting down the railroads. Surely there is a better way.

DPI and PCS can form one line of defense in a strategy of expected price stabilization. They are measures that can be put in place immediately at small sacrifice. They may not prove totally effective; perhaps another line of defense, involving price control or monetary/fiscal restriction, or a TIP or bonus plan, will still be necessary. Even so, it makes sense to do the simple, costless things today in the hope that the grave, costly steps may yet be avoided.

CHAPTER 13

Conclusions

THE PRESENT PARALYSIS of progressive economic opinion has, I believe, two main dimensions.

The first of these dimensions consists in an abdication of independent judgment on questions of macroeconomic policy. Progressives find themselves acquiescing in the arbitrary deficit reduction dictates of the budget process. In monetary matters, they are prostrate before the authority of the Federal Reserve. They are frustrated in their efforts even to raise the possibility of an incomes policy. They are passive in the face of the debt crisis, the terms-of-trade collapse of the developing countries, the movements of the foreign exchange rate—each the consequence of policy shifts, yet made to seem wholly beyond the power of policy to control.

This abdication is not accidental: it is the legacy of past political failures. Progressive opinion could not forestall the assertion of political autonomy of the Federal Reserve in the early 1950s. The collapse of the Keynesian fiscal order in the early 1970s took with it the open advocacy of setting the budget deficit so as to achieve economic and social goals. The failures of management and the shocks that swept away John Connally's programs also destroyed the general credibility of wage-price controls. There remains, after all this, no anchor for progressive macroeconomic opinion. When progressive statements that bear on the instru-

Conclusions

ments of macroeconomic policy are offered, the politician is tempted to see in them only issues of political preference, such as tax increases rather than expenditure reductions. Isolated voices, such as those of a James Tobin or a Rudiger Dornbusch or a Robert Eisner, are perceived in the political arena as expressing liberal sentiment; there is no political audience for the fully articulated alternative strategies that other economic professionals recognize in these contributions.

The second dimension of progressive paralysis consists of allowing constituency pressures to fix positions on microeconomic issues. Progressives too often favor social spending for humanitarian reasons only and investment spending primarily for the jobs it will create. Trade policies garner progressive support if they protect the current jobs of particular workers. Industrial policies are proposed that would transfer state power to joint boards of labor and business in existing heavy industry. Design of incomes policy is neglected because there is no constituency for it. The interests of those outside the U.S. political system, notably the struggling workers of the poor countries of the world, are systematically ignored, except sometimes on cynical occasions when their exploitation is raised to justify an additional measure of trade protection.

Behind both dimensions has been a fading from view of the concept of an economic goal, of the idea of definite standards for economic performance. The arithmomorphics of utility maximization teach that man is insatiable and that all satisfactions are relative—and if there is no limit on utility, how can there be such a thing as a satisfied objective? Economists have too readily applied this style of reasoning to macroeconomic conditions, with formidable influence over the style of political debate. *Full employment* and *price stability* have been reduced to the status of slogans—remote conditions that economic policy in the intermediate term no longer even pretends to aim for.

In the hands of those who lack economic vision, the political system has become largely, if not purely, a reactive agent—so much so that, as we have seen, much of its policy movement may readily be predicted. Policy moves to tighten when inflation rises and to ease when unemployment passes a critical threshold. Progressive opinion then becomes merely a reaction to these reactions. And in the meantime, remote from understanding, the cycles set off by reactive policy are wreaking cumulative destruction on the industrial structure, technological position and comparative standard of living of the United States.

Escape from mental passivity begins with reestablishing the link between goals and policy. I have tried, in the first instance, to show why, in their standard form, the old incantations about price stability and full employment will not serve. It is the internationalization of the American economy that has rendered the old goals in their old forms obsolete: the industrial integration that began in the 1960s and the financial integration that proceeded with great force in the 1970s. As a result, we are obliged to place the price competitiveness of U.S. export industries ahead of categorical price stabilization on some occasions, and on others obliged to consider the type and quality of jobs we generate ahead of the raw quantity.

I have tried, then, to formulate an economic strategy based on acceptance of, rather than resistance to, the global industrial role for which the United States is best suited. Our comparative advantage lies in the supply of capital goods to the investment sectors of the world economy. The foundation stone of the strategy then, is to restart world development, to begin again the surge that was halted by the global recession imposed by U.S. policy in the early 1980s and that has been suppressed in the succeeding years by the debt crisis.

From this basic goal follows a set of policies. Some are designed to foster and channel investment in those industrial sectors that need to be expanded. Some are designed to ease the transition, to manage the relative decline, of sectors that will need to contract. Some are designed to ease the political and social strains—particularly those caused by inflation—that industrial transition brings. Some, perhaps the most important, are intended to foster the growth of real income and the retirement of debt in those countries whose investment sectors must provide the growth of effective demand for the products of our capital goods industries.

In the 1970s, we learned that the business cycle generated in the pursuit of the traditional objective of price stability entailed massive adjustments in the structure of industry and the patterns of trade. We should have learned, too, from the later experience of the decade, that the United States could, in the end, profit from the adjustments if they were pursued aggressively enough. In the 1980s, however, we recoiled from the costs of so doing. The result of hanging up the trade-distorting business cycle in midstream, as we did from 1983 to 1987, has been to arrest the forward-moving phase of the adjustment. We now face a choice between pursuing an aggressive policy of catch-up—shock treatment—and accepting a permanent demotion in the hierarchy of industrial production.

Conclusions

The mechanics of shock treatment are wholly within the power of the policy instruments we already have. Fiscal and monetary actions are called for. What is holding up fiscal action is political obstruction, neither more nor less. What is holding up monetary action is, above all, a reluctance to move forcefully to liquidate the consequences of financial errors committed in the heat of the previous expansion. Both actions are an indispensable part of the cleanup required after the Reagan era.

Once the requisite fiscal and monetary steps are taken, further steps will be required to assure that they can be carried through. An inflation shock will result, but an inflation crisis can and must be avoided. The resolution of this paradox lies in splitting the shock from the propagation: in disposing of a necessary change in the general price level, led by the price of imports, in the shortest possible time.

The next phase of economic expansion cannot be made to last forever. But it can be nurtured so as to last a good long time. It must be led by governments capable of regulating their financial systems. Japan's role in raising its own consumption is not to be minimized. Nor is that of Europe. But the principal element must be the return of sustained, regulated growth in those economies that are prepared to feed on U.S. exports. These may include the giants of the developing world: China, India and, in a relaxed political climate, the Soviet Union. They must include Brazil, Mexico, Argentina and some of the smaller economies of Latin America. They should come to include others, notably in Africa, when and if appropriate political structures for the regulation of development can be put in place.

As the process of restoring progress toward development unfolds, the United States needs to acquire a renewed talent for smooth transitions. The problems here are manifold: in our financial system, our labor markets and our political system. In the financial arena, a strengthened grip of government on international flows is indispensable, and to establish this, again, the reorganization of certain banking institutions crippled by the debt crisis will prove necessary. New income support, retraining and community planning measures (some of which are provided for in proposed regulations affecting plant closings) can ease the transition for labor. Political steps should act to preserve the physical and social structure of communities affected by large industrial transitions—and not to obstruct those transitions or to protect particular jobs per se. Labor organizations must plan for a transition of the center of gravity of their power base to the advanced sectors and for a rising influence of those sectors in labor's policymaking apparatus. Most of all, a renewed and redesigned incomes policy must work to break the arbitrary influence of reference wages on inertial inflation and so insulate the U.S. political system from the destructive and reactionary consequences of inflation crises.

I have no illusion that the suggestions offered here are complete. Specialists in economic development will note that there is no discussion here of the problems of management of accelerated growth in the Third World, in countries where opportunities for mismanagement, larceny, capital flight and political disintegration are legion. Students of labor markets will note the cursory treatment of their field, as will specialists in the management of the banking system, and others, no doubt. Poverty and discrimination are not treated, nor is the fairness of the income distribution. It has not been my purpose to be complete. Rather, I have sought to sketch only the main factors, which are the macroeconomic, incomes and investment policy elements of U.S. strategy. Certainly, the application of the same goals to other fields would affect the design of policy in those fields. Perhaps through more complete investigation of these problems a new debate can be started.

I believe that the arguments of the preceding pages are rooted in a reasonable view of how the world works. Much space has been devoted to an examination of issues that readers, depending on their background, may have thought either obviously right or obviously wrong. The arguments about the importance of capital goods or the independent flexibility of monetary policy are examples. Yet too much economic writing is, in my view, executed from within the framework of one or another particular school and so starts from unexamined presumptions that much of a potential audience does not share. In this way, economic policy discourse cuts itself off from the possibility of proving widely persuasive.

I hope that I have evaded narrow classification and remained accessible to an audience of widely varying belief. I am, and am not, tolerant of some inflation. I believe, and do not believe, in the virtues of full employment. I argue here that a rise in the gross volume of profits and investment and a rise in the share of wages in incomes are compatible, achievable national goals. I have suggested that in some circumstances falling productivity growth and accelerated technological change occur together. There is, I hope, enough apparent paradox here to have kept readers interested and alert.

236

Conclusions

Some will question the political feasibility of my recommendations. In advancing my fiscal and monetary proposals, I have not tried to burst any bounds of past practice. In my judgment and for the broader purposes of proposed macroeconomic redirection, it is not necessary to do so. As a technical matter, the fiscal and monetary changes I advocate are straightforward; as political matters, there is demonstrated precedent for them.

It is doubtful whether I have been equally prudent on incomes policy and other matters of structural reform. The politics of incomes policy suffers from a structural defect: it is open for discussion only in emergencies, at which time the useful permanent options are not what sell.[1] It is sometimes necessary to patch a roof in heavy rain, but the task is always disagreeable and the result is often ineffective.

For this reason, roofs in the real world are repaired when the rain stops. I therefore have hope for useful structural reform. Such reform can reduce the risks of another inflation-generated political crisis, and this in turn would permit the natural ingenuity of the U.S. economy to realize its potential over a longer time. More broadly, structural reform can help return the United States to the cutting edge of rapid economic development and growth around the world. By dint of creative genius, we are best suited to this position and role.

This is a grand hope. It is based on confidence in the strength and resilience of the American economy and on faith in the continuing power of American policy. Yet for these as well there is both evidence and precedent. Within economics, the intellectual prestige of laissez-faire is fading once again. In politics, laissez-faire is already long dead; the only question is how the instruments of policy will be used. And there is reason for hope that, as the futility of the alternatives becomes clear, a political leadership willing to move forward boldly will be found. Indeed, such hopes are what make political life in the United States worth the price of participation.

NOTES

Chapter 1. Capital Goods

1. Representative business school titles include William Ouchi, *Theory Z.* (Boston: Addison-Wesley, 1981); and Ezra Vogel, *Japan as Number One* (Cambridge, Mass.: Harvard University Press, 1979). A post-Marxian perspective can be found in Samuel Bowles, David M. Gordon and Thomas E. Weisskopf, *Beyond the Waste Land* (New York: Anchor Press/Doubleday, 1983). Barry Bluestone and Bennett Harrison, *The Deindustrialization of America* (New York: Basic Books, 1982), presents a leftist but non-Marxian view. Robert Reich, *The Next American Frontier* (New York: Times Books, 1983), develops themes from the study of large organizations.

2. John Maynard Keynes, *The General Theory of Employment Interest and Money* (New York: Harcourt Brace, 1964), 32.

3. Professor William Baumol of Princeton University recently offered a characteristic statement of the economist's view in "America's Productivity 'Crisis': A Modest Decline Isn't All That Bad," *New York Times,* 15 February 1987, sec. 3, p. 2:

> At the heart of the debate about flagging United States "competitiveness" lies the anxious fear that the nation is suffering a long-term slowdown in productivity growth. This trend, in turn, is said to be creating chronic trade deficits and widespread unemployment as more efficient foreign manufacturers gradually supplant American producers—in short, the process of "deindustrialization." While anxiety may compel attention, however, it is not necessarily an aid to clear thinking.
>
> If we examine our current economic situation in the context of the last century of economic progress, the crisis seems not nearly so severe and the problems not nearly so intractable as some would have us believe. While our productivity growth rate does require careful attention, there is no basis for the fear that the nation has entered a period of permanent and disastrous decline.

Professor Baumol's position is typical of the professional mainstream in its careful reluctance to be drawn into apocalyptic polemic and also, more fundamentally, in the way it transforms the problem posed from the external to the internal perspective. Other recent works, including a notable one by Lester Throw, *The Zero-Sum Solution* (New York: Vintage Books, 1984), proceed in essentially the same way. This is in keeping with the basic intellectual structure of modern macroeconomics. Yet, as I shall argue in what follows, it provides misleading policy guidance for the internationalized economy, and works to deepen rather than relieve the tension between mainstream economics and the widespread public perception that something should be done about the competitive challenge.

4. A complete survey of the industrial policy dispute by R.D. Norton, "Industrial Policy and American Renewal" in *The Journal of Economic Literature* 24:1 (March 1986):1–40, highlights many books and popular articles but very few contributions by economists in academic journals. To be sure, a small number of mainstream economists with professional interests in policy have joined in. The Brookings Institution's Charles Schultze and Robert Z. Lawrence, to name two of the most prominent, have argued against the thesis that massive U.S. deindustrialization occurred in the 1970s and strongly against the assertion that manufacturing jobs were lost in this period due to increasing trade. See Lawrence, *Can America Compete?* (Washington, D.C.: Brookings Institution, 1984); and Schultze, "Industrial Policy: A Dissent," *Brookings Review* 2:1 (Fall 1983): 3. Corollary notions, such as that of a radical worsening in the U.S. earnings distribution or that of the disappearing middle class, have also been attacked by Lawrence in "Sectoral Shifts and the Size of the Middle Class," *Brookings Review* 3 (Fall 1984):3–11. Nor is a general Japanese superiority in manufacturing an uncontested fact; indeed, on average, labor productivity in Japan remains below that of the United States (as shown for the period through 1980 by Lawrence in *Can America Compete?* p. 33). Note should also be taken of investigations into the theory of strategic trade policy led by Paul Krugman. For a summary of Krugman's arguments, see "Is Free Trade Passe?" *Journal of Economic Perspectives* 1:2 (Fall 1987): 131.

5. In general, macroeconomic models deal with the broad flows of expenditure (consumption, investment, government), not with the mix of products and processes that provide the physical underpinning of such flows. Thus, the models presume, implicitly, that all the necessary elements of an industrial society, from raw commodities to capital goods, are present in the single economy under consideration. Indeed, such elements cannot be absent, as otherwise the economy could not function. Nor is their disappearance as a result of policy a possibility. Thus, in such a model, if a macroeconomic policy generating say high interest rates, recession and a fall in investment results in a slowdown of capital goods production and productivity growth, a change in policy generating recovery will subsequently speed up productivity growth. This involves a permanent sacrifice of potential production and income, but nothing has really been lost except time. Once the recovery is complete, economic expansion can proceed much as before. "Opening" a closed model in the conventional way does not change this situation, because such opening merely allows the incorporation of exports, imports and capital flows in their undifferentiated aggregates and at their money values. Once again, structure is ignored.

6. As pointed out forcefully in John Zysman and Stephen S. Cohen, *Manufacturing Matters* (New York: Basic Books, 1987).

7. The *World Development Report* for 1987 (pp. 202–203) distinguishes "low-income" countries with per capita GNP below $400; "lower middle income" ($401 to

Notes

$1,600); "upper middle income" ($1,600 to $7,450) and "high income" ($7,170 to $19,720).

8. In 1985 South Korea had a trade surplus of $4.3 billion with the United States and a deficit of $3 billion with Japan. See D. M. Leipziger et al., *Korea: Managing the Industrial Transition* (Washington, D.C.: World Bank, 1986).

9. David Ricardo, *Principles of Political Economy and Taxation,* Sraffa edition (Cambridge: Cambridge University Press, 1951), 69.

10. Joseph A. Schumpeter, *Capitalism, Socialism and Democracy* (London: George Allen & Unwin, 1976), chaps. 6–8.

11. See Brian Hindley and Alasdair Smith, "Comparative Advantage and Trade in Services," *World Economy* 7 (December 1984): 369.

12. Lester C. Thurow's *Generating Inequality* (New York: Basic Books, 1975), chap. 6, provides a lucid description of this process.

13. An interesting treatment of this issue appears in K. Kiljunen, "Industry and the Core-Periphery Concept," *CEPAL Review* 30 (December 1986): 97–115.

14. William H. Branson and Helen Junz, "Trends in U.S. Trade and Comparative Advantage," *Brookings Papers on Economic Activity* 2 (1971): 285–338.

15. Ibid., 337.

16. This is a major theme of the late Nicholas Kaldor. See, for example, "Interregional Trade and Cumulative Causation," *Economics Without Equilibrium,* Okun Lectures at Yale University, 1983, pp. 57–59. Paul Krugman, in "Trade, Accumulation and Uneven Development," *Journal of Development Economics* 8 (April 1981): 149–61, provides a simple, formal model of trade between a Northern economy whose manufacturing sector enjoys increasing returns and an agricultural South. The model shows how manufacturing will concentrate in the Northern economy. It is worth noting, too, that theory does not guarantee that the originating company will actually capture the excess returns from technological innovation. If competition arises quickly, these gains may instead be passed on to the consumer. Nevertheless, even in such a situation in a large developed economy, most of the consumers (themselves producers of consumer goods) will at first be domestic, and so they will capture a cost advantage from using a more efficient process until the diffusion of the innovation passes to the external market. Thus, for example, competition in the U.S.–dominated microprocessor market has meant much earlier diffusion of superior home and business computers in the United States than elsewhere, even though U.S. manufacturers of microprocessors are often in competitive difficulty. For a study of the U.S. merchant semiconductor industry, see Michael Borrus, Jim Millstein and John Zysman, *International Competition in Advanced Industrial Sectors: Trade and Development in the Semiconductor Industry,* a study prepared for the use of the Joint Economic Committee, U.S. Congress (Washington, D.C.: GPO, 1982).

17. Zysman and Cohen *(Manufacturing Matters)* present a table (p. 63) showing that Japan and Germany accumulated large trade surpluses in manufactured goods (capital and consumer goods together) in this period, while the United States did not. However, *competitiveness* is a matter of exports, not of the trade balance. U.S. *exports* kept pace with those of Germany and Japan; however, U.S. *imports* grew much more rapidly. High import growth happened because the United States allowed its standards of consumption to rise more rapidly than did the conservative governments in Germany and Japan. This was a good thing for American workers. And had the United States not done so, world economic growth would have been far lower and the Japanese export performance, in particular, would have been far worse.

18. In Robert Z. Lawrence, "Is Trade Deindustrializing America? A Medium-Term Perspective," *Brookings Papers on Economic Activity* 1 (1983):148.

19. Such adjustment problems included worker displacement in the highly visible steel, automotive and textile industries and attendant crises in local public finance.

20. This is true even though capital goods continue to dominate our export position. Using a slightly different measure from that of Lawrence, a 1986 Joint Economic Committee study estimates that U.S. high technology declined from a surplus of about a $27 billion in 1980 to a deficit of about $3 billion in 1986. See W.F. Finan, Perry D. Quick and Karen Sandberg, "The U.S. Position in High Technology: 1980–86," a report prepared for the Joint Economic Committee (Washington, D.C.: Quick, Finan and Associates, October 1986).

Chapter 2. The Age of Contradictions

1. Robert Triffin, *Gold and the Dollar Crisis: The Future of Convertibility* (New Haven, Conn.: Yale University Press, 1960).

2. Robert Mundell, "The Appropriate Use of Monetary and Fiscal Instruments for Internal and External Stability," *IMF Staff Papers* 9 (March 1962):70–77.

3. Raymond Vernon, "International Investment and International Trade in the Produce Cycle," *Quarterly Journal of Economics* 80 (May 1966):190–207.

4. Richard Cooper, *The Economics of Interdependence* (New York: McGraw-Hill, 1968).

5. Jean-Jacques Servan-Schreiber, trans. Ronald Steel, *The American Challenge* (New York: Atheneum, 1969).

6. Triffin, *Gold and the Dollar Crisis*, 10.

7. Takafusa Nakamura, trans. Jacqueline Kaminski, *The Postwar Japanese Economy* (Tokyo: University of Tokyo Press, 1981), chap. 2.

8. See William H. Branson and Helen Junz, "Trends in U.S. Trade and Comparative Advantage," *Brookings Papers on Economic Activity* 2 (1971); and Thomas Bayard, *Trends in U.S. Trade 1960–79,* Economic Discussion Paper No. 7, (Washington, D.C.: U.S. Department of Labor, Bureau of International Labor Affairs, October 1980), 27.

9. Yet, just how tenuous the simple Phillips curve relation was all along can be demonstrated with a simple regression exercise. If one estimates the rate of inflation as a function of the rate of unemployment for data from 1954 on, extending the sample one year at a time as new data becomes available, one finds that any (linear) association between the two variables is rejected until the sample is extended to include 1969. At that point, a strong and statistically significant effect appears. By 1971 the relationship is statistically insignificant once again.

10. Barry Bosworth and Robert Z. Lawrence, *Commodity Prices and the New Inflation* (Washington, D.C.: Brookings Institution, 1982).

11. As shown in figure 1-3A.

12. Robert P. Parker et al., "The National Income and Product Accounts of the United

Notes

States: An Introduction to the Revised Estimates for 1929–80," *Survey of Current Business* (December 1980):21–23.

13. John Kendrick and E. Grossman, *Productivity in the United States: Trends and Cycles* (Baltimore: John Hopkins University Press, 1980).

14. Edward F. Denison, *Accounting for Slower Economic Growth* (Washington, D.C.: The Brookings Institution, 1979) provides an exhaustive survey and a largely negative assessment of the various claims.

15. Ibid., 4.

16. An answer offered by Michael Bruno and Jeff Sachs, and widely taken up in the literature, attributes the productivity to the effects of import price shocks, which are analytically equivalent to "technical regress" in the framework that Bruno and Sachs use. This hypothesis has the merit of helping to explain why measured productivity growth fluctuated so sharply from one year to the next in the 1970s. However, it loses power in the 1980s, when sharp declines in real import prices failed to produce symmetric increases in productivity growth. Moreover, the technical regress analogy appears difficult to reconcile with the technologically based investment and export boom that the United States began to experience in the wake of the oil price shocks. See Michael Bruno and Jeffrey Sachs, *The Economics of Worldwide Stagflation* (Cambridge, Mass.: Harvard University Press, 1985). In a review article, John F. Holliwell summarizes: "Most of the more complete studies of stagflation and productivity decline attribute more weight to the changes in domestic and foreign demand conditions than to the direct effect of energy and other raw materials prices on producer decisions." Holliwell, "Comparative Macroeconomics of Stagflation," *Journal of Economic Literature* 26:1 (March 1988):26.

17. A comparable example is given by Albert Rees, "Improving the Concepts and Techniques of Productivity Measurement," *Monthly Labor Review* (September 1979):24.

18. "A Note on the Revision of Producers' Durable Equipment," *Survey of Current Business* (December 1985):16–17.

19. David V. Cartright, "Improved Deflation of Purchases of Computers," *Survey of Current Business* (March 1986):7–10.

20. A technical irony in the computer case occurs when the base year for the price index is shifted to 1982. Then the 1982 dollar value of computer sales (about $30 billion) becomes the real value of computer sales for that year. Deflating previous years' production now *reduces* the real estimates of output for those prior years, and so the "productivity gap" reemerges. But this raises an almost metaphysical question: in measuring consumers' welfare, is it more reasonable to regard a computer in, say, 1976 as an inferior version of the 1982 model or to think of the 1982 model as a vastly superior version of the 1976 model? Clearly, had the new index been in use in 1976, the real measure of computer output would have been far higher than it was, and the productivity growth gap would not have seemed nearly as serious as it did.

21. By Block's estimates, the undermeasurement of real output in capital sectors, together with undercounting of services output that occurs for similar reasons, can account for one-half of the aggregate slowdown of the productivity growth rate between the 1960–66 rate and that of 1973–79. This is virtually all of the slowdown in the later period not explained by the effects of the deep recession of 1973–74. Fred Block, "Post Industrial Development and the Obsolescence of Economic Categories," *Politics and Society* 14:1 (1985):71–104.

Notes

Chapter 3. What Reagan Did

1. Readers seeking a full account of these events are commended to David Stockman's memoir, *The Triumph of Politics* (New York: Harper & Row, 1986).

2. The official record on money growth is reviewed in the *1982 Report of the Joint Economic Committee, Congress of the United States, on the February 1982 Economic Report of the President* (Washington, D.C.: GPO, 1982), 69–79.

3. M1 was also affected by a special institutional factor, the introduction on January 1, 1981, of nationwide interest-bearing checking (NOW) accounts.

4. William Greider, *Secrets of the Temple* (New York: Simon & Schuster, 1987), provides a detailed inside look at the politics of monetary decision making in this period. Greider particularly concludes that the political pressure for recession was extremely strong: "Paul Volcker was often praised for his political courage, but in this case it might have taken more courage to resist" (p. 392).

5. Robert Eisner and Paul J. Peiper, "A New View of the Federal Debt and Budget Deficits," *American Economic Review* 74 (March 1984):11–29; Robert Eisner, *How Real Is the Federal Deficit?* (New York: Free Press, 1986). The basic point is made earlier in theoretical literature—for example, by William Buiter in "Measurement of the Public Sector Deficit and Its Implications for Policy Evaluation and Design," *IMF Staff Papers* 30:3 (June 1983): 317–25; and to policymakers by myself in *The Case for Rapid Growth*, Joint Economic Committee (Washington, D.C.: GPO, 1983), 63–66.

6. And revealed by Weidenbaum under highly amusing circumstances. *Hearings of the Joint Economic Committee*, June 9, 1982.

7. Greider, *Secrets of the Temple*, chap. 14, provides an account.

8. Exactly how quickly a rise in real wealth enters the flow of spending is a matter of dispute. Long-standing econometric estimates suggest a slow rate: between 3 and 6 percent per year. But if economic agents are constrained by an inadequate supply of credit, the immediate effects of a rise in real money on real spending may be much larger.

9. At which time price controls were in effect, giving each nominal dollar of money holdings more real purchasing power than it would otherwise have had.

10. A qualification concerns the effect of falling inflation on the demand for money balances held by the public. In times of high inflation, such as 1979–81, these are kept at minimum levels, since money holdings (which do not earn interest) lose value rapidly during inflation. Correspondingly, as inflation falls, the public becomes more willing to enjoy the convenience of money holdings, and this will diminish the effect of a rise in the real money stock on spending.

11. For example, Wing Thye Woo, "Exchange Rates and the Prices of Non-Food, Non-Fuel Products," *Brookings Papers on Economic Activity* 2 (1984): 511–36.

12. The activities of the ICC under Chairman Reese Taylor were aired and criticized by Republican and Democratic experts at a hearing of the Joint Economic Committee on November 17, 1981 See *Trucking Deregulation: Is It Happening?* (Washington, D.C.: GPO, 1982). Following extensive adverse publicity, the administration named two libertarian advocates of deregulation to the Commission.

13. Journalist Gregg Easterbrook provides a reliable account in "The Sky Isn't Falling," *The New Republic* (November 30, 1987): 18–23.

14. A compelling model of the dollar's effect on inflation is presented in Jeffrey Sachs, "The Dollar and the Policy Mix: 1985," *Brookings Papers on Economic Activity* 1 (1985): 117–85.

Notes

15. Peter Hooper and Barbara Lowrey, *Impact of the Dollar Depreciation on the U.S. Price Level: An Analytical Survey of Empirical Estimates,* Staff Study 103, Board of Governors of the Federal Reserve System, April 1979.

16. Volcker's testimony is reprinted in the *Federal Reserve Bulletin* 73:6 (June 1987):425–29.

17. It is true that the dollar's fall against the yen and the deutsche mark is important in restoring relative price competitiveness for U.S. sales in third-country markets, such as those of Latin America and East Asia, where the United States, Germany and Japan are in competition. Nevertheless, the continuing appreciation of the dollar against the currencies of those countries deprives them of the income effect that would otherwise increase their absolute purchasing power over U.S. products.

18. W. Michael Cox, "A Comprehensive New Real Dollar Exchange Rate Index," *Federal Reserve Bank of Dallas Economic Review* (March 1987): 1–15. Japan and Europe, whose currencies form the lion's share of the traditional trade-weighted currency index, count for just 42 percent of the Dallas comprehensive index and are the only currencies against which the dollar had fallen as of the end of 1986.

19. Sachs, "The Dollar and the Policy Mix." Sachs dates the "Mundell shift" from the beginning of the Reagan administration in 1981. However, given that close analysis shows restrictive fiscal and monetary policies working together until mid-1982 and joint easy fiscal and monetary policies for nine months thereafter, it is more persuasive to date the Mundell shift from May 1983.

20. The official accounts, on this matter as on so much else, are slightly misleading. U.S. overseas assets, which are mostly long-term, are booked at their acquisition price, or face value. Hence the recorded value of these assets did not appreciate in line with their market value in the inflationary 1970s, and so was understated in comparison with U.S. overseas liabilities newly booked (and accurately valued) after 1983. In terms of market value, the United States probably remained a creditor until well into 1986 or 1987.

21. Congressional Budget Office, *The Economic and Budget Outlook: Fiscal Years 1989–1993* (Washington, D.C.: CBO, February 1988).

22. In a column published on January 1, 1988, Leonard Silk of the *New York Times* was already quoting a warning from Harold Van Buren Cleveland, former chief international economist of Citicorp, that the "real choice" was between a mild recession in 1988 (to restore "confidence in the dollar") and a deeper recession that would be otherwise inevitable: "Paradoxically, a policy that gives priority to avoiding recession could bring a recession of unusual severity." Silk's column provides a good early warning of the drift of established thinking.

Chapter 4. The Nature of the Case for Price Stabilization

1. For a discussion of and references to empirical work on this issue, see Stanley Fischer, *Indexing, Inflation and Economic Policy* (Cambridge, Mass.: MIT Press, 1986), 20–26.

2. Estimates for 1976 by James D. Smith in Joint Economic Committee hearings of February 10, 1982, p. 204. Only corporate stock is more concentrated, 44 percent of it

being held by the richest 1 percent of the population. Estimates for other assets include real estate (13.1 percent), cash (11.1 percent), debt instruments (24.6 percent), and life insurance (8 percent). Note that some of the more widely held assets (real estate) are better inflation hedges than the most narrowly held ones.

3. The share of bondholdings of the top 1 percent of the population in 1976 marked a dramatic drop from the 1972 value of 60.1 percent, and Smith found a similar drop in share for corporate stock (from 62.6 to 44.2 percent). This could occur if new stocks and bonds were distributed to "inflation winners" outside the smallest circle of the traditional elite.

4. Lawrence Summers, in "The Non-Adjustment of Nominal Interest Rates: A Study of the Fisher Effect," National Bureau of Economic Research Working Paper No. 836, January 1982, shows that over the entire history of the known data, nominal interest rates have failed to adjust to changes in inflation.

5. In recent Latin American experience, high inflation has led to rapid expansions in bank branching and the provision of financial services. This causes real adjustment problems when governments move to end inflation and the public returns to holding cash. See Rudiger Dornbusch and Mario Henrique Simonsen, *Inflation Stabilization with Incomes Policy Support: A Review of the Experience in Argentina, Brazil and Israel* (New York: Group of 30, 1986).

6. Fischer, *Indexing, Inflation and Economic Policy,* 46. Fischer concludes with an estimate that 10 percent inflation in the United States imposes efficiency losses valued at about $8 billion as compared with zero inflation. This may be compared with the rule of thumb known as Okun's Law, which holds that to raise unemployment by 1 percent costs 2 to 3 percent in the growth rate of GNP. Point for point, then, if these estimates are accurate, the output losses from unemployment outweigh the efficiency costs of inflation on the order of 100 to 1. My own estimates in *The Case for Rapid Growth,* Joint Economic Committee (Washington, D.C.: GPO, October 1983), 24–27, suggest the continuing approximate validity of Okun's Law.

7. John Rutledge, *Outlook for Recession,* Joint Economic Committee hearing of October 21, 1981, pp. 32, 44. There followed an immediate exchange with the committee chairman, Henry Reuss:

> *Representative Reuss:* Well now, to examine that, is zero the optimum unemployment rate too?
> *Mr. Rutledge:* No, I would not say that.
> *Representative Reuss:* Did God switch signals on that?
> *Mr. Rutledge:* No. God never made a target for unemployment as far as I know, in the King James version, anyway.
> *Representative Reuss:* Speaking of theology is unsuccessful, at least in resolving this.

8. Frank Hahn, "Memorandum by Professor Hahn," in *Memoranda on Monetary Policy,* House of Commons Treasury and Civil Service Committee (London: HMSO, May 1980), 80.

9. For example, Brian Barry, "Political Ideas of Some Economists," in Leon N. Lindberg and Charles S. Maier, eds., *The Politics of Inflation and Economic Stagnation* (Washington, D.C.: Brookings Institution, 1985), 317: "Anti-inflationary hysteria is an opportunity to mobilize behind proposals that would, in calmer times, be widely recognized as reactionary twaddle."

Notes

10. John Maynard Keynes. *The Economic Consequences of the Peace* (New York: Harcourt, Brace and Howe, 1920), 149.

11. Ibid.

12. Eisaku Sakakibara et al., *The Japanese Financial System in Comparative Perspective,* a study prepared for the use of the Joint Economic Committee, (Washington, D.C.: GPO, 1982).

13. See Stephen S. Cohen, James K. Galbraith and John Zysman, "Credit Policy and Industrial Policy in France," in *Monetary Policy, Selective Credit Policy and Industrial Policy in France, West Germany, Great Britain and Sweden* a study prepared for the Joint Economic Committee (Washington, D.C.: GPO, 1981).

14. In particular, that group of the well-to-do with high incomes but relatively few savings and paper assets. Ronald Reagan, whose earnings came from honoraria and whose hostility to the income tax is legendary, was perhaps the archetype of this class.

15. Thomas Byrne Edsall chronicles the rise of the New Right in *The New Politics of Inequality* (New York: Norton, 1984). Thomas Ferguson and Joel Rogers explore the influence of property on the Democratic Party in *Right Turn: The Decline of the Democrats and the Future of American Politics* (New York: Hill and Wang, 1986).

Chapter 5. The Obsolescence of Full Employment

1. In technical terms, the debate has been about the shape and slope of the Phillips curve and about the slope of the social welfare indifference curves. If the Phillips curve is very steep (in the limit, vertical), a fall in unemployment can be purchased only by a large (in the limit, unbounded) increase in inflation. If the indifference curves are very flat, society is willing to accept large increases in unemployment in return for small declines in inflation. Thus steep Phillips curves and flat social indifference curves define the conservative position.

2. See chapter 9.

3. For a brutal indictment of the optimists, see R.E. Lucas, "Tobin and Monetarism: A Review Article," *Journal of Economic Literature* 29:2 (June 1981): 558–85.

4. Axel Leijonhufvud, *Keynes and the Classics,* IEA Occasional Paper No. 30 (London: Institute for Economic Affairs, 1971), 10.

5. In particular, the essential role of price control in making wartime stabilization effective often slipped the minds of some who were thinking through a free market prototype for postwar Keynesian macromanagement.

6. *Historical Statistics of the United States, Colonial Times to 1970,* part 1 (Washington, D.C.: U.S. Department of Commerce, Bureau of the Census, 1975), 126, 127.

7. One may contrast this literature with the arguments of Samuel Bowles, David M. Gordon and Thomas E. Weisskopf in *Beyond the Waste Land* (New York: Anchor Press/Doubleday, 1983), which focus on a breakdown in the cooperation of *workers.* This argument, with its very different cultural implications, has attracted much less attention.

8. Michal Kalecki, "Political Aspects of Full Employment," in his *Selected Essays on*

the Dynamics of the Capitalist Economy (Cambridge: Cambridge University Press, 1971), 138.

9. Ibid., 138, 142–43.

10. The theory rests on the observation that wage contracts rule in the labor market, making it impossible for labor markets to clear as rapidly as rational expectations theory tends to assume. In this situation, increases in nominal aggregate spending with effective demand will not simply raise wages and prices, but will also stimulate employment and output, even if all economic agents are behaving in a rational way. Stanley Fischer of MIT and Martin Baily of the Brookings Institution have been prominent exponents of this position.

11. Robert Eisner, *How Real Is the Federal Deficit?* (New York: Free Press, 1986).

12. William H. Beveridge, *Full Employment in a Free Society* (New York: Norton, 1945), 18.

13. Herbert Stein, "Economic Growth as an Objective of National Policy," statement to the Joint Economic Committee, January 9, 1986.

14. *Economic Report of the President* (Washington, D.C.: GPO, 1987), 211.

15. G. Cain, *Married Women in the Labor Force* (Chicago: University of Chicago Press, 1966), 2.

16. George Perry, "Changing Labor Markets and Inflation," *Brookings Papers on Economic Activity* 3 (1970): 141.

17. Measured as average hourly earnings in the private nonagricultural sector for production or nonsupervisory employees. Data are from the *Economic Report of the President* (Washington, D.C.: GPO, 1988), 298.

18. *Employment and Training Report of the President* (Washington, D.C.: GPO, 1976).

19. Thomas Schelling, *Micromotives and Macrobehavior* (Cambridge, Mass.: Harvard University Press, 1978), 91–115.

Chapter 6. Profits and Productive Investment

1. Frederick Engels, "Socialism, Utopian and Scientific," in Karl Marx and Frederick Engels, *Selected Works* (New York: International Publishers, 1972), 434.

2. Joseph A. Schumpeter, *Capitalism, Socialism and Democracy* (London: George Allen & Unwin, 1976), 67.

3. For a reader, see David Colander, ed., *Neoclassical Political Economy* (Cambridge, Mass.: Ballinger, 1984).

4. Paul Krugman, "Is Free Trade Passe?" *Journal of Economic Perspectives* 1:2 (Fall 1987):131–144, provides a summary. It is interesting that Krugman, a consummate neoclassicist *cum* American Keynesian, leaves the consequences of his argument for the theory of distribution unanalyzed. Patrick Conway and William Darity explore the grim consequences of increasing returns for distribution in "Growth and Trade with Asymmetric Returns to Scale: A Model for Nicholas Kaldor," an unpublished 1987 paper.

5. Samuel Bowles, David M. Gordon and Thomas E. Weisskopf, *Beyond the Waste Land* (New York: Anchor Press/Doubleday, 1983), chap. 6.

Notes

6. Michal Kalecki, "The Determinants of Profit," in *Selected Essays on the Dynamics of the Capitalist Economy* (Cambridge: Cambridge University Press, 1971) chap. 7.

7. Robert Eisner, *How Real Is the Federal Deficit?* (New York: Free Press, 1986), chap. 11.

8. All the accounting relationships still hold, but now capitalist consumption is less in money terms than it would have been otherwise (because goods are cheaper), while real and money investment is greater. Since these two variations offset each other, profits are therefore the same as in the flexprice case. One might ask, *why* don't consumer goods prices rise with demand far enough to eliminate excess demand and choke off the need for new investment? Fundamentally, they cannot do so, so long as competition holds between consumer goods producers. For with competition, too high a price will induce entry by a new firm with superior capital equipment and lower costs, destroying the profitability of the existing producers. The theory of *limit pricing*, another technical subject, deals with the conditions under which such entry is encouraged or deterred.

9. A more detailed exposition of this process can be found in Hyman Minsky, *Stabilizing an Unstable Economy* (New Haven, Conn.: Yale University Press, 1986), chap. 7.

10. Paul Baran and Paul Sweezy devote the heart of their *Monopoly Capital* ([New York: Monthly Review Press, 1966], chaps. 4–7), to an analysis of the absorption of surplus in unproductive activity in sales efforts, civilian government and military activity. Their use of the term, which encompasses actions by the state as well as by corporations, is broader than mine.

11. But see Edward Wolff, *Growth, Accumulation, and Unproductive Activity: An Analysis of Postwar U.S. Economy* (New York: Cambridge University Press, 1986).

12. *Economic Report of the President* (Washington, D.C.: GPO, 1987), table B-22.

13. Robert Reich, *The Next American Frontier* (New York: New American Library, 1982), chap. 8.

14. Michael Piore and Charles Sabel, *The Second Industrial Divide* (New York: Basic Books, 1985), chaps. 10, 11.

15. Barry Bluestone and Bennett Harrison, *The Great U-Turn* (New York: Basic Books, 1988), 193–95.

Chapter 7. Industrial Intervention

1. Community preservation, not deindustrialization, is the strong underlying theme of Barry Bluestone and Bennett Harrison's brief for industrial policy, *The Deindustrialization of America* (New York: Basic Books, 1982).

2. Extensive hearings on industrial policy were held in 1982–83 by the Joint Economic Committee and separately by the Economic Stabilization Subcommittee of the Committee on Banking, Finance and Urban Affairs, U.S. House of Representatives. Five congressional manifestos on the topic appeared between 1982 and 1984: *Report of the Joint Economic Committee on the 1982 Economic Report of the President; Rebuilding the Road to Opportunity: A Democratic Direction for the 1980s* by the Committee on Party Effectiveness, House Democratic Caucus (September 1982); *Jobs for the Future: A Democratic Agenda* by the Senate Democratic Caucus; *Forging an Industrial Competitiveness Strategy*

by the Subcommittee on Economic Stabilization; and *Renewing America's Promise: A Democratic Blueprint for the Nation's Future* by the National House Democratic Caucus. These were a more unified effort than they may appear, because the same staff was in many cases responsible for several of these documents.

3. Specifically in R. D. Norton, "Industrial Policy and American Renewal," *Journal of Economic Literature* 24:1 (March 1986):1–41.

4. See, for example *Business Management Practices and the Productivity of the American Economy,* Hearings before the Joint Economic Committee, U.S. Congress, May 1, 1981, testimony by Robert Abernathy and William Hayes of Harvard Business School. Their article, "Managing Our Way to Economic Deadline," appeared in the *Harvard Business Review* 58:4 (July–August 1980):67.

5. For a survey of selected credit-oriented industrial policies in Europe, see *Monetary Policy, Selective Credit Policy and Industrial Policy in France, Great Britain, West Germany and Sweden,* a study prepared for the use of the Joint Economic Committee, U.S. Congress (Washington, D.C.: GPO, 1981). The Joint Economic Committee also published a study by Eisuke Sakakibara, Robert Feldman and Yuzo Harada, *The Japanese Financial System in Comparative Perspective,* a study prepared for the use of the Joint Economic Committee, U.S. Congress (Washington, D.C.: GPO, 1982).

6. A brief history of the RFC by James M. Bickley, "An Evaluation of the Reconstruction Finance Corporation with Implications for Current Capital Needs of the Steel Industry," can be found in George Sternlieb and David Listokin, eds., *New Tools for Economic Development: The Enterprise Zone, Development Bank, and RFC* (Piscataway, N.J.: Center for Urban Policy Research, Rutgers University, 1981), 144–62.

7. This type of argument was commonly made by Charles Schultze. See his article, "Industrial Policy: A Dissent," *Brookings Review* 2:1 (Fall 1983): 3.

8. *Hard Choices: A Report on the Increasing Gap Between America's Infrastructure Needs and Our Ability to Pay for Them,* a study prepared for the use of the Subcommittee on Economic Goals and Intergovernmental Policy of the Joint Economic Committee, U.S. Congress (Washington, D.C.: GPO, 1984). The study comprises a report and twenty-two appendices covering participating states.

9. The paper by Aoki ("Intra-firm Mechanism, Sharing and Employment," mimeo, 1986) describes this system well. See Chapter 11, note 16.

10. *Report of the Joint Economic Committee, Congress of the United States, on the February 1986 Economic Report of the President* (Washington, D.C.: GPO, 1986).

11. This is a note from personal experience. I served as staff economist for the House Banking Committee at this time.

12. Specifically, the radical appreciation of the dollar cheapened Chrysler's input costs relative to its sales prices, and in combination with a restructuring of the company, this restored profitability. It is a reasonable guess, based on my review of the company's plans submitted to the Treasury from 1979 to 1981, that without the change in economic conditions Chrysler would not have survived.

13. *1982 Joint Economic Committee Report,* 112–16.

14. *Case Studies in Public/Private Cooperation to Revitalize America: Coal. Report of the Joint Economic Committee,* U.S. Congress (Washington, D.C.: GPO, 1982).

15. *Case Studies in Private/Public Cooperation to Revitalize America: Passenger Rail. Report of the Joint Economic Committee,* U.S. Congress (Washington, D.C.: GPO, 1981).

Notes

16. A detailed treatment is given in the author's Ph.D. dissertation, "A Theory of the Government Budget Process," Yale University, 1981.

Chapter 8. The Case for a Limited Tax Shock

1. Congressional Budget Office, *An Analysis of the President's Budgetary Proposals for Fiscal Year 1988* (Washington, D.C.: CBO, 1988). These and subsequent budget numbers include the social security accounts and projected surpluses therein.

2. However, in some particulars, CBO has departed from this rule. In the early 1980s, baseline forecasts presumed a 5 percent after-inflation growth rate in the defense sector on the ground that such growth was (as reflected in budget resolutions of the time) established congressional policy.

3. Mark Kamlet, David Mowery and Tsai-Tsu Su, "Whom Do You Trust: An Analysis of Executive and Congressional Economic Forecasts," *Journal of Policy Analysis and Management* 6:3 (Spring 1987): 365–84.

4. Robert Eisner, *How Real is the Federal Deficit?* (New York: Free Press, 1986), chap. 2.

5. The government debt held by the Federal Reserve does correspond to the value of money held by the public, which also depreciates with inflation. However, changes in the real value of money are better treated separately, under the rubric of monetary policy.

6. Using an inflation rate lower than that forecast by CBO reduces the estimated value of the inflation tax and so makes partial (and perhaps inadequate) allowance for the fact that (as most economists believe) the drag on the economy created by reductions in real wealth is less than the drag created by direct reductions in money income.

7. A third adjustment favored by some (Robert Eisner and Robert Heilbroner, in particular) concerns the treatment of capital spending in the federal budget. Such "investment" expenditures, amounting to nearly $200 billion annually, are not counted as deficits (losses) when made by private corporations, but are so counted in the public sector. Still, for purposes of fiscal policy, it is current expenditure flows rather than expected future benefits that are important. And so, for our purposes, it is not inappropriate to group capital outlays with current expenditures, just as both investment and consumer spending are counted as additions to GNP.

8. What, then, is the relationship between the all-government, price-adjusted deficit and real growth? How much real growth can a nominal deficit stabilized at 2 percent of GNP sustain? There is no airtight answer to this question, since much depends on monetary policy and on the world situation. Still, rough estimates based on past historical conditions may be sought econometrically. Robert Eisner and Paul J. Pieper have published one such estimate in the *American Economic Review.* This estimate, while offered quite tentatively, suggests that a price-adjusted budget *in balance* is roughly right when the target growth rate is between 4 and 5 percent. Since this is a good target growth rate, we will adopt it. It is consistent with the general outline of fiscal strategy given here. See Robert Eisner and Paul J. Pieper, "A New View of the Federal Debt and Budget Deficits," *American Economic Review* 74: (March 1984): 24–26.

Notes

9. This issue was discussed repeatedly between Henry Reuss, as Chairman of the Joint Economic Committee in 1981–82, and Federal Reserve Chairman Paul Volcker. See, for example, *The Future of Monetary Policy*, Hearings before the Joint Economic Committee, U.S. Congress, June 2, 8, 10 and 15, 1982, p. 462.

Chapter 9. Real Money and Real Interest Rates

1. William Greider, *Secrets of the Temple* (New York: Simon & Schuster, 1987), chaps. 7–10, provides a detailed and fascinating history of the politics of monetary decision making.

2. Joint Economic Committee, U.S. Congress, *Report on the February 1982 Economic Report of the President* (Washington, D.C.: GPO, 1982), 87–97.

3. However, the rate at which an increase in real wealth is spent will be slower compared to that of an increase in income achieved by government spending or transfers. Just as individuals do not immediately convert stock market gains to cash, they do not hold real money balances constant and attempt immediately to spend an increase.

4. Details of the estimating equation, known technically as a response or reaction function, are as follows:

$$GRLFM2 = .16 \times GRLGNP - 1.22 \times INFL$$
$$(1.40) \qquad (5.95)$$

$$+ 1.88 \times UNEMP \ \& \ -4.83 \times VOLCKER$$
$$(4.66) \qquad\qquad (3.94)$$

GRLFM2 is the growth rate of real money, measured as M2 divided by the price level. GRLGNP is the growth rate of real GNP. INFL is the rate of inflation (CPI index). UNEMP is the rate of unemployment, and VOLCKER is a dummy variable for the period after mid-1979. The equation is estimated on quarterly data from 1970:1 through 1985:4. R^2 is .58, indicating that 58 percent of the quarterly variance in real money growth rates is explained by the equation. The Durbin-Watson statistic is 1.5, indicating the probable presence of other systematically-related variables. T–statistics are in parantheses.

5. In statistical terms, this is a shift in the intercept term.

6. In the wake of the stock crash, American Keynesians came strongly to the view that an immediate dollar depreciation on the order of 30 percent was needed. This view was expressed to the Joint Economic Committee in early November by Paul Krugman, to the House Banking Committee by Martin Feldstein and Herbert Stein, and in public forums by James Tobin, Robert Eisner and others.

7. Testimony of Martin Feldstein, Committee on Banking, Finance and Urban Affairs, U.S. House of Representatives, October 29, 1987.

Notes

Chapter 10. World Growth and the Debt

1. New orders for capital goods comprised about 26 percent of all new orders for goods in the United States in 1986 (down from 29 percent in 1980). About 66 percent of U.S. merchandise exports are manufactures, and about 60 percent of those are capital goods (most of the rest being intermediates). Thus about 40 percent of merchandise exports, or about $90 billion worth, consist of capital goods, including automotive. Taking exports away from domestic capital goods production and adding imports leaves about $320 billion of domestic capital goods sales in 1986 against $812 billion of noncapital durable goods, or a ratio of about 2.5 to 1. Taking account of the output of non-durable goods ($1.06 trillion) gives a ratio of 6:1, but the latter are less capital intensive, so the truth lies in between.

2. Presently, as the above figures show, about 30 percent of U.S. capital goods production is exported. Data on exports-to-shipments ratios for particular industries that produce capital goods range from a quarter up to about one-half for 1984, but these ratios would be higher in 1987 after the large export growth of that year.

3. The same applies to Korea, Taiwan, Singapore and Hong Kong; though those countries are not in any debt crisis, they would quickly lose their world position if they lost price competitiveness in U.S. markets.

4. Overseas Development Council, *Agenda* (Washington, D.C.: Transaction Press, 1988).

5. The Bradley plan was presented to an international meeting of private and public sector officials at Zurich, Switzerland, in July 1986.

6. Democratic senator Paul Sarbanes of Missouri and Congressman John LaFalce of New York are sponsors of legislation to this effect.

7. Proposal made by Lorie Tarshis in *Challenge* 30:2 (May–June 1987):18–23.

8. As proposed in March 1988 by James D. Robinson, chief executive officer of the American Express Corporation, in a speech to the Overseas Development Council, Washington, D.C.

9. Excellent analyses have been made by Anatole Kaletsky, *The Costs of Default* (New York: Twentieth Century Fund, 1985), and by Jeffrey Sachs and Harry Huizinga, "U.S. Commercial Banks and the Developing Country Debt Crisis: The Experience Since 1982," mimeo, prepared for the Brookings Panel on Economic Activity, Washington, D.C., September 9–10, 1987. Sachs and Huizinga particularly dissect the question of bank behavior and incentives discussed here.

10. This plan, presented by Finance Minister Luis-Carlos Bresser-Pereira, is said to have been devised by Jeffrey Sachs.

11. Lance Taylor, Marshall Lectures at Cambridge University, mimeo, May 1987.

12. Manuel Pastor, "Current Account and Debt Accumulation in Latin America: Debate and Evidence," mimeo presented to the American Economics Association, December 1987.

Notes

Chapter 11. Incomes Policies

1. An excellent history is by Hugh Rockoff, *Drastic Measures: A History of Wage and Price Controls in the United States* (Cambridge: Cambridge University Press, 1984).

2. Controls thus may *either* speed the adjustment of prices to a lower stimulus from the fundamentals, and so reduce the output cost of disinflation (if the fundamentals are brought into line in a comprehensive anti-inflation strategy), *or* they may merely delay the adjustment of prices to the higher levels dictated eventually by unreconstructed inflationary fundamentals. Either produces a direct effect on prices.

3. Certainly Nixon's controls failed if the test is their long-term staying power.

4. The definitive theoretical treatment remains John Kenneth Galbraith, *A Theory of Price Control* (Cambridge, Mass: Harvard University Press, 1952).

5. A useful econometric evaluation of the Nixon controls is by Alan S. Blinder and William J. Newton, "The 1971–1974 Program and the Price Level: An Economic Post-Mortem," *National Bureau of Economic Research*, Reprint No. 210 (Cambridge, Mass.: NBER, 1981).

6. Two book-length surveys of TIP proposals are Arthur M. Okun and George Perry, eds., *Curing Chronic Inflation* (Washington, D.C.: Brookings Institution, 1978), and David Colander, ed., *Incentive-Based Incomes Policies: New Developments in TIP and MAP* (Cambridge, Mass.: Ballinger, 1986).

7. A formal model incorporating the cost of credibility has been provided by David Backus and J. Driffill, "Inflation and Reputation," *American Economic Review* 75:3 (June 1985): 530–38.

8. As they certainly were, for example, in early 1982, when the Federal Reserve's refusal to ease its targets generated justified fears that they intended to prolong the 1981–82 recession. See the *1982 Joint Economic Report* and William Greider's *Secrets of the Temple* (New York: Simon & Schuster, 1987).

9. For documentation on this point, see Milton Friedman, "How to Give Monetarism a Bad Name," and Beryl Sprinkel, "Money Growth Targets and Federal Reserve Accountability," in James K. Galbraith and Dan C. Roberts, eds., *Monetarism, Inflation and the Federal Reserve*, essays prepared for the use of the Joint Economic Committee (Washington, D.C.: GPO, 1985).

10. The phrase means rapid disinflation at a low output cost and was coined by the late William Fellner. The concept is discussed in Herbert Stein, "Views of Inflation in the United States," *Occasional Paper 3* (New York: Group of 30, 1980).

11. Jack E. Triplett, "Can TIP-MIP-MAP Proposals Work? Lessons from the Council on Wage and Price Stability," in Colander, ed., *Incentive-Based Incomes Policies*, 177–200.

12. Richard Jackman and Richard Layard, "Is TIP Administratively Feasible?" in Colander, ed., *Incentive-Based Incomes Policies*, 95–110.

13. James K. Galbraith, "Political Problems of Incentive Anti-Inflation Plans," in Colander, ed., *Incentive-Based Incomes Policies*, 231–36.

14. Martin Weitzman, *The Share Economy* (Cambridge, Mass.: Harvard University Press, 1984).

15. Lester C. Thurow, *The Zero-Sum Solution* (New York: Simon & Schuster, 1985), 160–63.

16. Masahiko Aoki argues in an interesting recent paper that in Japan, where bonus

Notes

schemes are part of a general relationship of shared and balanced objectives between workers and capitalists, the "sharing aspects" of the employment relation lead firms to restrict their own size, and so require less formal vertical integration than would otherwise be the case. Thus major automobile producers in Japan rely far more heavily on subcontractors than is the case in the United States, and the employees of those subcontractors enjoy fewer benefits and lower pay compared to workers in the central enterprise. See Aoki, "Intra-Firm Mechanism, Sharing, and Employment: Implications of Japanese Experience," mimeo, 1986. Paper prepared for the World Institute of Development Economics Research (WIDER), Helsinki, Finland.

17. Koji Taira, "Japan's Unemployment: Economic Miracle or Statistical Artifact?" *Monthly Labor Review* 106: 7 (July 1983):3.

18. Adrian Wood, *A Theory of Pay* (Cambridge, Mass.: Cambridge University Press, 1978).

Chapter 12. National Expectations: A Proposal

1. In 1985 there were about 3 million federal civilian employees, 3.2 million in the armed services, 37 million civilian and military retirees, 37 million receiving Old Age, Survivors and Disability (OASDI) benefits under Social Security, 10 million recipients of Aid to Families with Dependent Children (AFDC), and 4 million receiving veterans' benefits. In arriving at a rough figure of 60 to 70 million persons, allowance is made for substantial overlap between these categories. In addition, there are about 14 million employees and 18 million retirees in the state and local government sectors who could easily adhere to the federal system in the matter discussed later.

2. Stanley Fischer, *Indexing, Inflation and Economic Policy* (Cambridge, Mass.: MIT Press, 1986); and Rudiger Dornbusch and Mario Henrique Simonsen *Inflation Stabilization with Incomes Policy Support* (New York: Group of 30, 1987).

3. In statistical terms, freedom from systematic error is referred to as having a predictor that is an "unbiased function" of the true course of events, while the range of random error can be measured by the standard deviation of the forecasts.

4. The story is told in David Stockman, *Triumph of Politics* (New York: Harper & Row, 1986) 196–209.

5. The link between expected and actual inflation may be modeled in a variety of ways, depending on one's view of how the economy functions. Depending on one's choices, the precise welfare manifestations of a change in *ex ante* inflation expectations will vary. Thus, if one adopts a wage-cost markup pricing model, in which the expected inflation rate helps to determine wage settlements for the forthcoming year, a change in the expected rate of inflation may change money wage demands, money wages, prices and inflation directly, with no spillover to real wages, real effective demand or employment. Alternatively, in a monetarist framework, in which the exogenous growth of the money stock is driving the inflation rate, a shift in *ex ante* inflation expectations (with no change in the rate of money creation) may have transitory real effects (a fall in such expectations may increase labor supply and output, other things equal) but no permanent effects on the price level. That

is, under one model, changing inflation expectations affect price setting; under the other, they affect market clearing. Yet both models agree that over the long run one cannot do better than predict the inflation rate accurately. Therefore the choice of model is substantially irrelevant to the problem we face here. The problem under either choice is how to optimize the prediction of inflation.

6. For a discussion of reference wages and pattern bargaining, see Michael Piore, ed., *Inflation and Unemployment: Structuralist and Institutionalist Views* (White Plains, N.Y.: M.E. Sharpe, 1979). The theoretical dynamics of this process are set out in Adrian Wood's *A Theory of Pay* (Cambridge, Mass.: Cambridge University Press, 1978).

7. Households do not normally compute price indices from information available on supermarket shelves, and so can have little accurate sense of general price changes from local information.

8. And perhaps also to review large expansions of fringe and pension benefits not counted under the standard.

9. See Colin Crouch, "Conditions for Trade Union Wage Restraint," in Leon N. Lindberg and Charles S. Maier, eds., *The Politics of Inflation and Economic Stagnation* (Washington, D.C.: Brookings Institution, 1985), 105–39.

10. This is, however, somewhat risky, since there is no guarantee that the pace of inflation within the year will be smooth from month to month. If, for example, prices jump by 6 percent in May and stabilize thereafter, the whole of April's adjustment will be required to offset the real income loss over the year. Moreover, in the case where actual inflation outruns the DPI adjustment, there is a permanent income loss in subsequent years, since the next year's DPI loss will be geared to expected inflation and will not routinely compensate for past inflation.

11. And in any event, the windfall received in years when inflation is less than the index may be considered as insurance against occasional adverse shocks.

12. In a private letter dated October 25, 1985. Used with permission.

13. It is a fact from the literature of highway safety that the number of fatalities falls as the concentration of speeds, measured as the proportion of cars driving between, say forty-five and sixty miles per hour, rises. See Thomas H. Forester, Robert F. McNown and Larry D. Singell, "A Cost-Benefit Analysis of the 55 MPH Speed Limit," *Southern Economic Journal* 50:3 (January 1984):631–41.

Chapter 13. Conclusions

1. George Perry makes this point nicely in "Lessons from the Postwar Policy Period," Brookings General Series Reprint No. 423 (Washington, D.C.: Brookings Institution, 1986).

INDEX

Index

Index

Index

Index

Index